A glossary of computing terms

A glossary of computing terms

Eighth edition

Edited by
The British Computer Society Schools Committee
Glossary Working Party

Arnold Burdett

Diana Burkhardt

Alan Hunter

Frank Hurvid

Brian Jackson

John Jaworski

Tim Reeve (Chairman)

Graham Rogers

John Southall

LONGMAN

on behalf of the British Computer Society

Addison Wesley Longman Limited
Edinburgh Gate, Harlow
Essex CM20 2JE, England
and Associated Companies throughout the world

First published by the British Computer Society 1977
Fourth, fifth and sixth editions published by Cambridge University Press
Seventh edition published by Pitman Publishing 1991
Eighth edition published by Longman Group Limited 1995
Second impression (Reprinted with corrections twice) 1996
Fourth impression 1997

British Library Cataloguing in Publication Data
A catalogue entry for this title is available from the British Library

ISBN 0-582-27544-X

Produced by Longman Singapore Publishers Pte Ltd
Printed in Singapore

Contents

How to use this glossary   vii
Introduction   ix
Acknowledgements   xi

Part A   How Computer Systems Are Used   *1*

A1   Data Processing   *2*
A2   Word Processing   *8*
A3   Spreadsheets   *13*
A4   Communications   *18*
A5   Databases and Information Retrieval   *24*
A6   Graphics and Design   *28*
A7   Modelling and Simulation   *33*
A8   Virtual Reality   *36*
A9   Control   *38*
A10   Numerical and Scientific Computing   *42*
A11   Sound   *49*
A12   Hypertext and Hypermedia   *60*
A13   Computer Assisted Learning and Training   *62*
A14   Artificial Intelligence and Expert Systems   *66*
A15   User Interface   *70*
A16   User Documentation   *86*
A17   Computer Personnel   *90*
A18   Law and Administration   *94*

Part B   What Computer Systems Are Made Of   *99*

B1   Types of Computer   *100*
B2   Peripherals   *105*
B3   Memory   *109*
B4   Display Devices   *125*
B5   Printers   *133*
B6   Networks   *143*
B7   Communications Devices and Control Devices   *153*

Part C   How Computer Systems Work *161*

C1   Systems Design and Life Cycle   *162*
C2   Systems Documentation   *171*
C3   Management and Manipulation of Data   *182*
C4   Programming Concepts   190
C5   Programming (Flow of Execution)   *204*
C6   Programming (Subprograms)   *211*
C7   Program Syntax   *219*
C8   Program Documentation   *226*
C9   Developing, Testing and Running Programs   *238*
C10 Programming Languages   *248*
C11 Data Representation   *257*
C12 Numeric Data Representation   *270*
C13 Systems Software   *279*
C14 Machine Architecture   *291*
C15 Interfaces and Buses   *306*
C16 Physical Components   *311*
C17 Communications Technology   *315*
C18 Truth Tables and Logic Gates   *328*

Part D   Appendices   *345*

D1   Acronyms and Abbreviations   *346*
D2   Units   *357*

Index   359

How to use this glossary

Each term which is defined appears in the comprehensive index, and many users will make this their main method of access to the definitions.

All definitions are preceded by a readily picked out **bold** heading.

Many definitions include associated terms, in these cases the principal definition is immediately followed by an *italic line* which lists terms whose definitions are included in the main term. Terms defined in this embedded way are printed in ***bold italic*** type. For example, on page 11, the definition of 'Non-breaking space' reads:

Non-breaking space
>*including: pad character*
>is the ... ...sometimes called a ***pad character***, which will...

Where there are alternate terms with the same meaning, the one judged to be least common, is in an *italic line* after its more common synonym . In addition, some definitions contain 'nested definitions' which are set out in the form of sub-paragraphs. In all cases the defined terms have been printed in ***bold italic*** to make them easy to find. For example, on page 30, the definition of 'Graphics tablet' contains the alternative term *graphics pad* and the terms ***Stylus*** and ***Puck*** nested within it:

Graphics tablet
>*also known as: graphics pad*
>*including: stylus, puck*
>is a device ... ...
>
>***Stylus*** is the name ......
>
>***Puck*** is a ... ...

Two forms of cross referencing have been used:

(1) 'see above' or 'see below' – used when the term referred to is to be found in the same section, and

(2) 'see page nn' – used when the term referred to is to be found in another section or another part, or occasionally, when a term is a long way away in a large section.

Terms that are being referenced are put in *italics* to draw attention to them, for example, the definition of 'Micro-spacing', on page 11, includes:

'..inserting small amounts of *soft space* (see above) in order to…'

Where the reference to an associated term is suggested, it is usually in the form of a separate sentence: 'See also *this term*, page nn.'

All acronyms and abbreviations used in definitions, and many others, are collected together alphabetically in Section D1.

Introduction

The story of the origins of the *Glossary* have been included in the introductions to previous editions. It is still worth reprinting part of the Introduction to the sixth edition.

> *When a conference of the Regional Examining Boards, meeting in 1974, invited the British Computer Society to produce a standardised list of terms for use in computer studies courses and examination syllabi, the Working Party thought in terms of a 'once-off' document containing about 100 terms. There were no O-level courses, only one A-level examination and a small number of CSE syllabi in existence, and those schools involved in computer studies relied on batch processing using punched cards or, for a few fortunates, an on-line terminal connecting them to the local authority computer. Microcomputers were just beginning to appear.*
>
> *As soon as work on the first edition of the* Glossary *commenced, it was decided to include a simple and concise definition of each term that was unique to computing as well as a list of preferred terms and so the first edition appeared in 1977 containing some 430 terms of which 260 were defined.*

The *Glossary* proved so popular that it was obvious that further editions would be needed to include the new terms appearing almost daily due to the rapid development of the technology and the increasing use of computers in education.

Previous editions found wide acceptance at universities, colleges and industrial training departments as well as in schools and the *Glossary* has been a definitive reference specified in many examination board syllabuses. With the advent of the National Curriculum, the firm establishment of GCSE and the review of A Level and AS level syllabuses as well as other courses at a variety of levels, the working party has tried to ensure that the *Glossary* meets the needs of students following courses leading to these examinations.

It has been the policy to update the *Glossary* every three years or so. In this the eighth edition, all definitions have been revised and the organisation of the whole *Glossary* has been restructured. Terms have been arranged within three distinct thematic parts. Each part is divided into sections containing groupings of associated terms. Since the terms have been grouped, it is hoped that readers will also browse within sections and make use of the general introductions to each section. This background information to the subject topics should illustrate to students the use of some of the vocabulary of computing in context.

The Working Party is conscious of the need to provide definitions which cover the use of terms in the context of large computer systems as well as the world of microcomputers, even though for many school and college students large computer systems are outside their practical experience.

The current emphasis on communications – the 'super highway' and other associated concepts – presented a serious challenge for this edition. There is a long-standing vocabulary of communications but there has recently appeared a whole new range of terms, many of which may not survive the life of this edition. We have made decisions about which terms to include and time alone will tell whether we were right. Other terms have been considered but not included since it was judged either that their use in schools and colleges was not yet justified or that the terms themselves lacked consistent use, in the world of computing.

It must be stressed that it is not intended that the *Glossary* should be used as a textbook. Although many groups of definitions have been expanded to provide more than just a bare definition, in the hope of providing a wider and clearer understanding of the term, these expanded definitions cannot cover all the aspects appropriate to any topic. A standard text should always be consulted for fuller explanations.

The Working Party would welcome offers from teachers willing to involve their students in a review of this edition. Comments on this edition and contributions or suggestions for future editions will be gratefully received and should be sent to the Registrar, BCS, 1 Sanford Street, Swindon SN1 1HJ, or to any of the members of the Working Party through BCS.

Acknowledgements

The Working Party has appreciated the help it received from those members of the BCS Schools Committee who made comments and suggestions about material to include in this edition. We are greatly in the debt of three members of the Society – Dennis Blackwell, John Haynes and Aline Cumming – who took the trouble to read the whole of our draft manuscripts, suggesting improvements and pointing out our many mistakes. All of their corrections and many of their suggestions have been incorporated into the final version; any remaining mistakes or imperfections are entirely ours.

Our editor at Pitman for the seventh edition, John Cushion, became very much an *ex-officio* member of the working party and, even though reorganisation in the publishing world produced a change of publisher, he has remained in close and friendly contact throughout the final preparation of this edition. We have enjoyed his company and benefited greatly from his wise advice.

Finally our thanks to those who have hosted our meetings and to BCS staff who have copied and distributed material for us.

Part A:
How Computer Systems Are Used

A1	Data Processing	2
A2	Word Processing	8
A3	Spreadsheets	13
A4	Communications	18
A5	Databases and Information Retrieval	24
A6	Graphics and Design	28
A7	Modelling and Simulation	33
A8	Virtual Reality	36
A9	Control	38
A10	Numerical and Scientific Computing	42
A11	Sound	49
A12	Hypermedia Systems	60
A13	Computer Assisted Learning and Training	62
A14	Artificial Intelligence and Expert Systems	66
A15	User Interface	70
A16	User Documentation	86
A17	Computer Personnel	90
A18	Law and Administration	94

This section contains terms which may be met by any computer user working with applications in any of the areas covered. Some sections in Part A are concerned with general issues and others with well defined areas of computer use. Some sections contain terms which might have been placed in Part B or even in Part C, but they were kept with other related terms for completeness; this is particularly true of the sections covering sound and user interfaces, which have become more prominent aspects of computer use since the previous edition was published. Some terms have references to terms in Part B or Part C which will provide readers with pointers to other associated terms and concepts.

A1 Data Processing (DP)

Other concepts related to the design and implementation of systems to carry out commercial data processing are found in several later sections, especially C1 Systems Design and Life-cycle, C2 Systems Documentation and C3 Management and Manipulation of Data.

Data Processing in its broadest – and technically correct – sense covers every task which a computer carries out. Traditionally its meaning has been restricted to those particular computing applications and activities concerned with business and commerce.

The term has tended not to be used when describing the processing of scientific data where complex mathematical calculations are performed. In many business applications, relatively straight-forward tasks are carried out on relatively small amounts of data for each transaction but repeated routinely for each of a very large number of individual records in the same run. Typical of such application areas are accounting, payroll, record keeping, route planning, stock control. Nevertheless, with business operations becoming more complex – particularly where large scale modelling is involved – the dividing line between business and scientific processing is not so clear-cut as it previously appeared. In addition to its meaning as an operation, 'data processing' is also used as the title of the section of an organisation which carries out this area of work.

The user organisations typically associated with these traditional data processing applications are banks, government departments and a whole range of businesses. For any particular application type (for example, payroll), there is often a standard type of package, although there may be many variations of it available. Also, although all users will need to use a particular type of package to do the same job, they may require a specific version because they have different hardware or operating systems or because they need to use the package in association with another application area.

Associated with this area of computing are particular programming languages (COBOL is a prime example) and techniques (for example, database management).

Within most commercial organisations there will be a Data Processing Manager and a small team of support staff who will have overall responsibility for seeing that the system provides a satisfactory service to the users (individuals or departments). However, the individual departmental users are responsible for defining those data processing tasks which the system is required to carry out for them, while the maintenance of all the system – hardware and software – is likely to be done on contract by outside people.

Article number
including: ISBN, UPC, EAN
is the number given to a particular product (e.g. the **International Standard Book Numbers (ISBN)** found on a book). This is often printed together with its bar-code representation, so that it can be read both by people and automatically by a *wand* (see page 106) or some other *point-of-sale terminal* device (see page 150). The numbers are usually structured, and there are international agreements on how the numbers should be constructed for various types of goods. Two common forms of numbering system are the **Universal Product Code (UPC)** and the **European Article Number (EAN)**.

Audit trail
is a record of the file updating that takes place during a specific transaction. It enables a trace to be kept of all operations on files.

Bar code
is a pattern of parallel black-and-white lines used to represent a code number, which can then be read automatically. It is often used by shops to identify a product at the cash-desk so that its price can be found automatically from a computer, as an alternative to a cash-till operator entering the price directly through a keypad.

Computer Bureau
is an organisation which offers a range of computing services for hire (for example, data preparation, payroll processing). Bureaux usually offer two types of service: they provide computing facilities for organisations which do not have any of their own and they also offer specialist services covering vital common operations (for example, payroll) to organisations which do not have the appropriate piece of applications software.

Control total
is the sum resulting from the addition of a specified field from each of a group of records, for example adding tax deductions in a payroll program.It is used for checking data.

Data capture

is the action of collecting data for use in a particular computer process. This may be done automatically, as in the continuous monitoring of temperature in a chemical process, or manually as in gas meter reading. See also *data capture* in A9 Control, page 39.

Data preparation

is the translation of data into machine-readable form.

Direct Data Entry (DDE)

is the input of data for batch processing using a key-to-disk unit. The data may be validated while held in a temporary file before being written to the disk for subsequent processing.

Encryption

is the technique of encoding data to make it meaningless to those who do not know how to decode it. See also *encryption* in A18 Computer Law and Administration, page 96.

File

in data processing. is an organised collection of related records, see also *file*, page 185.

Grandfather, father, son files

are the three most recent versions of a file that is periodically updated. They are retained for security purposes.

Information

is the meaning given to structured data by the context in which it is interpreted.

Information processing

is the organisation, manipulation and distribution of information. As these activities are central to almost every use of computers, the term is in common use to mean almost the same as 'computing'.

Information technology (IT)

is the application of appropriate (enabling) technologies to information processing. The current interest centres on computing, telecommunications and digital electronics.

Kimball tag

is a small punched card attached to merchandise, which is detached when goods are sold, to provide machine-readable sales data.

Master file

is a file of data which is a principal source of information for a job. It can be updated or amended as necessary. In a batch processing system a *transaction file* (see below) is used to update the master file. See also *master file* in C3 Management and Manipulation of Data, page 185.

Transaction file

also known as: update file, changes file
is a collection of records used in batch processing to update a master file. See also *master file* (above) and in C3 Management and Manipulation of Data, page 185.

Turnaround document

is a document that, after being output by the computer, can be used to record additional data. All the data from that completed document can then in turn be input to the computer.

Validation

including: data vetting
is the checking, by the computer, of data at the input stage to detect any data that is incomplete or unreasonable. Methods used include *control totals* (see above), *check digits*, *hash totals*, *range checks* (see below) and *data types* (see page 265). It is also known as *data vetting*.

Data verification

including: verifier
is the act of checking transferred data – usually at the stage of input to a computer – by comparing copies of the data before and after transfer (for example, repeating the keyboard operations to check that the data has been correctly transferred in a key-to-disk system). Where a separate device performs this task, it is called a *verifier*.

Management Information Systems (MIS)

are designed to provide small amounts of management-level information – such as summaries of the larger amounts of data which individual user departments might require. This type of information may typically be used by managers as an aid to monitoring budgets or assessing sales targets.

Decision Support Systems (DSS)

are refined *management information systems* (see above) where the emphasis is on providing senior management with key information for strategic decision making. Such systems use sophisticated analysis techniques and may include *expert systems* (see page 68).

Archive file

is a file containing data that is no longer in current use but which must be kept in long-term storage as it may be required at some future date, for example certain accounts information required for audit purposes. For security reasons, archive files are usually kept away from the computer system to which they belong.

Backup file

is a copy of a file, to be available in the event of the original file being corrupted or lost.

Check digit

is an extra digit, or other character, derived from the original digits (usually by summing these in a number base which is different to that of the actual number). It is then attached to the original number as a means of later checking its validity.

Hash total

including: check sum

is a control total, which has no external meaning, for example in a payroll program the sum of the employee numbers. Also known as a *check sum*.

Hashing

is the process of generating a number, usually by some calculation on the values in a field, record or area of store regardless of their meaning. This number could then be used as a *hash total* (see above), as a position in a table, a position on a disk, etc.

Range check

is a validation method where the data is rejected if its value is outside specified limits.

Reference file

is a special type of master file which during normal use is read-only and is used to contain data which does not normally change. A special program would be used when the data needs altering. An example is the 'price file' in a supermarket point-of-sale system: the computer finds out the cost of each item sold during the day, but the file is only updated when prices change perhaps once a day or once a week.

A2   *Word Processing (WP)*

For details of printing and display devices used in word and document processing applications, see sections B4 Display Devices and B5 Printing Devices.

Word Processing is the application of computing to the editing, formatting and production of typed letters and documents, including the addition of stored text (for example, for personalised circulars). A system dedicated to this application is often referred to as a **word processor**. An alternative to a word processor when only very limited formatting is needed is a text editor.

Document Processing is an extension of the formatting functions which have been common to word-processing packages for some years, in order to allow the integration of non-textual characters into the layout. Associated with this extension has been the use of bit-mapping or pixel mapping to take advantage of the ability of extremely high definition monitors and of laser-printer techniques to produce fine lines, graduated density and (where necessary) apparently continuous spectrum colour.

Typical document production will include diagrams, graphic characters, numeric, picture representation and symbols as well as text. The software associated with Document Processing needs to be able to manipulate areas of the document as if it were a single entity – analogous to alphanumeric character manipulation in text processing.

A general requirement of computers which run document processing systems is an abundance of memory and a fast processor.

Cut & paste
including: clipboard, notepad
is the technique of transferring a section of data (text in a word processor, or diagrams and text in a page make-up package) from one part of a document to another part of the same document, or to another document. In some systems the data is held in a temporary storage area called the *clipboard* or *notepad*. Data held in these storage areas will normally remain there until overwritten by new data, so allowing one exact copy of the original to be pasted in more than one place.

Dictionary

is the list of allowable words which can be used in a particular application. Although most applications contain a standard dictionary, sometimes there is a facility to allow an individual user to create a separate personal dictionary which is then referred to if a particular word entered by that user is not found in the standard dictionary.

Desk-top presentation

is the use of graphics, charting and page make-up software, together with high-quality output devices, to produce sophisticated information displays. These will normally be seen on screen or printed out onto paper. However, using specialised devices, the information can also be output directly to overhead projector foil, onto photographic film to provide high-quality slides or even projected directly onto a cinema-style screen, for use in lectures and demonstrations.

Desk-Top Publishing (DTP)

is the use of a *page make-up system* (see below) and high-quality output devices to produce material which can be used directly as the first stage in the production process for printed leaflets, manuals, books, magazines, reports, etc.

Export

including: import

is to create a file using one piece of software so that it can be read by a different piece of software. *Import* is the corresponding read process to accept a file produced by some other software. Often there is a specific version of a particular package whose file and data formats are chosen by its manufacturer to be the standard version for exporting from and importing into that package.

Using these formats reduces the problems of data transfer between different software applications.

Hard space

including: soft space

is intended space that the user has explicitly typed (such as the space between two adjacent words). *Soft space* is inserted by software to even out the look of a line in order to create justified text. Because the user may later alter the formatting of the text, these 'extra' spaces must be remembered by the software, so that they can be removed where necessary. Reformatting justified text does not remove hard spaces.

Justification

including: left justification, right justification, full justification, centring
is the arrangement of characters so that they align with margins. This may
occur on the screen or on a printer, or may be required when setting out data in
columns or as forms.

```
Left justification is the normal method of aligning
continuous text, with an even left-hand margin. This
often leaves an uneven right-hand margin since each
printed line is likely to contain characters, (for
example words, spaces and punctuation marks) which
occupy different lengths of line.

 Right justification is normal for columns of numbers,
  although it is sometimes seen in text. Here, an even
 right-hand margin is created. This may well result in
 a ragged left-hand margin, since each printed line is
     likely to contain characters (for words, spaces and
   punctuation) which occupy different lengths of line.

Full justification (sometimes simply referred to as
justification) has even margins at both left-hand and
right-hand ends of the line. It is created by the
(automatic) insertion of extra spaces (soft spaces)
between  words  once  a  line  of  approximately  the
correct length has been entered.
                     Centring,
          which is often used for headings
                        and
              similar displays,
     places the characters symmetrically between the
                      margins.
```

Figure A2.1: Different justification styles

Line break

is the place where a line of printed text ends. Word processors normally break
lines only between words or, if sufficiently sophisticated, by inserting hyphens
at appropriate places.

Mailmerge

is the process of combining a document (often a letter), and a data file (often a
list of names and addresses), in such a way that copies of the document for
different people are suitably different. In its simplest form, this is merely
ensuring that letters have the correct style and title for the addressee and that

the address is inserted into the appropriate place. More complex uses can include inserting whole paragraphs into standard letters or documents. The process remains the same for all applications; a document is set up which has marked places within it at which data from other files is inserted.

Micro-spacing

is a feature available on some printers to print fully justified text by inserting small amounts of *soft space* (see above) in order to spread the total amount of added space evenly across a line. This ability is particularly necessary when proportional fonts (where characters occupy different widths of printed space) are being used and fully justified text is still required.

Non-breaking space

including: pad character

is the type of space (such as that in "Henry IV") which occurs between words that should not appear on separate lines. Many word processors allow the user to type a special combination of keys to insert such a character, sometimes called a *pad character*, which will print as a space, but will not be allowed as a line break.

Overtype

sometimes: overwrite

is to replace text on a screen with other text entered from the keyboard (or possibly read from a file) during the process of entering or editing a document.

Page make-up system

allows on-screen combination of graphics and text. The software allows easy manipulation of the layout to produce a professional-looking result that can be reproduced for leaflets, manuals, magazines, etc.

Spelling checker

is a program which is normally used with a word processor or desk-top publishing system to check the spelling in a document. Each word in the document is checked against the *dictionary* (see above). If it does not appear in the dictionary then the user is told this. The word may be correct (but not in the dictionary) or it may be wrongly spelt. Some programs even check the spelling as the document is typed in.

TeX

including: Latex, Metafont

is a specialised text processing system devised by the American mathematician and computer scientist Donald Knuth. It allows much greater control over the display of mathematical and scientific formulas than conventional word processors and is often used by academic authors submitting technical manuscripts to journal or book publishers. The power of TeX makes it a difficult language for beginners, and a number of alternative user interfaces, such as *Latex*, have been designed – this offers the facilities for the production of a number of common types of scientific document without the user needing to write pure TeX. As well as the text-processing features of these languages, there is an associated type-face definition system called *Metafont*.

Text editor

is a program for creating and amending text. It is designed to be used for preparing the source text of programs and for editing text files. It can have similar editing functions to a word processor but requires a more formal approach than is usual in word processing if formatting is to be retained.

Thesaurus

is a dictionary arranged by meaning instead of spelling. A computer-based thesaurus used in conjunction with a word processor allows a user to select a word in the text, and to be offered a range of words with similar or related meanings. Using one of these instead of the original word can enhance the writer's prose style.

Word wrap

is a facility available in many word processing packages which breaks lines automatically between words. When the text being typed on the line reaches beyond the right-hand margin, the whole of the last word is transferred to the beginning of the next line.

WYSIWYG (What You See Is What You Get)

(pronounced 'wizzy-wig') refers to a screen display which matches the eventual printed output in layout, highlighting and underlining, font, etc. Such displays are particularly helpful in applications such as *desk-top publishing* (see above) and *spreadsheets* (see A3, page 13).

A3   *Spreadsheets*

Spreadsheets are an important and powerful use of the computer. A spreadsheet is based on the idea of the computer looking like a large sheet of squared paper with the added advantage of being able to do arithmetic.

Figure A3.1: A spreadsheet

The squares are usually called cells (sometimes slots) and each is identified by its column label (often a letter or letters) and its row label (often a number). In the example the cell with hello in it has address F5, where F is the column label and 5 is the row label. The contents of a cell may be one of several types:

- a heading or message
  this is just plain text - i.e. a collection of characters.
- a number
  it is important to realise that there is a difference between a number as text and a number that is required for calculation – most spreadsheets allow for the conversion between a number as text and a number in a form suitable for calculation.
- a formula that represents a calculation;
  in this case what is seen in the cell is the result of the calculation rather than the formula itself. An example of a formula may be one that adds the contents of two cells together and multiplies the result by 3:

  3*(A21 + B21)

  (If A21 contains the number 5 and B21 contains the number 6 then the cell containing the formula above will display the number 33. It still contains the formula after the calculation has been done, so that if the contents of A21 or B21 change then a new calculated value will be displayed.)

- an instruction

  an example would be an instruction that takes the contents of a cell (a number) and uses it as a product code. The instruction then causes a table of product codes, prices and descriptions elsewhere in the table (or even possibly a different spreadsheet) to be searched and when the correct product code is found the description is inserted in the current cell which contains the instruction. In another cell would be an instruction to do the same but to insert the price.

Figure A3.2 is an example of a spreadsheet showing how many French francs one would get for different amounts of English money.

	A	B	C	D
1	Exchange Rate			
2	11.50	Pounds	Francs	
3		0	0.00	
4		5	57.50	
5		10	115.00	
6				

NOTE:
Cells C3, C4 and C5 each contain a formula:
in C3 it is B3*A2
in C4 it is B4*A2
in C5 it is B5*A2

Figure A3.2: *A spreadsheet for currency conversion*

In this spreadsheet you can see numbers (for example, in cell B4), labels or headings (for example, in cell C2), and the result of applying a formula (as in cell C4). However, a spreadsheet need not be used for just doing the original calculation, it will also respond to changes in the data. It is this ability to respond to *'what if'* questions that makes a spreadsheet such a powerful business tool.

What if the rate of exchange altered? You can cope with this by simply re-typing the exchange rate in cell A2 and the freshly converted amounts of francs would appear in column C.

What if the amount of pounds that you wanted to exchange was not in the table?

Type the amount in place of the zero amount in cell B3 and the converted amount will appear in cell C3.

In the above example the formulae used in column C are all very similar, but not quite identical; they all use A2 but this is multiplied by the appropriate entry in column B. On most spreadsheets there is no need to type each formula in individually: by replication you can repeat them automatically and make the system keep the reference to A2 every time but alter the reference to column B. Many spreadsheets also have a facility to take a set of figures and convert them into some type of graph (such as a pie chart, a line graph, or a bar chart).

The printing out of a spreadsheet can pose problems. Some software will just print out everything that is being used. However, most allow the user to indicate the cells that are to be printed out; many allow the cells to be printed out in a different order from their 'natural' one so that parts of the sheet that are separated by a lot of rows/columns can be printed close together. Some spreadsheets even allow the sheet to be printed sideways to allow for a wide sheet to be printed. A further complication in printing is what should be printed out for some of the cells - should it be a formula or the result of the formula? Again, many spreadsheets allow the user to choose.

The use of spreadsheets has been extended beyond just numbers. Imagine a list of names and addresses; each one might consist of (say) four entries: (a) the name, (b) the house number, (c) the road and (d) the town. Each entry could be put into a different column and each row hold a different name and address, as in Figure A3.3.

	A	B	C	D	E
1	Name	No.	Road	Town	
2	Mr Smith	1	Acacia Avenue	Birmingham	
3	Mrs Jones	2	High Street	Luton	
4	Ms Black	77	Sunset Road	Liverpool	
5	Miss World	12	Hillside	Leicester	
6					
7					

Figure A3.3: *A spreadsheet used as a database*

So you can use a spreadsheet as a simple database. Further to this, some spreadsheets can be used as word processors (in fact the draft of this text was prepared on such a spreadsheet). Usually this means that the text is set out in one column of the spreadsheet, but the other columns can be used as well. This becomes even more powerful when you wish to include some calculations in your text as there are no calculations for the user to do since the spreadsheet will do them all!

Cell

also known as: slot

including: address, column, row, block

is the 'square' on a spreadsheet in which only a single entry can be placed, sometimes called a *slot*. The single entry can be either a number, a group of words or a formula. It can be referred to by its *address* in the spreadsheet using the *column* and *row* labels. The column label refers to a vertical group of cells and the row label refers to a horizontal group of cells (see Figure A3.3). If we have a rectangular grouping of the cells this is termed a *block*. Usually the block is identified by giving the addresses of the upper left cell and the lower right cell of the rectangle, for example A3F12 would have 6 columns (A to F) of 10 rows (3 to 12).

Formula

is the way a calculation is represented in a spreadsheet. As well as numbers a formula uses the address of cells to identify other values to be used - the result is then displayed in the cell in which the formula was placed. If any of the cells referenced in the formula change in value then the result of the formula is changed to reflect the altered values.

For example, if the first side of a rectangle is in B3 and you wished to find the second side of the rectangle (in C3, say) whose sides always add up to (say) 12, the formula in C3 might be:

$$(12 - 2*B3)/2$$

Function

is a special type of formula used in a spreadsheet. It has usually been set up to represent a formula that may be too complex or too long to expect an ordinary user to enter, or it may be just very useful. Examples of this might be:

SUM()   a function to calculate the sum (i.e. the total) of a row or a column or a block of cells.

MEAN()   a function to calculate the average (mean) of a row or a column or a block of cells.

FIND()   a function to find where, in an area of the spreadsheet, a particular value is to be found.

Recalculation

is the term used to describe the process whereby the spreadsheet recalculates the values that may have altered because of the last input of data. The process of recalculation can be automatic - done after each and every entry in the spreadsheet - or it can be manual, whereby the user decides when it should be done and presses a particular set of keys to have the recalculation done. The advantage of having it set to manual is that the entry of data is quicker as the user does not have to wait for the updating (which can take an appreciable amount of time if the spreadsheet is large); the disadvantage is that the user has always to indicate when the recalculation should be done. It is sometimes important to know the order of the recalculation - whether it is by row (i.e. the first row, then the second and so on) or by column (i.e. the first column, then the second and so on). With many spreadsheets it is possible to alter the order of calculation.

Replication

including: absolute reference, relative reference

is the process of copying a formula from one cell to another. As a formula usually involves references to cells this means you should be aware of whether you want to keep the exact same reference to the cell (this is termed an *absolute reference*) or whether you want the reference to adjust itself according to either the row or column movement (this is termed a *relative reference*). An example of this is when you have a formula in cell A12 that calculates (say) the sum of a row of figures – something like SUM(A1...A10) – and this is then replicated into cell B12. Generally you will want the result to represent the sum for row B; if you tell it that A1 and A10 are relative then this will happen.

Spreadsheet

is an applications package usually used to display financial or statistical information. It takes its name from the way data is arranged on the screen in rows and columns, as in the traditional layout of figures in account books. The user can specify that numbers displayed in particular positions are to be dependent on entries in other positions, and are to be recalculated automatically when these entries are changed. Hence the effects of changes to one data item on, for example, totals, sub-totals, 'profits' and 'VAT' can be explored.

A4 Communications

Other related terms may be found in sections B6 Networks,
B7 Communications Devices and Control Devices and
C17 Communications Technology.

The internal architecture of a computer involves electronic signals being passed from component to component. It is a natural extension of this idea to send signals *out* of the computer, to another computer, perhaps thousands of kilometres away. The technology to achieve this is discussed in section C17. On an electronic scale, the distance of a few metres to your printer is so large that it raises a new set of problems (is the printer actually switched on? – what does the computer do if it isn't?): these problems are surprisingly not made *much* more severe if the printer is across the other side of the Atlantic. So it seems quite natural for a number of computer applications to have been developed that involve communication and information-provision over large distances.

Many of the applications have become so much a part of modern industrialised societies that it takes us aback to realise that they involve computing technology – taking cash from a cash dispenser in the middle of the night in a strange town, sending a fax, reading the sports results on Teletext, and so on.

Bulletin board
including: system operator (sysop), Campus 2000
is the electronic equivalent of a notice-board, carrying short items that may be of interest to a wide number of people. Bulletin boards are sited on a computer, and the users access the computer by a *network* (see page 144) or *electronic mail* (see below). They can leave messages for anyone to read, review messages left by other users and sometimes take copies of software that has been placed on the board. The organiser of such a board is traditionally known as the *system operator* or more familiarly as the *sysop*. Larger bulletin boards are run by organisations such as newspapers, computer manufacturers or universities, and offer comprehensive information services as well as an opportunity to read or post messages. A popular large board accessed by many schools because of its educational focus is *Campus 2000*.

Figure A4.1: A typical bulletin board screen

Cellular phone

is a portable radio-telephone that can be used while moving around (for example, in a car). The country is divided into overlapping cells, each a few miles in diameter and centred on a low-powered transmitter/receiver. When a call is made, it is handled by the nearest transmitter, but automatically switched to an adjacent cell (without a break in the call) if the handset moves out of range.

Computer conferencing

makes use of *electronic mail* (see below) to allow a group of people with a common interest, but geographically separated, to share advice, opinions, information and so on. The users are organised in a 'conference' and are able to examine messages left by other users, add their own comments, and generally participate in the work of the group. This is very similar to the idea of a *bulletin board* (see above), but there is a suggestion in a computer conference that users are all on an equal footing, and are all expected to contribute equally.

Computer-Supported Co-operative Work (CSCW)

including: work group

It is too early to tell whether this unwieldy description will find a permanent place in computer terminology: it describes the use of networked computer systems to enable **work groups** of employees to share documents, diaries and other computer files.

Closed User Group (CUG)

Not all information services on a *Viewdata* system (see below) are available to all subscribers. Commercial businesses, for example, may choose to provide information only to registered dealers or sales representatives: such a group is known as a 'closed' user group.

Electronic Funds Transfer (EFT)

including: debit card, EFTPOS, cash dispenser, automatic teller machine (ATM)

is the use of computer networks to transfer money. This may be done between banks, as an alternative to sending a cheque or a bankers' draft, especially where international transfers are involved. Most large companies now pay their employees by electronic transfer of funds into their personal bank accounts. Increasingly, it is being used in retail stores as an alternative to payment by credit card or cheque: the purchaser offers a *debit card* which is processed in the same way as a credit card, but which initiates the transfer of money from the purchaser's account directly to the shop's account. In this use, it is normally known by the cumbersome title of *Electronic Funds Transfer at Point-of-Sale* (*EFTPOS*). The same principles are involved in a cash withdrawal from a *cash dispenser* or *automatic teller machine (ATM)*.

Electronic mail ('E-mail')

including: mailbox, JANET, Internet

is the sending of messages from user to user on a computer network. The message is stored in the recipient's *mailbox* until the next time that they use the computer, when they will be told that there is a message waiting, and can inspect it, print it out or reply. Because it is relatively cheap, and because the sender and the recipient do not both have to be using their computers at the same time, it is a popular way for schools and colleges to communicate with colleagues in other countries. There is an encouraging amount of international co-operation between the larger networks, which allows messages to be sent internationally through *gateways* (see page 152) between networks. The *Internet* is one such super-network. The principal academic network used for E-mail between British Universities and colleges is *JANET (Joint Academic Network)*. Figure A4.2 shows how E-mail messages are passed, by describing the routing information that accompanies a typical message.

```
Date: Tue, 12 May 92 16:06:31
To: j_jaworski@open.ac.uk
From: linda_hof@ca.sfu
Subject: politics
```

Tuesday afternoon, 4.06pm Pacific Standard Time – Linda Hof sends a message about 'politics' from her terminal in Simon Fraser University in Canada ('ca.sfu') to John Jaworski in England: his E-mail address 'open.ac.uk' will allow the message to be routed to the UK, to the 'academic community', and finally to the Open University.

```
Received: from mpx8529.educ.sfu.ca by whistler.sfu.ca (5.65/SFU-2.0)
        id AA05341;
  Tue, 12 May 92 16:06:31
```

Linda is using the mpx8529 system in the education faculty. The message first goes to the main university computer, called 'whistler'; an identification number is attached to it.

```
Message-Id: <9205122306.AA05341@whistler.sfu.ca>
```

The Simon Fraser University computer adds some more identification to the message, so it can be traced back if it fails to be delivered correctly. This computer connects directly to the Internet which links it to the UK. The message is sent, split into small packets of data, and reassembled in the UK.

```
Received: from [128.189.32.1] by vax.NSFnet-Relay.AC.UK via NSFnet with SMTP
  id aa06724; 13 May 92 0:04 BST
```

Just after midnight, British Summer Time (about two minutes before it left, which means that somebody's clock was set badly!) the message arrives in the UK. [128.189.32.1] is the Internet identification of the Simon Fraser Computer on the network. The NSFnet-relay computer is the 'gateway' to the Internet for the UK

```
Received: from vax.nsfnet-relay.ac.uk by sun.nsfnet-relay.ac.uk
  with Internet SMTP id <sg.28177-3@sun.nsfnet-relay.ac.uk>;
  Wed, 13 May 1992 00:12:48 +0100
```

It is transferred from the gateway computer to a local Sun machine that will distribute the message in the UK – this takes about 8 minutes!

```
Via: UK.AC.NSFNET-RELAY; Wed, 13 May 92 0:15 GMT
```

And finally, about half an hour later, it arrives at the Open University computer; it will be in John Jaworski's mailbox when he next logs in.

```
From:   CBS%UK.AC.NSFNET-RELAY::CA.SFU::LINDA_HOF 13-MAY-1992
        00:15:13.24
To:     j_jaworski
CC:
Subj:   politics
```

Figure A4.2: The life story of an E-mail message

Facsimile transmission (Fax)

including: junk fax, fax groups

is the use of regular voice-quality telephone lines to send copies of documents, which may include drawings as well as text. The sender inserts the document into their own fax machine, and dials the receiving machine, which must be available at that time, and not busy sending or receiving another fax. The two fax machines need to be compatible. In order to simplify the process of identifying compatibility, fax machines are classified into *groups* with different technical specifications. The two machines need to belong to compatible groups.

The sending machine scans the paper on a line-by-line basis, and transmits the information to the receiving machine, which recreates the document using photocopier technology (for this reason, many fax machines can also operate as photocopiers). Many computers that can be connected to the telephone lines can send faxes directly, without the need to generate a paper copy first: this simplifies the problem of finding the receiving machine busy, as the computer can simply try again later, without human intervention – unfortunately, this also allows unscrupulous advertisers to fax large quantities of *junk fax* mail to unsuspecting recipients.

Minitel

The French telecommunications agency has replaced printed telephone books by an on-line computerised directory enquiries service, called 'Minitel'. Simple terminals with screens are widely available in public places, and personal equipment may be bought or rented. As well as telephone information, a wide variety of commercial and public information is available and theatre and travel tickets can be purchased, as well as more conventional ordering of goods. This is essentially a public *bulletin board* (see above).

Telecommunications

a general term describing the communication of information over a distance. The method of communication is normally via a *cable* (see *wire connector*, page 156) or electro-magnetic radiation. See also *wireless communication*, page 157.

Tele-commuting

is the use of information technology to allow people to work in their own homes, while still being in easy contact with the office. Typically, this involves use of *electronic mail* and *fax* (see above), as well as allowing remote users access to a central computer or network.

Tele-conferencing

including: video-conferencing

is the use of communication links to conduct meetings between people who are geographically separated. The links might be voice-only, or might include pictures, when it is usually referred to as *video-conferencing*.

Videotex

is the overall name given to systems that supply information on television screens. See *Teletext* and *Viewdata*, below, for fuller descriptions.

Teletext

including: Ceefax, Oracle

is a system that uses part of the broadcast television picture unseen to the regular viewer, to supply a variety of information, such as news stories, weather forecasts, train cancellations and so on. With a specially equipped TV set, the viewer can press buttons on a remote control handset to replace the TV picture by simple text pages. Each page is numbered, and all the pages are transmitted in sequence. A particular choice of page is requested by entering the number, after which there is a slight delay until that page is next transmitted; this waiting time limits the number of pages that realistically can be provided. Some pages are linked, and allow the viewer to pass from one page to another more rapidly. All TV channels in the UK offer this service; the BBC version is known as *Ceefax*. The commercial channels were originally known as *Oracle* until the name 'Teletext' was adopted as a brand name. Because the viewer cannot talk back to the provider of the pages of information, this is only a one-way information service. See also *Prestel*, below.

Viewdata

including: Prestel

is the general name given to a *Teletext*-like system (see above) which displays 'pages' of textual information on a television screen, but uses regular phone lines, rather than a broadcast television signal, to transmit information. It is then possible for the user to interact with the system, supplying information, requesting searches of the data, or even ordering goods and services by supplying credit-card information. Because pages are only transmitted after a specific request, very large collections of data can be offered, without penalty to other users. The best-known such system is the UK *Prestel* viewdata system.

A5   *Databases and Information Retrieval*

Although a computer can store enormous amounts of data, this data is useless without appropriate links between individual data items – imagine, for example, what a (printed) telephone directory would be like if it was simply two separate listings of telephone subscribers and their numbers, without the connection that is made by the printed layout between a particular subscriber and their own telephone number! The data is also useless if it cannot be easily retrieved when required — imagine the telephone directory in random rather than alphabetic order!

So too with computerised collections of data. These are generally referred to as **databases** and can vary between a simple name-and-address listing and a massive collection of structured data that provides information to a large business. It is easy to be deceived when one is experimenting with techniques for accessing databases: if a demonstration database can be constructed with tens (rather than millions) of entries, many of the techniques can seem unnecessarily long-winded – if you were certain that your data would never extend to more than 100 entries, it would be sensible to store it in a simple table, as part of your program; when it grew, despite your plans, to 1,000,000 entries no table would be capable of holding it, and it would be necessary to use a disk, and your program would need to use sophisticated methods of disk management.

Because of the need to access this large collection of data in an efficient manner, random access storage devices, such as disks, are essential for a database system.

Large databases usually have many potential users, and so operating system problems of allowing simultaneous use of the same data files arise – the solution to these problems are usually embedded in a complex piece of software, known as the **database management system (DBMS)**.

Not all users will be experienced with computers – often it will be necessary to provide simple **query languages** that allow questions to be asked in something close to English.

Database
sometimes, but infrequently, two words: data base
is a (large) collection of data items and links between them, structured in a way that allows it to be accessed by a number of different applications programs or *query languages* (see below). The term is also used loosely to describe any collection of data.

Data model

including: entity, attribute, entity-relationship diagram, relation
The designers of a large database will normally construct a diagram of the
planned database, known as a data model. This will show the things
represented in the database (the *entities*) and the information held about them
(the *attributes*). For this reason, a data model is sometimes known as an
entity-relationship diagram. The *relations* between entities will be marked,
and from this model, the most efficient arrangement of the data will be worked
out. Figure A5.1 explains a small portion of a data model. See also the *entity-
relationship diagram*, Figure C2.1, page 172 .

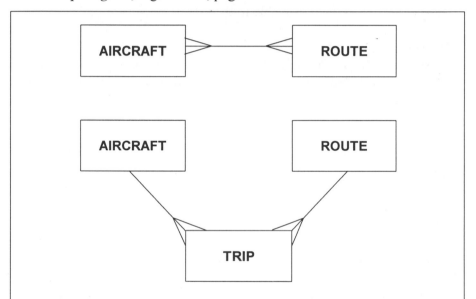

In the top diagram, two entities, **aircraft** and **route** are identified.
Attributes are not shown, but might include the plane number, its type,
passenger capacity and so on, for the aircraft, and the starting point and
destination for the route. There is a relation between these entities: an
aircraft can be used on many routes, and a route can be travelled by
many aircraft. Such 'many-many' relations are not easy to implement in a
database, so the designer breaks this relation, invents a new entity called
trip which represents one specific journey over that route by one specific
aircraft. One aircraft now makes many trips, but each trip is only made
by one aircraft. Similarly, one route has many trips over it, but each trip is
over just one route. Two such one-many relations are more efficient to
implement.

Figure A5.1: How a data model helps in designing a database

Database Management System (DBMS)
is the complete collection of software that manages access to, and updating of, a database.

Data dictionary
sometimes known as: data directory
is a file containing descriptions, and other 'bookkeeping' information about the data held in a database. It is not usually accessible to users

Distributed database
is one where several computers on a network each share part of the data and co-operate in making it available to the user.

Flat file
is a database held in a single file – this allows only a very simple structuring of the data, which can only be considered to be on a single level (hence 'flat').

Hierarchical database
is one where the data is held in a *tree* structure (see page 260) and can be thought of by users as existing on any one of a number of levels.

Information retrieval
or: data retrieval
is the process of extracting meaningful information from stored data; usually the term is used where the collection of stored data is large, typically a database.

Normal form
is a way of structuring the data in a database according to theoretical rules, in order to avoid problems of inefficiency in accessing and maintaining the data.

Query language
Database users without computer expertise might be offered the facility to interrogate the database through a query language. For a fuller description see *query language*, in C10 Programming Languages, page 253.

Relational database

including: table, view

is one where the data is structured as a series of *tables* and the (relational) database management system provides tools for joining tables together and selecting items from within tables. In this way, each user can be given a different *view* of the data. Relational databases are especially powerful, because the method of storing data in tables makes no assumptions about how the applications programs will access the data, and hence does not restrict the queries in any way.

Schema

including: data description language, subschema

Managing the large amounts of data of different types stored in a modern database requires that descriptions of the data items are held, as well as the data items themselves. This description is usually referred to as the *schema*. The description will be in a *data description language*. The *database management system* (see above) may re-format the data before presenting it to the user, and will make use of individual *subschemas* that describe how that particular user sees the data.

A6   *Graphics and Design*

Other related terms may be found in section B4 Display Devices

The display screen of most computer systems uses the same technology as television. Therefore, it is capable of displaying *pictures* as well as text – indeed, text is simply a rather specialised form of picture. Because of this technology, there are many computer applications that use computer power to generate graphics.

Sometimes, the graphics may be an end in themselves, with **painting** or **drawing** packages available to illustrators, to enable them to compose and edit high-quality images. Most computer games are now set in a graphical environment, with exciting animated graphics to underline the action.

Other packages use graphics as part of the design process for books and other printed matter – adding illustrations or decorative borders. In some cases, a photograph (or even 'live-action' video) can be 'retouched' electronically, to add, remove or re-colour some elements of the picture. Many TV graphics are nowadays generated purely electronically.

In other applications, the processing power of the computer is used for calculation, as well as for the pure drawing.

Figure A6.1: *Computer aided architectural design*

Computer aided design packages are used in fields as diverse as architecture and electronics: a builder may design a building on the computer, and call up an itemised list of all the materials to be used in the construction – the length of pipes, cables, amount of masonry and so on. Or the designer of an electronic printed-circuit board may position the main components to his or her liking, and allow the computer to suggest how the connections should be made, to achieve an efficient design.

Clip art

While computer graphics packages allow the user to draw their own illustrations, many publishers offer computer disks full of professionally-drawn pictures that can be edited to suit an individual user's needs. These are popularly known as 'clip art' because of the way in which they are 'clipped' out of the file and 'pasted' into your own drawing.

Figure A6.2: *Clip art*

Computer Aided Design (CAD)

including: drafting

This is the use of a computer system to produce drawings or 'blueprints' as part of the design of some construction project; this might be the civil engineering design of a motorway, the layout of components on a printed circuit board, or the drafting of furniture positions in an office or a home — to give just three common examples. This computer aided ***design*** phase is also sometimes known as computer aided ***drafting***. Most modern CAD packages also use the design data as the basis for calculations — for example, of costs, mechanical stresses, quantities needed, etc. With the information available from the design stage, it is possible in many cases for the computer system to control the manufacturing process as well. See also *CAD/CAM*, page 39.

Computer animation

is the creation of apparent movement through the presentation of a sequence of slightly different still pictures. The screen display of a computer is re-drawn every 1/25th of a second, at least, whether it has changed or not, because of the television technology used in display devices. With a fast computer, it is possible to generate a new picture in this time, so that an impression of movement can be created, in the same way as a cinema film creates the illusion of movement from still pictures. Computer animation packages are now routinely used in the television and film industry, particularly where they can mix 'live action' with computer-generated images.

Computer graphics

is the use of the computer to display pictorial information. This can be as simple as a line drawing or chart, or as complicated as an animated sequence of pictures. The output might be shown on the computer screen, printed out as hard copy, or transferred directly to videotape.

Digitizer

also known as: scanner

Many graphics images begin life as drawings on paper and must be converted into a form that a computer graphics package can use. A digitizer scans a drawing and turns it into a *bit map* (see page 298); this captures the image, but for CAD packages it is necessary to have information about the precise position of important points and lines.

Graphics tablet

also known as: graphics pad
including: stylus, puck

is a device used to input line drawings into a computer. The user draws with a *stylus* on a flat pad or tablet (sometimes called a ***graphics pad***), either copying a drawing or working freehand.

Stylus is the name for devices used for drawing on a graphics tablet. The movement of the stylus is detected by the tablet and its software in one of a variety of ways, for example through the use of a wire matrix in the pad or by sensing the angular movement of an arm supporting the stylus. A stylus may be pressure sensitive, producing a darker or more intensely coloured line if pressed firmly.

Puck is a small disk-shaped device, which is moved around on the tablet (or pad) to trace a drawing.

The position of the stylus or puck on the tablet is input to the computer and used to position a cursor on the screen. Subsequent movement causes a drawing on the screen which matches the movements on the tablet. These devices are generally preferred to a mouse for computer drafting packages.

Drawing package

including: line art

Computer graphics packages with the word 'draw' in their titles tend to be of the sort known as *vector graphics* packages, where the instructions for drawing certain basic shapes, such as lines, rectangles, circles and so forth, are stored, rather than the picture itself. These basic shapes, or 'objects', can easily be moved around the drawing, or laid on top of other objects; because of the way they are constructed, they do not interfere with one another, and can be thought of as existing in separate 'layers'; text in drawings would be stored as shapes – each letter a separate object. Because most 'line art' of this sort tends to have only a few elements, there is a considerable advantage in that less storage is needed, as compared to a *painting package* (see below). Scaling the picture up or down in size would not alter the clarity of the drawing. See also *vector graphics,* page 129.

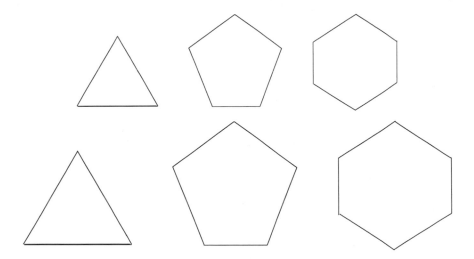

Figure A6.3: *Typical output from a drawing package, at two scalings*

Painting package

Computer graphics packages with the word 'paint' in their titles tend to be of the sort known as *raster graphics* packages, where a picture is held as a *bit map* (see page 298) – that is, the state of each individual *pixel* (see page 127) is stored. Text in such a picture would be stored as a bit map. Such drawings use a lot of storage space, because even 'blank' portions of the picture contribute to the size. They can also appear jagged when scaled up or down in size. However, for freehand drawings, and areas of tone, such packages are better than *drawing packages* (see above). See also *raster graphics,* page 128.

Figure A6.4: Typical output from a painting package

A7　Modelling and Simulation

Imagine having to design and build a new bypass to divert traffic round a town. Before starting on such a venture it would be wise to check on the cost and compare that with the advantages to be gained. Although it is quite possible to produce accurate costings, it is harder to work out how wide the bypass should be (should it be dual or single carriageway, for example) or what route it should take to reduce the traffic flow through the town. By the time the road is built the money will have been spent and the bypass may not be effective. When data on current traffic flow has been collected and likely future traffic requirements have been assessed a model can be produced. **Modelling** attempts to show what is happening now and the results of the intended alterations. The model produced is a mathematical description of the rate of traffic flow at all points of interest. The details of this model can be changed, for example by increasing the expected amount of traffic, to see whether this causes any problems. Once the model has been tested with these conditions it can then be judged how good the proposed changes would be. The bypass could then be built, with the likelihood that it would be worthwhile, or it could be abandoned, as not useful enough, having only had the cost of the exploration.

It is when you want to test and use a mathematical model that a computer would be used. The computer can quickly carry out the necessary calculations (many of which are repeated but quite simple) and show the results using tables of numbers or diagrams. **Simulation** is the running of the design.

Weather forecasting uses a computer simulation. Data is gathered from many sources at different times and from this the computer predicts what weather we are likely to expect in the near or far future. From experience we know that accuracy can vary from being very good to being dramatically wrong. The prediction can only be as good as the model. Economic forecasting is also performed in a similar way, but often lacks the accuracy of even a weather forecast.

Any model is limited by human understanding and the need for it to be sufficiently simple to allow results to be calculated in a reasonable time.

Computer simulations are also used in training. A flight simulator is used to prepare pilots to cope with anything from standard flying and landing, to dealing with emergencies without putting anyone's life at risk. A flight simulator can range from a simple screen display to a full-size mock-up of the flight cabin with movement effects.

In education, computer simulation can be used to show a process that would normally be impossible to demonstrate because it would be too dangerous, too expensive or would take too long. In a simulation dealing with a nuclear reactor station, alterations could be made that would not be allowed at a visit to such a station! Similarly, in the field of genetics, alterations could be simulated on a reasonable timescale rather than waiting months or years for even simple processes to be checked.

In silicon chip design, a simulation is used to show how the circuitry would behave. The design is adjusted until the required response is achieved. This saves the expense and time of producing, testing and having to change a series of prototypes. In these circumstances **emulation** software could be used to check computer behaviour for various programs before the new chip becomes available.

Model

A model is a sequence of ideas that attempt to represent a process realistically. At some stage these ideas are expressed mathematically as a set (or collection) of equations. The accuracy of this model is limited by the knowledge of the process being modelled, the time available to produce the model, the availability of input data and how quickly results are required.

Modelling

Modelling is representing a process. This is done by using a series of mathematical ideas that approximate to how the real process behaves. Ideally, this approximation should be very close to the actual process.

Simulation

Simulation is the use of a computer program to predict the likely behaviour of a real-life system. A mathematical model of the system is constructed and written in the form of a program that can be run.

Emulation

Emulation should be more than simulation. This should mimic exactly the behaviour of the circumstances that it is emulating. An emulator of computer B run on computer A could allow computer A to run further software in the same way as computer B. This is done so that major changes in machine design can use previous versions of software, to extend the range of software run on a computer or to check on the behaviour of a computer that has yet to be built. Unless an emulator is run on a much more powerful computer than the original, the emulation will tend to run at a slower rate than on the computer that is being emulated. See also *emulator* in C13 Systems Software, page 284.

A8   Virtual Reality

Virtual reality systems transport the user into an environment created by the computer. Computer-controlled graphics are used to generate realistic scenes with which the user can interact.

To provide realism and to prevent distraction from the immediate environment, the user may wear a headset. The headset incorporates earphones to play the appropriate soundtrack directly into the ears, while small video screens, in goggles covering the eyes, ensure that the only images seen are those generated by the computer.

When the head moves, the simulation changes the image in response to where the user is now 'looking'. This gives the illusion of moving through the scene. The use of the headset provides a powerful psychological effect, giving a strong feeling of realism. An alternative to using a headset is the use of wrap-around displays with stereo sound for group participation.

To increase further the feeling of experiencing the simulated environment, a *data glove* can be worn. This is an input device that enables the position of the fingers and the orientation of the hand to be sensed by the computer. It provides the opportunity for the user to point at or 'touch' objects, which will produce some response from the system.

Full virtual reality is a technology that is still in its infancy; it is very demanding in its requirements for resources. It needs high-quality three-dimensional graphics. The need for immediate and smooth change of scene requires fast processing. There are also enormous storage requirements. However by using CD-ROM and accepting lower standards of visual presentation on a screen, low-quality virtual reality can be produced to run on relatively modest computer systems; these products are being sold as virtual reality.

Data glove

is an input device worn on the hand of a user of a virtual reality system. Typically, it enables the position of the fingers and the orientation of the hand to be sensed by the system. In most systems, when the user 'touches' a simulated object, there is no physical sensation returned to the hand. Greater realism is possible in systems which do provide this kind of feedback.

Headset

is an input and output device, like a helmet, worn by a user of a virtual reality system. It gives the wearer the impression of being within the computer-generated scene, with sound provided through headphones and vision through small video screens in goggles worn over the eyes. The headset senses changes of position of the head and inputs this to the computer so that the simulation can be changed appropriately. Since the user is isolated from sounds and visions, other than those provided by the virtual reality system, there is a very strong sense of being within the simulated environment.

Virtual reality system

also known as: VR system

is a computer system that provides a simulated environment by three-dimensional graphical images and an appropriate soundtrack. It gives the user the impression of being within the environment. The graphical images are often of rather poor quality but these are expected to become more realistic as advances in the technology are made.

A9   Control

*Other terms related to the use of computers in controlling
processes and devices will be found in B7 Communications
Devices and Control Devices and C17 Communications
Technology.*

The use of computers to make machines do what we want them to - called
control - grew out of the extensive use of mechanical devices and electro-
magnetic switches (relays). In telephone exchanges, traffic lights and lifts,
control used to be achieved by the use of mechanically operated switching
systems. Other methods were designed to control the operation of machines,
made up of devices which reacted to conditions in the environment such as
temperature, pressure, speed, position. Large manufacturing plants were built
controlled by these methods.

The development of microprocessors and microcomputers made it
possible to improve the reliability of existing systems and to make them
more flexible. In a modern airliner the computer system is capable of
controlling take-off and landing as well as automatically maintaining course,
speed and altitude. The computers used in cars take over part of the control
of the car engine from the driver. The operation of washing machines and
video equipment is frequently managed by microprocessors.

Control may be exercised remotely, in which case control signals are sent
from the controller to the device. These signals may be transmitted in any of
the ways which are used to pass data for example through wires, or as radio
or infra-red signals.

Control systems may be either passive or re-active. In a **passive system**
the controlled device, once it has been set going, will perform a
predetermined set of activities regardless of the circumstances. A **re-active
system** will vary its behaviour in response to different situations. By using
programmable chips, connected to suitable sensors, it is now common for
systems to respond to the information provided by these sensors. Combining
control and observation, through the use of sensors, has made it possible to
extend the scope of automatic **process control**, for example in the
manufacture and packaging of chemical products.

Automation
is the use of machines or systems to perform tasks normally performed or
controlled by people.

CAD/CAM

including: computer assisted manufacturing (CAM)

is the use of the output from a computer aided design (CAD) process as input to control a **computer assisted manufacturing (CAM)** process. This can be an integrated process in which the manufacturing happens automatically and is important in the development of new products. See *computer aided design*, page 29.

Data capture

including: data logging, sampling

is the **sampling** (collection at specified intervals) of output from external sensors (see also *polling*, page 304). This data may be used to control a process. **Data logging** is the capture and storage of data for later use, thus data captured in a control process may be logged for later analysis of the process.

Feedback

including: closed loop feedback, open loop feedback

is the use of data from sensors as input to the controlling program. In this way the result of previous actions becomes input which contributes to selecting the next action. If the response to the feedback is automatic (there is no human operator involvement), the process is called **closed loop**; if an operator is involved, it is called **open loop**. In most situations where feedback is used to control position, for example stacking boxes on shelves, the correct position is achieved by an iterative process, in which a move is followed by a position check, each move bringing it closer to the required position, until the correct position is reached.

Fly by wire

is a method of controlling an aeroplane in flight. The flaps, rudder and other control surfaces of the aeroplane are operated by motors. These motors are controlled by (electrical) signals which are created as a result of actions by the pilot. This kind of flight control system involves the use of computers to analyse the pilot's intentions and thus work out the right amount of movement of the control surfaces; the computers can over-ride the pilot in situations which would endanger the aeroplane.

G-code

is a form of *intermediate code* (see page 252) which can be used by the control systems of machine tools.

Numeric control

also called: computer numeric control (CNC)

generally refers to the automatic control of machines such as lathes and milling machines. Some numerically controlled machines simply obey a preset program of instructions, while more advanced machines can react to *feedback* (see above) from *sensors* (see page 160).

Paper tape

including: paper tape punch, paper tape reader

is sometimes still used as the means of program and data input to machine tools. A pattern of holes punched in the tape is used to represent the data. In order to prepare the tape a **paper tape punch** is attached to the computer on which the program and data are prepared while a **tape reader** is used as an input device to the machine tool.

Figure A9.1: Punched paper tape

Process control

including: integrated manufacturing

is the automatic monitoring and control of an industrial activity by a computer that is programmed to respond to the *feedback* (see above) signals from *sensors* (see page 160). The operation controlled may be as small as a single machine packing boxes or as extensive as the control of an automated bakery, where the mixing, cooking and packaging are controlled within a single **integrated manufacturing** process.

Robot

including: robot arm

is a computer-controlled mechanical device which is sufficiently flexible to be able to do a variety of tasks. Robots are frequently used to do jobs where consistent performance is required (such as paint spraying motor cars) or where there is some danger to humans performing the task (such as the handling of toxic materials). A **robot arm** is a relatively simple fixed robot capable of picking things up, positioning them, etc.

Telemetry

    is the use of communications (usually radio) and measuring sensors to achieve control of machines and instruments at a distance. For example, the control of satellites and space probes, or the monitoring and control of the performance of formula 1 racing cars, where the technicians can adjust the engine control system on the car from the pits while the race is in progress.

A10   Numerical and Scientific Computing

The first computers were seen simply as calculating devices, able to carry out lengthy and tedious mathematical calculations without error and at high speed. They made existing trigonometric and logarithm tables unnecessary, as computers were able to calculate values when needed, as fast as they could look up stored values – although at that stage, the individual scientist did not conceive of a personal computer, and continued to work with portable calculating devices such as slide rules and tables.

The focus of computing has now shifted away from the purely numerical, but nevertheless there are still major uses for mathematical programming. The statistical analysis of large amounts of data involves considerable amounts of computation, as well as the ordering and sorting of the data.

Another area involving numerical computing is the deciphering of codes – **cryptanalysis**. Strictly, a *code* is any scheme for substituting one representation of data for another, as in *character code* (see page 267). The correct term for a coded message, where the intention is to conceal information, is a **cipher**.

The process of enciphering messages – **cryptography** – also involves numeric computing because it is usual to turn textual messages into numbers (A=01, B=02, CAT=030120 etc.) and to perform mathematical operations on the resulting large numbers, in order to turn them into a cipher.

Some of the techniques encountered in numerical uses of computing belong to the mathematical branch known as **numerical analysis**. Some of these techniques are defined below. In calculating the values that appear in mathematical tables, the computer often uses power series; sometimes a calculation is done in an indirect way, using **iteration**, where a 'trial' answer is repeatedly refined, until it is approximately correct.

Algorithm
is a specific procedure that will either accomplish some computing task, without taking forever, or at least report back that it is unable to do so. It is thus roughly equivalent to a computer *program* (see page 219), although strictly speaking a computer program that appeared to go into an infinite loop would not be an algorithm, because you could not be certain that it would not eventually find an answer.

Combinatorics
including: enumeration
is the branch of mathematics to do with counting or ***enumerating***. In using computer systems to search for alternative routes through a road network, for example, it will be important to ensure that all possible combinations are considered, and that extra work is not done by considering routes that have already been looked at. Combinatorial *algorithms* (see above) are designed to take care of details such as this.

Cryptanalysis
including: cipher, cipher breaking
is the '***breaking***' of ***ciphers***. Nowadays, this is almost always done by computer. Captured cipher messages are analysed to see if patterns emerge that will indicate the method of coding, after which further analysis may indicate the precise *key* (see *cryptography*, below) used in the enciphering.

Cryptography
including: cipher, secret messages, key
is the science of sending *secret messages*, or ***ciphers***. In communicating by code, it is usual for everyone to use the same method, but to have some personal (and secret) ***key*** that modifies the method in a way that makes the message remain secure, even if the method is known. Generally, textual messages are converted into numbers before being enciphered, resulting in a very large number of perhaps a hundred or so digits. The method is an *algorithm* (see above) that processes that number but uses the key number as a vital part of the calculation. See *public key cryptography* below.

Data Encryption Standard (DES)
is a standard method of encrypting data, developed by the US government. The method specifies how a *key* (see *cryptography* above) is used to encode the message in a standard way. It is believed that the method alone is secure enough, without knowledge of the key, for it to be published. Making the method publicly available means that computer manufacturers can develop software and hardware for easy implementation of the method.

Iteration (mathematical)

is a mathematical procedure for solving equations, where an initial estimate is made of the answer, and the result of using this (possibly quite poor) guess is used to improve the answer. If this process is repeated, or re-iterated, enough times, the desired answer can be found to any degree of accuracy. See Figure A10.1 for an example of iteration. See also *loop,* page 204.

CALCULATING A SQUARE ROOT

We know that the square root of 2 is 1.414214 to 6 decimal places. An iterative method of calculating this is to take a guess (even a very bad guess) such as 3. If this first guess is then used as x in the calculation:

$$y = \frac{1}{2}\left[x + \frac{2}{x}\right]$$

*you get an answer y=1.833, which is **closer** to the known answer than the original guess. The value of this method is that if you then repeat the calculation, using 1.833 as the guess, the next **iterate** is closer still, 1.46212. In fact, after only two further iterations, the method is giving the known answer correct to six decimal places. Finding the formulas that 'work' in these situations is part of **numerical analysis**.*

Figure A10.1: *An example of iteration*

Public key cryptography

including: RSA algorithm, one-way functions, trapdoor functions
Some mathematical operations are easy to do, but in practice impossible to undo. As a simple example, it is easy to multiply together 11 and 13 to get 143, but it takes an amount of trial-and-error to work back from 143 to the (only) factors 11 and 13. If the numbers involved had hundreds or thousands of digits, rather than just two, the amount of trial and error involved would mean that even a fast computer might be unable to find the factors in an acceptably short time. Such operations – easy to do, and impossible to undo in a realistic time – are known as ***one-way functions***. If the operation is one like the multiplication above, where some secret knowledge (like the numbers 11 and 13) provides a short-cut, they are known as ***trapdoor functions***. These can be used as the basis for a simple but secure coding system, as shown in Figure A10.2. The best-known such function was developed by the

mathematicians Rivest, Shamir and Adleman, and is, unsurprisingly, called the *RSA algorithm*.

📖	A public directory is published – for everyone in the code system, it tells the whole world what **key** is used to send messages to that person. This is a (big) number that can be used to encode messages. The *de*coding part is secret: only one person knows that!
📄	I want to send a message to you. I write my message out, substituting A=01, B=02 etc. and get a (long) number which represents my message.
📄 ⇨ 📄	Now I look up your key in the public directory and use it to turn my message into another long number – this is done in a way that no-one except you can decode – even *I* can't, unless I look back at my original message.
📄 ⇨ 📄	You receive my message, and using your very secret decoding method, turn it back into the original message.
	How do you know that the message was *really* from me? Anyone could look up your key in the public directory and send a misleading message that claimed to be from me! I can *prove* it was from me, like this:
📄 📄	With my message, I include my name and address, but before I code this, I use my own secret de-coding key to turn the name and address part into a scrambled version.
📄 📄 ⇨ 📄 📄	Now I code the whole message – the message itself *and* the previously scrambled name and address.
📄 📄 ⇨ 📄 📄	You receive this two-part message, and use *your* secret de-coder to extract the plain message and the scrambled name and address. You read the message, and need to check that it is from me.
📄 ⇨ 📄	You take the scrambled part, look me up in the directory and see what my public coding key is. Using this will unscramble the name and address, and you are confident that it *was* from me, because I am the only person in the world who knows what my *de*-coding key is.

Figure A10.2: *How a public-key cryptosystem works*

Monte Carlo method

A whimsical name which comes from the use of chance (usually *random numbers* – see below – rather than roulette wheels) in simulation. In exploring the behaviour of a complex system (which might be chemical, physical, biological, human, etc.), the overall behaviour of the system may be too complicated to specify confidently in mathematical terms. If the many small decisions in the system *can* be easily specified, then the behaviour of the system can be simulated, using random numbers to model a large number of small decisions. For example, migration of people between towns in the UK might be too complicated to specify mathematically, but information *is* available on how many people move from London to Edinburgh (say) each year. The overall behaviour of the population can be explored by selecting one resident of London, and generating a random number to see if that individual will stay or move, and if so, where to. By repeating this for the whole population of the UK, predictions about future population trends will be possible, even if the mathematics is not fully understood.

Numerical analysis

is the branch of mathematics that studies the methods (such as *power series, iteration, recursion*) mentioned in this section. Numerical analysts are interested in methods of computing, but are not necessarily heavy users of computers in practice.

Power series

Some mathematical quantities (like π) can be computed using a series such as:

$$\pi = 4\left(\frac{1}{2} + \frac{1}{3} - \frac{1}{2^3.3} - \frac{1}{3^3.3} + \frac{1}{2^5.5} + \frac{1}{3^5.5} - \cdots\right)$$

Depending on how accurate an answer is needed, more or less of the terms being added together can be included. If you stop computing the series above after four terms, the answer 3.117284 is accurate to (only) 1 decimal place — if more are needed, adding in (say) four more terms increases the accuracy to 3 decimal places. *Numerical analysis* (see above) is the branch of mathematics that is used to design suitable power series.

Recursion

is a mathematical way of defining a computation in terms of a reduced version of itself. This may seem like a paradox, but because this method is close to the way some mathematical operations are programmed in a computer, it can be very efficient. See Figure A10.3 for two examples.

USING RECURSION

Factorials

The factorial of a number, written as 7!, 3! and so on, is defined as:

$$7! = 7 \times 6 \times 5 \times 4 \times 3 \times 2 \times 1$$
$$3! = 3 \times 2 \times 1 \qquad \text{and so on.}$$

Factorials often turn up in **combinatorial algorithms**. *Another way of defining a factorial is to say that:*

$$7! = 7 \times 6!$$
$$3! = 3 \times 2! \qquad \text{or, in general, } n! = n \times (n-1)!$$

Thus, each factorial is defined in terms of a smaller factorial. This is a **recursive** *definition. To make this work, it is necessary to give the smallest factorial 1! a specific value (in this case 1 itself).*

Sorting

A list (of numbers, or words — anything) often has to be sorted into order (numerical or alphabetic, say). One way of defining the process **recursively**, *in a way that can be easy to program, is as follows:*

> *Find the earliest item in the list;*
>
> *print that out, and remove it from the list;*
>
>> *now repeat the whole process, but using the new, shorter, list.*

In a similar way to the factorial example above, it is necessary to program the computer to stop taking items off the list when you have shortened it so far that there is nothing left!

Figure A10.3: Two examples of recursion

Prime numbers

are numbers like 7, 19, 23 and so on, which have no factors other than themselves and one – that is, they cannot be made by multiplying other numbers together (as 24 can be made by multiplying 6 x 4, or 3 x 8, and so on). Prime numbers are important in computing because they form the basis of ciphers (see *cryptography*, above), and also because searching for new prime numbers is a good test of mathematical programming techniques. Other uses of prime numbers are in the design of *hashing* algorithms (see page 188), and (pseudo) *random number generation*, see below.

Random number generation

including: pseudo random number generator

Many *simulations* (see page 34) on a computer need to make use of random numbers, in a similar way to 'tossing a coin' in order to make a decision. Most programming languages include a random-number function, that gives the user a suitable number, as if it had been chosen at random — numbers between 1 and 6, for example, to simulate the throw of dice in a game. Because computer programs cannot be truly random, a *pseudo random-number generator* is used, which gives numbers with the appearance of being random. See *Monte Carlo method,* above, for more information.

A11   Sound

*Other related terms, especially those concerned with modulation, may be found in section C17 Communications Technology. Note that, throughout this Glossary, the spelling '**analog**' has been preferred to the alternative '**analogue**'.*

This section is concerned with the use of computers to generate, store, communicate and manipulate sound.

Most of the terms used when working with computer-generated sound belong to the terminology of music or sound. There are however some terms whose use in a computing context need to be defined.

Electronic reproduction of natural sound has been available for many decades. The ability to generate natural sounds electronically – **sound synthesis** – was developed long before computers. Sound is produced by the continuous vibration of air. This means that it has analog properties. A microphone converts sound energy (air vibrations) into electrical energy (fluctuating voltage and current). In the opposite process a loudspeaker converts electrical energy into sound. These are both analog devices, since they create or use varying electrical energy. The earliest forms of sound synthesis worked by creating and manipulating varying electrical currents, they worked entirely on analog principles. With the use of digital computer techniques the more recent digital audio systems have been developed. These systems use digital methods to create, process and store sounds but receive analog input from microphones and produce analog output for loudspeakers.

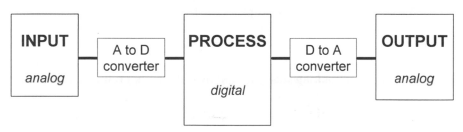

Figure A11.1: *A sound system*

The electrical output from microphones is analog (that is, it consists of a continuously fluctuating voltage). It has to be converted into a digital form if it is to be stored on a digital device (for example, a compact disk) or if it is to be transmitted or manipulated in a digital form. Loudspeakers or headphones require analog signals. The conversion of analog (sound) signals to digital is achieved by a sampling process while the conversion of digital to analog is achieved by adding the values of the bits in the digital representation.

Both analog and digital methods are used to transmit, record, manipulate and create sounds. Digital methods involve the use of computers (or microprocessors) to manipulate data. Thus many pieces of digital musical or sound equipment will contain microprocessors.

The use of computers to create sounds involve sound or speech synthesis. Many microcomputers have (or can be fitted with) appropriate chips so that they can output speech; for example the computer can 'speak' words as well as display them on the screen. The use of voice input is being developed, but there are difficulties yet to be overcome before it can be the normal method of communication between people and computers. As far as the computer is concerned sound is just another form of data which it can create, store, manipulate or output, provided the right input and output devices are available and connected. The manipulation of sound data may be done by software or by hardware within the computer or attached to the computer.

Sound synthesis

also known as: sound generation
including: analog and digital sound generation, subtractive synthesis,
Frequency Modulation (FM), Phase Distortion (PD), Linear Arithmetic
(LA), additive synthesis
is the use of electronic devices for creating sounds, sometimes called *sound generation*. The sounds may be generated using either analog or digital techniques. Electronically generated sound can create notes which are like those produced by a variety of musical instruments.

Analog sound generation has been used for a very long time (well over 50 years). Usually, the sound is produced by starting with a complex waveform, containing many harmonics, which is produced by an oscillator. Electronic filter circuits are then used to modify the sound by removing some of these harmonics. This process is called *subtractive synthesis*.

Digital sound generation is a recent development in which numbers representing sound waves are manipulated. A variety of methods are used to create the sounds, some of them unique to a particular manufacturer. The most commonly used synthesis methods are:

Frequency Modulation (FM) in which the digital representation of a number of pure waveforms are combined with each other to create a complex compound sound.

Phase Distortion (PD) in which the digital representation of a waveform is modified, by speeding up the rate at which the wave is generated, to produce a complex waveform. This complex waveform is then modified as in an analog synthesiser.

Linear Arithmetic (LA) in which sampled sounds are used as well as pure tones as the start of the process. Arithmetic operations are then carried out on the values of the bit patterns representing the sounds. (See *sound sampler*, below.)

Additive synthesis is a computer software method in which the user selects a mixture of harmonics and the computer calculates the values for the waveform at very small successive time intervals. In all cases the digital values for the sound are turned into sound signals by a digital-to-analog converter. Different methods of creating sounds produce different qualities of sound.

Music synthesiser

including: synthesiser, analog synthesiser, digital synthesiser, multi-timbral synthesiser, polyphony

is an electronic device for creating sounds. It is often called just a *synthesiser*. The sounds may be generated electronically using either analog or digital techniques (see *sound generator*, below). Most synthesisers have a piano-style keyboard and need to be connected to an amplifier with loudspeakers for the sounds they produce to be heard.

Analog synthesisers are usually intended to be used as musical instruments to be played, and most do not have the ability to store the sounds they create.

Digital synthesisers generally incorporate some form of digital storage and frequently have a built-in store of ready-made sounds. Digital synthesisers generally offer a much greater variety of sounds and a wider range of manipulation options than analog synthesisers. For example, a *multi-timbral synthesiser* can play two or more different sounds at the same time, or produce a number of different notes at the same time (*polyphony*), or a combination of both of these capabilities in the same synthesiser.

Envelope

including: ADSR (attack, decay, sustain, release)

is a shape which is used to describe the changes in volume (amplitude), pitch (frequency) and timbre (quality) of a note as it changes with time. The form of sound envelopes are normally used in *sound synthesis* (see above). One commonly used way of describing a volume envelope is known as *ADSR*, an acronym for Attack, Decay, Sustain and Release.

Figure A11.2: Volume envelope

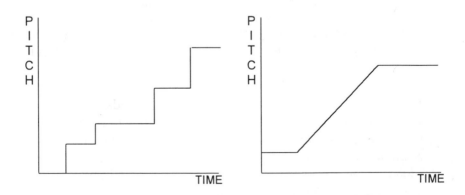

Figure A11.3: Two pitch envelopes

Attack is the rate at which an envelope rises to its initial peak before starting to decay. For example percussive sounds (piano or drums) have a high attack rate for their volume (amplitude). *Decay* is the rate at which an envelope falls from its initial peak to a steady (sustain) level. *Sustain* is the level at which an envelope remains whilst a key is still pressed after the initial attack and decay stages. *Release* is the rate at which an envelope fades away from its sustain level when the key is released.

MIDI (Musical Instrument Digital Interface)

including: MIDI standard, MIDI channel, MIDI code.

A musical instrument digital interface, MIDI (frequently, but incorrectly, referred to as a MIDI interface) is a particular form of serial *interface* (see *interface*, page 300 and *interface card*, page 308) built into or added to the parts of an electronic music system. The interface allows electronic music data to be passed in both directions between parts of the system. The links between parts of the system are called *MIDI channels*.

The form of the interface and the structure of the data are defined by the *MIDI standard*, which was agreed between the major manufacturers of electronic musical instruments in 1983. The standard defines the codes (*MIDI codes*) to be used for musical data, for example the pitch of a note and its volume. These codes allow music data to be passed between devices from different manufacturers in the same way that *ASCII codes* (see *character set*, page 267) allow alphanumeric data to be passed between different computers.

Music keyboard

including: keyboard

Any electronic music device which is controlled by a keyboard similar to a piano is called a music keyboard or a *keyboard*. The keys, which are arranged like the black and white keys on a piano, are frequently supplemented by switches, sliders or other ways of setting and changing the electronic signals produced by or used by the device.

Sound controller

including: audio controller, musical instrument controller

is a hardware device which controls sounds generated by a sound source. Controllers usually do not produce sounds themselves, though they may be made to look like (and be used like) a musical instrument, for example a piano keyboard or a guitar. These are called *musical instrument controllers*. Some controllers use joysticks, sliders or wheels. These may be built into other controllers or attached to a musical instrument. Control of sounds is usually achieved by using *MIDI codes* (see *MIDI*, above). There are also *audio controllers*, which can generate (MIDI) control signals from audio sounds. With an audio controller looking like a microphone, a user can sing into it while 'playing' a synthesised sound from a connected sound generator, and thus control the sound produced.

Sound generator

also known as: sound source

is a digital device capable of producing sounds as part of an electronic music system; it is sometimes called a *sound source*. A range of such devices exist, which create sounds similar to those produced by particular musical instruments, such as drum machines, electric guitars or electronic organs. *Music synthesisers* (see above) are an example of a sound generator with a piano-type keyboard which is used to play them, but most sound generators have no direct means of being played as if they were musical instruments. Some have a collection of pre-defined sounds and some have synthesising capability. If the sounds can be altered then there will be controls to do so. The sounds may be accessed via MIDI, to be used as input to a sequencer or a music controller, or the device may be attached to a computer as a dedicated peripheral.

Sound sampler

including: sampling rate, sampling resolution

is an example of a *digital sampler* (see page 160), in which the device receives sound signals from a microphone (or other sound source) and analyses them. It makes and stores the digital measurements from this analysis. By performing this process of analysis, measurement and storage very quickly and very frequently, the sampler converts the signal into a digital representation of the sound.

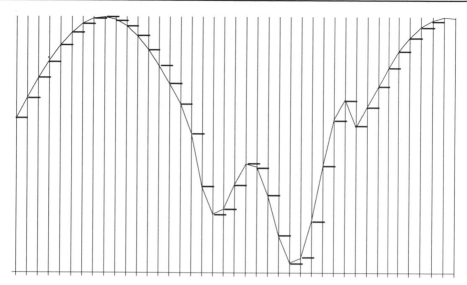

Figure A11.4: A continuous waveform with sample levels

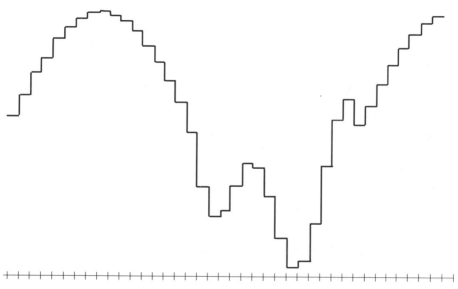

Figure A11.5: The sampled waveform from Figure A11.4

The succession of values from this sampling can be processed, stored or fed through a digital-to-analog converter to reproduce the sound. Sound sampling is the standard method of capturing sound for storage or manipulation in digital form.

The quality of sound produced using a sound sampler depends upon the *sampling rate* and the *sampling resolution.*

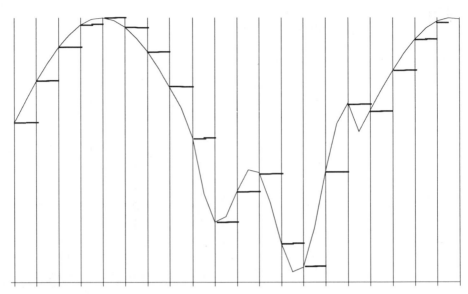

Figure A11.6: *The same waveform, sampling frequency halved - resulting in much cruder sound quality*

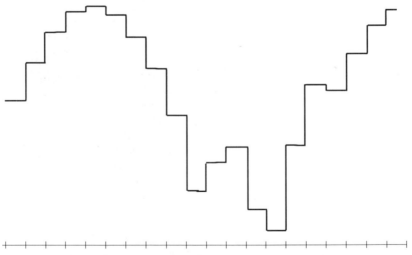

Figure A11.7: *The sampled waveform from Figure A11.6*

Sampling rate is the frequency at which samples are taken and is usually twice the maximum frequency of the sound being sampled.

Sampling resolution is the number of bits used for data storage, which is 16 bits for CD players but may be only 8 bits in some personal computers.

Sound mixer

including: channel, music channel

is an operator-controlled electronic device for combining sound signals. The operator selects how input signals are to be combined to form one or more output signals. The paths or connections for input and output signals are known as *channels* or *music channels*.

Sound processor

is the general term for electronic sound equipment which can take a sound signal as input, modify the signal and output the new signal. The processing may use either analog or digital techniques, but the use of digital methods is now more common. Most sound processors have a particular function, for example echo units, reverberation units, graphic equalisers, noise reduction units. All of these work in *real-time* (see *sequencer*, below).

Sound processing software on a suitable computer can do the same things that individual sound processing items achieve. Thus a computer may be used as a general-purpose sound processor.

Computer-based music system

including: digital sound system

is an arrangement of electronic music devices and a computer linked together so that music and other sounds, such as speech and singing, can be captured, stored, manipulated, generated or reproduced. These systems will probably contain both digital and analog components. Where only digital processing components are used it is referred to as a *digital sound system*.

Music work station

is a collection of connected music-generating and sound-manipulating equipment. A typical arrangement will include a keyboard, a synthesiser and a sequencer. They are increasingly likely to include a computer with appropriate software. See *computer-based music system*, above.

Sequencer

including: real-time entry, step-time entry

is a digital device which can store a set of representations of notes, rhythms and other musical data for replaying at a later time. It may also include facilities for editing or for producing repeated patterns. Sequencers may range from the very simple, capable of storing only a small number of notes or a single chord, to the complex, capable of simultaneously handling many independent musical parts. Sequencers are often built into *synthesisers* (see *music synthesiser* above) and drum machines or other electronic music devices. One example of the use of a sequencer is to play a piece of stored music at different speeds without the distortion of pitch, which happens if the speed of a tape recorder is varied. Another is to change the sound of a series of notes previously entered, rather like changing the colours of parts of a computer-generated picture with an art program.

Music parts can be entered into a sequencer in one of two ways, *real-time* or *step-time*.

Real-time entry is when the musical information is provided by playing the notes with the correct relative time intervals. They need not be the actual intervals since the sequencer can modify the speed (tempo).

Step-time entry is when the time interval between each note is defined by the person entering the musical information.

SMPTE codes

SMPTE is an acronym for the Society of Motion Picture and TV Engineers (USA). The codes are an agreed set of standards which make it possible to synchronise sound and video signals.

Speech recognition

including: voice print

is a process of analysing a spoken word and comparing it with those known to the computer system. The use of *voice prints* (like finger prints, each person's voice is unique) for security purposes is increasing. It is already possible to use voice input to computers. However, the differences between the same words spoken by different people still make this an unreliable process requiring substantial memory and processing power.

Speech synthesis

including: speech synthesiser, phoneme

is the production of sounds resembling human speech by electronic methods.
This is achieved either by the use of computer software or through hardware,
a *speech synthesiser*. A speech synthesiser is a piece of hardware, usually
built into a computer. It is an output device that generates sound in response
to input data, usually in the form of alphanumeric characters. The sound is
produced either by selecting an appropriate sound from a collection of stored
sounds or by breaking down the input data into its individual speech
components, called *phonemes*, for example the vowel sound in 'meet' or
'meat', which are output in sequence.

A12   *Hypermedia Systems*

Hypermedia systems are interactive computer systems which are concerned principally with the storage of data (and its associated information retrieval) for reference purposes. They are usually organised so that the user can obtain information in a number of ways. Often called **hypertext** systems, they store text in such a way that users are able to construct their own links between different parts of the text. The multi-level approach to text acquisition, storage, analysis, comparison, retrieval and editing includes a comprehensive command structure which allows users to move through a document. This may be achieved by the use of pre-programmed links, through techniques such as *browsing*, or by searching for specific words. The system will remember the path taken.

Hypermedia is an extension of hypertext and also includes related graphics (still, animated and moving video) and sound.

The data is held in a non-linear structure using nodes and, for each node, a small number of links (typically 2, 3 or 4) are available to related nodes. Using on-screen menus, often presented on a menu-bar, it is possible to move through the system in a variety of search patterns. Starting with a main index, the user can choose a path which introduces the context of a particular subject and then, having noticed some point of special interest, can change the search pattern to follow the context of that new subject. The system might also allow the user to search for associated themes by using key words in the particular screen being displayed at that time.

The change in the type of information generated by calls into such a system can be dramatic. For example, in a system which was apparently associated with an art gallery, the user might choose to look at information about one particular artist which could include a screen display of that artist's pictures. Then, seeing a subject of interest depicted in one of the paintings, choose to look at paintings by other artists on the same subject. If the subject happened to be people playing musical instruments, the next step might be to choose to hear some music associated with those instruments. This might then lead to a topic dealing with the production of sound, and then to information about the physics of wave motion.

The usefulness of such a system is dependent on the type of data structure which it employs, the size of the database and the access time. The ease of use might be related to the physical process of using the menus, where a touch-screen might have considerable advantages over a mouse or the arrow keys.

Multimedia

is the presentation of information by a computer system using graphics, animation, sound and text. The data may be stored in a variety of ways using conventional computer storage devices, together with a picture database on CD-ROM. Output might be through VDUs, sound-generators and laser projectors.

Integrating a tutor program could allow the system to be used as a training resource. The performance of the user could then be monitored by recording the choices made in response to questions and evaluating this response using an expert system. This performance output might then be sent to a remote trainer who would assess the trainee's progress.

Interactive video

involves the use of a computer linked to a large capacity data store such as a Compact Disc (CD) to provide random access retrieval of images (including stills and continuous video) and sound. Data, once recorded, is not easily changed or added to and access times can sometimes appear long. However, any disadvantage arising is generally outweighed by the amount, variety and quality of data which can be retrieved from one active device.

HyperCard

including: card, stack

is an application-building tool provided with Apple Macintosh computers which allows for interactive storing and retrieving on-screen *'cards'*. These can contain text, graphics, sound and video clips, and are grouped together in one or more related *stacks*.

Browse

is a feature of hypertext systems which allows users to build their own route through an application rather than following a pre-determined one. The route so chosen may be remembered by the system so that it can be re-traced back to the starting point of that route. Browsers are particularly useful in such applications as computerised manuals, computer aided learning packages and large databases.

Video clip

is a short section of film or video stored in digital form (both sound and pictures). It is easily incorporated in computer displays and hypermedia systems. The video clip would normally be stored in compressed form, otherwise the storage cost would be prohibitive. See also *video data compression*, page 327.

The foundations of computer assisted learning were laid during the early 1960s with the development of **programmed learning systems**. These early systems did not use any form of computer technology (the micro-computer was not to appear for many years) but were either paper-based or used electro-mechanical devices known as **teaching machines**.

A basic principle of programmed learning was one of 'value added'. Before any teaching programme was constructed, a pre-test and a post-test for the unit to be taught were written. A learner would sit the pre-test, undergo the programmed instruction and then sit the post-test. The value added to the learner could then be deduced by comparing the two scores. It was assumed that the learner could never be at fault. If the improvement in score was only small, then it was assumed that there was a problem with the programmed instruction.

The programmes could be either linear or branching. A **linear programme** would be a sequence of very small learning steps punctuated by a test question. The learner would know at once if they had answered correctly or not, but there would be no remedial instruction. A **branching programme** would not let the learner continue to the next step if a test answer was wrong. In this case one of several remedial instruction paths were followed depending on the nature of the error.

Some of the teaching machines were multimedia, controlling slide projectors and tape recorders. They were all expensive and unreliable. The paper form of the techniques were more successful. Books were written as branching programmes.

This approach to learning had some success with well defined skills or confined areas of training. The armed services based many of their instructional manuals on programmed learning principles and for a time it seemed that the Royal Air Force could have a significant influence on the educational system. Attempts to write programmes to deal with areas that required a creative and critical approach were poor and by the end of the 1960s interest in the approach had diminished.

Once the micro-computer arrived, the same principles were revived under the title of **Computer Aided Learning (CAL)**. Although now the technology was no longer a problem the learning programmes were just as difficult to write. The early CAL systems did little better than the programmed learning systems. One major useful contribution to learning was the development of *adventure* games. Another was the use of controllable computer simulations of situations which were too costly or too dangerous to create in real life. The general approach started to become effective when video and CD-ROM images could form part of the instructional material. It is now understood that an effective learning system must have the ability to adapt in a major way to the response of the learner. This can happen if the system is able to learn about the learner. **Expert systems** can do just this but, as with all effective software, they are expensive and difficult to write.

The processing speeds and data capacity of computers are ever increasing. Coupled with the development of even more adaptive software, it is to be expected that CAL will move onto the more creative areas of learning.

If the computer has so far proved to be limited in its role as a teacher it is much more effective as a manager of the learning process. **Computer Managed Learning (CML)** is very much concerned with the recording of what a learner has achieved and directing the learner to the next unit of study. Computers are good at recording well-structured data and making decisions based on well defined rules; CML is essentially recording and branching. The growth of a modular approach to learning courses has been made practical by the use of CML systems.

Authoring language
including: authoring system
is a programming language for the creation of instructional material that uses a *Computer Aided Learning* approach (see below). An *authoring system* is a computer system that is able to execute an authoring language.

Adventure game
is a computer game in which the player explores a computer-generated environment, usually having to solve puzzles in order to make progress. Early adventure games (named after the first one, which was called simply 'Adventure') used only text; the player typed instructions such as 'GO SOUTH', 'OPEN DOOR', 'PICK UP GOLD', and the computer responded with a description of the new scene. Later games make substantial use of graphics, and may be playable over a network with several players taking part.

Because of their problem-solving nature and the way in which they stimulate the imagination, adventure games have been widely and successfully used in education.

Computer Aided Learning (CAL)
including: Computer Based Training (CBT), Computer Managed Instruction (CMI), Computer Managed Learning (CML)
is the use of a computer to provide instructional information to a student, pose questions and react to the student's response.

> *Computer Based Training (CBT)* is the use of a computer as an instructional system in a training environment. The approach is the same as computer assisted learning but the learning area is confined to a well defined training objective.
>
> *Computer Managed Instruction (CMI)* is the use of a computer to manage a student's progress through a course of instruction. The student's performance is recorded by the computer and new modules of instruction are defined or delivered as determined by the curriculum. A computer managed instruction system may or may not contain computer assisted learning material.
>
> *Computer Managed Learning (CML)* is the use of a computer in a similar fashion to computer managed instruction, but with additional emphasis on providing help which depends upon the responses given by the student. Some computer managed learning systems can build up a detailed learning profile for each student. This profile can be used for both reporting and directing the studies of an individual student.

Buggy
is a simple robotic device exclusively used in a computer education context. The device can move in two dimensions and supports light and touch *sensors* (see page 160). The student can program the device to exhibit certain behaviour or the device could form part of a multimedia *computer managed learning system* (see above).

Many buggies are controlled by an external general-purpose computer. This allows the use of a variety of programming languages to construct the controlling programs.

Turtle
is a simple robotic device initially designed to exploit the graphical aspects of the programming language LOGO (see page 254). It is designed to have a pen attached to it so that a hard copy of its walk can be recorded. Students can program the device with any suitable language but it could form part of a *computer managed learning system* (see above) associated with certain aspects of learning mathematics.

Roamer

including: Bigtrack

is a simple robotic device exclusively used in the computer education context. Unlike many *buggies* (see above) Roamer has a computer built into it. This computer controls the movement of Roamer by responding to a sequence of instructions. These instructions form a program which the student has stored in the device by the use of a set of keys which are part of Roamer. *Bigtrack* is a device that has a similar educational purpose to Roamer but it moves by laying tracks (like a tank) rather than wheels.

A14   Artificial Intelligence and Expert Systems

Artificial intelligence (AI) is a recognised discipline within computer science. It attempts to design software (sometimes with associated hardware) that behaves in a way which, if it were human behaviour, would be described as intelligent.

The earliest artificial intelligence systems, in the 1960s, concentrated on such activities as playing chess and proving (mathematical) theorems. However the techniques built up are now being applied to aspects of behaviour not normally thought of as requiring great intelligence, such as recognising objects, understanding simple text, speech recognition and general visual interpretation.

These activities although often relatively straightforward for people are, in fact, not so straightforward for computers. It is a challenging problem to write programs for a computer to perform these activities - so much so that we are still far from successfully writing the programs, except in the most simple cases.

One recent development in artificial intelligence is neural networks. These draw from and emulate the structure of the brain in terms of neurons. The networks are made to 'learn' from training sessions and then repeat what has been learnt when given new data.

An **expert system**, sometimes known as an **Intelligent Knowledge Based System (IKBS),** is an example of an 'intelligent' system applied to a real life application. The computer performs at or near the level of human experts.

Examples of expert systems include PROSPECTOR, which advises geologists when they are out in the field. The system asks for certain data about the environment where the geologist is considering drilling bore-holes and provides advice based on this data and on 'knowledge' already stored in its knowledge base.

Other well known expert systems include XCON, which gives advice on how to configure a VAX computer system – that is , how to make sure the correct units are specified and how they should be connected together for a certain application. There are a number of systems in the medical area; one of the better known is MYCIN, which gives advice on which drugs to use for certain types of bacterial infection.

Artificial intelligence (AI)

is the study and development of computing applications for tasks which would be described as requiring intelligence, if they were done by people. Many of these applications involve systems capable of learning, adaptation or self-correction.

Cognitive science

covers a wide range of subjects which are concerned with the thinking processes (cognition) and are, to a great extent, people-oriented. Some, such as *artificial intelligence* (see above), computer vision and *human-computer interaction* (see page 71), are concerned with computers. Others are concerned with how people function; for example, cognitive psychology which includes the study of the mental processes of memory, language processing and vision. Some cognitive scientists find it helpful to describe how humans function in terms of a computer model of information processing.

Neural net

is artificial intelligence software which allows a system to learn to recognise features or characteristics of situations which are input to it. The technique is based on a model of the logical properties of interconnected sets of nerve cells.

A neural net is made up of a network of very many junctions, or nodes. Each of these nodes will 'learn' features according to its input. Once the learning phase is completed, the neural net can be used to recognise features of the same type that were presented to it.

Neural nets have been used for visual recognition and also for financial prediction.

Pattern recognition

is the process of identifying objects in a digitised picture, or in some cases digitised sounds, through analysis of the digital representation of the objects and comparison with stored knowledge about similar objects.

Cybernetics

including: robotics

is the study of the control of processes by a computer, for example an industrial process or a robot. **Robotics** is the study and design of robots. See also *control,* page 38, and *robot,* page 40.

Expert system

also known as: (Intelligent) Knowledge Based System (IKBS), (KBS)
including: knowledge base, knowledge engineer, knowledge acquisition,
knowledge elicitation, inference engine, heuristics, explanation, rulebase,
shell

is an application of artificial intelligence to a particular area of activity where traditional human expert knowledge and experience are made available through a computer package.

Knowledge base is that part of an expert system which holds knowledge about the application area (or domain), such as drug side effects. Much of the knowledge is held as **IF ... THEN ...** type rules. For example:

```
IF a patient has high blood pressure
AND is anaemic
THEN avoid the use of a certain kind of
drug.
```

From time to time the knowledge base is updated.

Heuristics are rules which are not derived purely from logic but are derived from the experience of a person. These are known as 'rules of thumb'. Many of the rules in an expert system are of this type.

Rulebase is the part of the knowledge base which is made up of all the rules known to the expert system.

Knowledge engineers are the people who collect the information in the knowledge base. This information is collected from a variety of sources in a variety of ways, one of the most important is collecting information through talking to experts. The collected knowledge is then formulated as a set of rules and facts.

Knowledge acquisition or *knowledge elicitation* is the process of gathering information for inclusion in a knowledge base.

Once the knowledge base has been constructed, the expert system is ready to be interrogated or consulted. The system requests the user to provide information and then searches the knowledge base to find appropriate advice for the user.

Explanations can be requested by the user. The system will provide the user with the reasoning behind the advice given. This is often in the form of a list of the rules tested by the system.

Inference engine (or ***inference processor***) is a piece of software in an expert system which does the searching of the knowledge base. Searching the knowledge base uses standard searching methods which are independent of the application, for example a top-down or a bottom-up search.

Shell is a piece of software, which is an 'empty' expert system without the knowledge base for any particular application. The user enters the appropriate rules and facts.

Expert systems have a clearly identifiable internal structure, which is illustrated in Figure A14.1.

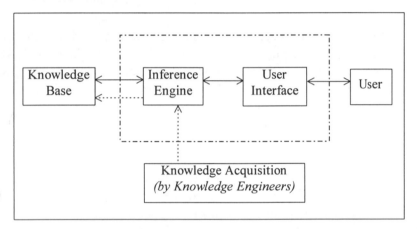

Figure A14.1: *An expert system structure*

The User communicates with the system through the User Interface, which passes requests for advice to the Inference Engine. The Inference Engine processes the request, obtaining information – rules and facts – from the Knowledge Base as required and finally returns the answer to the User Interface, and hence to the User.

In the Knowledge Acquisition phase, the Inference Engine stores the information from the Knowledge Engineers in the Knowledge Base.

A15　User Interface

Cooks usually try to make their meals tasty and attractive as well as nutritious. In the same way, software writers try to make their products attractive to the user as well as being effective and easy to use. Much time and effort is spent on designing ways in which the user interacts with the computer and the software. Most software users are more concerned with what a package can do than with how it works. They expect to be able to see and understand what the software can do, they want to be able to communicate their instructions easily and have quick and understandable responses from the computer.

As the scope of computer applications has increased and the number of computer users has also increased, a variety of ways have been evolved for communication between the user and the computer; this is called the **user interface** or **user environment**. There are fashions in user interface design, just as there are in car or clothes design, but what is important is that the interface should achieve its objectives as efficiently as possible.

All user interface designs are limited by the capabilities of machines and people. Each design seeks to make the most of the strengths and avoid the weaknesses of computer equipment and its users. Aspects of computer hardware, for example processing speed, memory capacity, input and output devices, restrict what software can achieve. Speech is the most common form of communication between people but the development of methods of communication between people and computers through speech has not yet produced cheap and reliable systems for everyday use. Communication through text is limited by the speed at which people can read text which is presented on a screen and type responses accurately on a keyboard. Recent improvements in hardware have greatly enhanced the graphics capability of small computers. Many software designers have chosen graphical ways of presenting the activities or concepts available for selection at any time: icons (small pictures with an easily understood meaning) are widely used, since graphical information is independent of the user's language and can be used wherever the meaning of the icon is understood. All user interface designs are compromises between what it is desirable to provide and what it is possible to achieve.

It is the combination of those parts of the hardware and software of a system with which the user interacts which make up the user interface. User interfaces are described in a variety of ways, whose names highlight their main features; for example, **graphical user interface (GUI), menu selection**

interface, windows environment, forms dialogue. There is no single kind of user environment which suits all applications or all users; the choice of an appropriate user interface depends on the amount of information to be presented or elicited, the experience of the users and their familiarity with the particular software.

Since taste and personal preference largely determine people's reactions to different user environments, there will always be scope for variety in their design. For those people who spend a long time working at a computer it is very important that the user interface they experience makes a positive contribution to their efficiency. It is increasingly common for the user to be able to adapt (**customise**) the facilities provided by the system to fit the situation in which the system is used.

Where there is an unusual user environment, such as where provision has to be made for disabled people, special arrangements are often made. These may include the provision of customised input and/or output devices, such as touch sensitive keyboards, and the appropriate additional software.

Human-Computer Interaction (HCI)

sometimes: interface rather than interaction
including: Graphical User Interface (GUI), Man-Machine Interface (MMI), user environment
is one of a number of terms used to describe the communication between people and computer systems. Other terms for this are: ***Man-Machine Interface (MMI)***, ***user interface*** and ***user environment***. Any of these terms is likely to be used in discussions of how people and computer systems interact and the ease of use of a system.

One way of classifying interfaces is by the style of communication they provide. Some are purely textual whilst others, known as *Graphical User Interfaces (GUI)*, replace some or all of the words by icons. See also the introduction to this section.

Keyboard

including: qwerty keyboard, numeric keypad, function key, embedded keyboard
is the typical input device used with all general-purpose computers. A keyboard will have a number of keys, which is not the same for all computers nor is the arrangement the same.

Part of the keyboard is likely to be arranged in the same way as a traditional typewriter; this is called a *qwerty keyboard*.

Part of the keyboard may be a block of keys for the digits 0-9, possibly including the arithmetic symbols for add, subtract, multiply and divide, and an enter key; this is called a *numeric keypad*.

In addition to the keys for letters, numbers and punctuation marks, a typical keyboard will have special keys including, at least, enter (or return), escape (esc), control (ctrl) and some *function keys*. What these keys do will depend on the software being used rather than the hardware.

It is sometimes possible for the user to assign part of the keyboard for special purposes. This part of the keyboard is called an *embedded keyboard*. For example, keyboards with a restricted number of keys, such as laptop computers, allow a group of the keys to be assigned the role of a numeric keypad if the user wishes.

WIMP environment (Windows Icons Menus Pointer)

from: Windows Icons Menus Pointers
is a method of accessing the computer making minimum use of the keyboard by using a *mouse* (or similar device) to move a *pointer* over *icons* or text *menus* displayed on the screen. For example, selecting an icon may open a *window* and start a task. For definitions of these individual terms see below.

Window

including: active window, pane
is a temporary area opened on the screen displaying the activity of a program. There can be several windows on the screen at any one time which can be moved if required or removed completely (restoring the original information on the screen). At any one time only one window will be *active*, that is accessible for input by the user. Things may be happening in other windows, for example a clock may be showing the time, but this does not mean that the window is active. If several activities are being run at the same time, each will be in a separate window but only one can be worked on at a time. It is possible to have more than one window visible and shift from one task to another by moving the cursor from one window to another. A window may be divided into parts, called *panes*, which can be used separately; for example, headers and footers in a document.

Icons

also spelt: ikons

are small pictures or symbols, with an easily understood meaning, displayed on the screen as a method of offering a choice of activity. A pointer is moved to a selected icon using, for example, a mouse, cursor control keys or a light pen, and the activity is started by clicking a mouse button or pressing an appropriate key. This method has advantages over text-based input for inexperienced users. Icons can be independent of the user's language, provided the symbols are generally recognised.

Menu

including: action bar, menu bar, pull-down menu, pop-up menu, status bar

is a range of options offered to a computer user so that a choice can be made. A menu may simply be a screen display which lists a number of choices. The user is expected to press an appropriate key to select one of them; one of the choices offered is likely to be another menu. Sometimes a special panel appears when a choice has to be made. This hides part of the screen, but the screen is restored to its original state after the choice has been made.

Menu bar or **action bar** is a line of titles for menus across the screen (usually at the top, but sometimes at the bottom). These are the menus which the user can choose at that point. Clicking when the *mouse pointer* (see below) is on the appropriate word, or else pressing an appropriate key, selects a menu. The choice is usually displayed as a *pull-down menu*.

Pull-down menu is a menu that appears on request after its title has been selected from the menu bar. It gets its name because it usually appears immediately below the menu title.

Pop-up menu is a menu that appears on the screen wherever the user happens to have positioned the cursor. It may be called up as the result of pressing a *hot key* (see page 79), or because the program needs to offer the user a choice as a result of what is being done at that instant.

Status bar is a line of information displayed on the screen, usually either at the top or at the bottom, which shows some of the conditions in the task at the moment, such as the page and line number in a word processing application.

Menu selection interface

is a form of user interface in which the computer displays a list of options from which the user must make a choice, either by typing the code displayed against the option, or by moving a highlight to the option (using cursor keys, a mouse or a trackerball) and then pressing a particular key or clicking the mouse button. The response may be to carry out the choice, to request further information (using any of the communication styles) or to report an error. See also *WIMP environment*, above.

Pointer

also known as: mouse pointer
including: cursor, cursor movement key, arrow key, caret
is an icon (sometimes in the form of an arrow) on the screen. It moves around the screen in response to the movements of a mouse (or other similar device), or the use of keys. The pointer often changes its shape depending on its position on the screen, or the situation in an application. When the pointer indicates a position in text it is usually called the *cursor*.

Cursor is the screen symbol which indicates where on the screen the next action will begin. To make it easier to find and follow in text handling situations, the cursor may be made to flash on and off or the present position might be emphasised by using *highlighting* (see below). When entering text, the cursor automatically advances to the next typing position after a key is pressed. Actions other than entering text require the movement of the cursor about the screen. These movements are controlled by a mouse (or other similar device), or by the *cursor movement keys*.

Cursor movement keys (up, down, left or right), which are sometimes referred to as the *arrow keys* (↑, ↓, ←, →), are one way of directing the movement of the cursor about the screen.

Caret is the name for a symbol used by printers to show that text needs inserting; for this reason the name is used for the screen cursor for inserting text which is often in the form of a 'I'. Unfortunately, *caret* is also the correct name for the character ^ which is one of the symbols available on many keyboards.

Highlighting

including: inverse video

is changing the appearance of a part of a screen display by altering it in some way so that it stands out; for example by changing colour arrangements or by putting shading around an area of the screen. One commonly used method involves the use of ***inverse video***, in which black becomes white and colours change to the colour represented by the inverse bit pattern, for example the inverse of 00011011 is 11100100.

Highlighting changes:

HIGHLIGHT   into   HIGHLIGHT

Mouse

including: mouse event, mouse button

is a computer input device, usually connected to the computer by a thin cable. Using a hand to move the mouse in contact with a flat surface causes a cursor, or pointer, on the display screen to move. A mouse has one, or more, finger-operated press switches, called ***(mouse) buttons***. When a mouse button is pressed it causes a 'click' sound and passes a signal to the computer; the same thing happens when the switch is released. What effect these have will depend upon where the pointer is on the screen and what software is being used. Mouse operations, such as *clicking* (see below), dragging (see *drag*, below) or combining these with the use of keys on the keyboard provide a wide range of possible options at any moment. Actions, such as pressing or releasing the mouse buttons, are sometimes called ***mouse events***. See also, *event*, page 194. One alternative to a mouse is a *trackerball* (see below).

Trackerball

sometimes called: trackball

is an input device which is used to do the same things as a *mouse* (see above). It is a ball, set into a cup, which can be made to roll in any direction by using a finger or the palm of a hand, depending on the size of the ball. The movements of the ball are mirrored on the screen by a pointer and finger-operated switches work in the same way as *mouse buttons* (see above). Trackerballs are now sometimes mounted on *laptop computers* (see page 100), being easier to use in this position than a mouse.

Clicking

including: double clicking

Pressing a mouse button is called clicking, because this usually produces a 'click' sound. If the user clicks when the pointer controlled by the mouse is on an *icon* (see above), or a *screen button* (see below), then the operation represented by that icon (or button) is selected. For example, clicking on the picture of the flag of a country may cause its national anthem to be played.

Some software expects the mouse button to be pressed twice in quick succession which is called **double clicking**; a single click may have one effect while double clicking may have another.

Dialogue box

including: text box, list box

is a window which appears when information about a choice is needed, or when options have to be selected. For example, choosing PRINT from a FILE menu may cause a dialogue box to appear, requiring answers to such questions as the name of the file, how many copies, etc. Normally, a dialogue box will offer the chance to cancel the request as well as the option to proceed. Dialogue boxes are intended to make it easy to obtain the necessary information quickly.

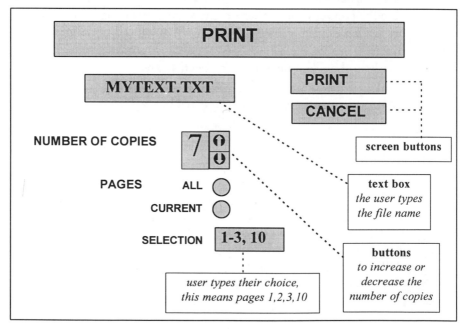

Figure A15.1: Dialogue box

In the dialogue box, shown in Figure A15.1, the **text box** for typing the file name, **MYTEXT.TXT**, could be replaced by a **list box**, in which the application shows a list of file names from which the user selects with the pointer.

Some list boxes stay the same size, others drop down to show several items.

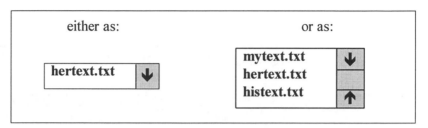

Figure A15.2: List box

See also the diagram, Figure A15.5, in *conversational interface,* page 80.

Screen button

is the name given to an area of the screen which is used to select an action. Selection is usually achieved by moving the pointer to the button and then pressing (and releasing) a *mouse button* (see above). A screen button may be an icon or the picture of a button switch with an icon or a word on it. See also *toolbar*, below, and *dialogue box*, above.

Drag

including: drag-and-drop editing

is the use of a mouse (or other similar device) to move an area of a screen display, which may be text or some part of a graphic display, bodily from one location to another. Before such movement can take place, the area concerned has to be defined in some way such as *highlighting* text (see above), or marking the boundaries of a graphics item. Moving things around in this way is sometimes referred to as **drag-and-drop editing**, which may also be used to copy, as well as move, part of a screen display. One example of dragging is moving the icon for a file from one sub-directory to another as a way of repositioning the file within the directory; another would be moving a graphic item from an application running in one window on the screen to a different application running in another window. Drag is sometimes used to mean moving the mouse while holding down a button.

Scrolling

including: scroll bar

is the action of 'rolling-up' a screen. As each new line appears at the bottom, the existing top line disappears off the top. Where an application occupies more than a single screen, it is usual to provide a *scroll bar* to move the displayed portion of the application up or down the screen (vertical scrolling) and sometimes left and right across the screen (horizontal scrolling, see Figure A15.3).

Figure A15.3: Scroll bar

Toolbar

including: tool, toolbox, toggle

is a line of *screen buttons* (see above) which represent the actions, *tools,* that are currently available to be carried out within an applications package or a system. For example, clicking on an icon for a brush in a drawing program will select a paintbrush tool. It is normal to make the icons behave like press switches (buttons), so that it is possible to see which tool has been selected or if the tool is still selected. Clicking on a selected tool again will cancel the selection; this means that the switches are *toggles*, changing each time they are 'clicked'.

Figure A15.4: Toolbar

Toolbox is sometimes used to describe a collection of *utility programs* (see page 280).

Hot key

also known as: quick key

is a function key or a key combination (frequently combining *control* or *alt* with other keys), which causes an action (such as calling up a menu, or running another program) whatever the user is doing. The name suggests the urgency of beginning a new action without fully breaking off from the existing task, or without the need to progress through a sequence of menus. The uses of *function keys* (see page 71) are sometimes defined as a menu on the screen or may be defined on a *keystrip* (see page 88) for the application.

Macro recording

is the action of recording a sequence of keystrokes, which achieve a particular purpose, and saving the recording for future use. By assigning a *hotkey* (see above) to stand for this recorded sequence (see *macro,* page 213), it is possible to make frequently required actions easier to perform. For example, a single key combination could be used to type the whole of a frequently used phrase.

Interactive computing

including: conversational mode

is a mode of operation in which the user and a computer system are in two-way communication throughout the period of use. In practice, most personal computer applications are interactive, whereas some applications on terminals attached to large central computer systems, for example in supermarket branches, are still run in batch mode with data and command instructions supplied through the terminal. (See also *batch processing,* page 166.) When a terminal user on a network appears to be in continuous communication with the central computer, getting replies almost immediately, it is described as ***conversational mode***.

Command line interface

including: command sequence

is a form of user interface in which the user types commands for the computer to carry out. As the term suggests, the command is usually restricted to a single line of text, which may consist of any sequence of acceptable commands. The user has to know the conventions of the *command line interpreter* (see page 281). The commands may be combined to make up a ***command sequence***, which can make this a convenient way of getting the computer to perform a sequence of actions (see *macro,* page 213). This form of interface can be efficient in the hands of experienced users, but can be very frustrating for those who do not know the right commands to use.

Conversational interface

is a form of user interface in which the computer and the user appear to be holding a conversation or dialogue, using the screen for output and the keyboard for input. The user may be seeking information from the computer, but the computer may need to ask its own questions before it is able to provide the answer to the question originally asked. The example below, which could be a dialogue about a request to print a file, gives an indication of the kind of communication that might be experienced:

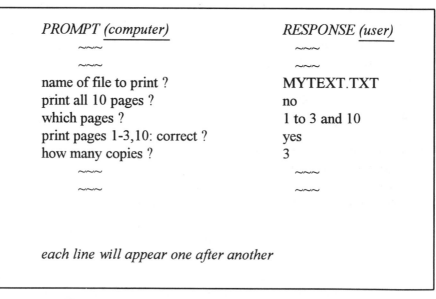

Figure A15.5: Conversational dialogue screen

Forms dialogue interface

including: response field

is a user interface in which the computer outputs separate prompt (see below) and response fields for a number of inputs.

Response field is the place in a dialogue screen (Figure A15.6) where users may type their responses, in any order. There may be automatic movement of the cursor, depicting the entry point, from response field to response field. The process is similar to filling in a form on paper and allows the entries to be changed at any stage until the 'execution' key or button is pressed.

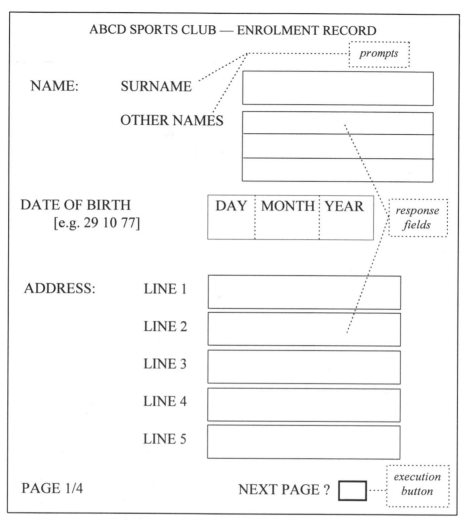

Figure A15.6: *Forms dialogue screen*

Wildcard

is a symbol used in some commands or search instructions to stand for a range of characters. For example, **?** is often used to stand for any single character, hence the command `type d?????.doc` would cause all files of type `.doc` whose names have five characters beginning with a **d** to be typed. The character ***** is usually used to stand for any group of characters (or perhaps none), hence the command `delete *.*` may be unwise, since it could cause all files to be deleted.

Directory

including: sub-directory, directory file, folder

is a group of files or a group of files and **sub-directories**. A sub-directory is a directory within a directory, its contents may be files or other sub-directories or both. A directory is held, in the form of a list of file and sub-directory names (the **directory file**), on the backing store to which it refers; stored with it will be information needed for files to be retrieved from the backing store. A directory file is sometimes referred to as a **folder**. Directories are usually represented in a tree structure (see *tree,* page 260), as shown in Figure A15.7. See also *file,* page 185.

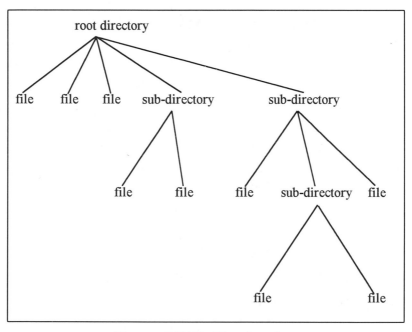

Figure A15.7: *Directory tree*

Error message

is a message to the user indicating that something has gone wrong; it may include instructions on what action is needed. Well designed applications packages will include comprehensive error detection routines and helpful error messages. These routines will detect errors resulting from user mistakes, such as letting the printer run out of paper or failing to put the right disk into a disk drive, as well as errors occurring in the system itself.

Password

including: logging in (log in, logging on, log on), logging out (log out, logging off, log off), personal identification device, (PID), personal identification number, (PIN)

is the sequence of characters, known only to the user and the computer system, that must be presented as part of *logging in* to a computer system with security protection before it will allow a user access to the system. Some parts of the system may have additional passwords.

Logging in (*also known as: log in, logging on, log on*) is the procedure that has to be followed to gain access to and begin a session on a *multi-access* system (see page 166) with security procedures.

Logging out (*also known as: log out, logging off, log off*) is the correct procedure to be followed when ending a session on a multi-access system.

In addition to using passwords, some systems also have some kind of 'electronic key', such as a cash card for bank systems, which has to be used with a password. This is sometimes referred to as a *personal identification device, (PID)*.

Personal identification number (PIN) is a number used as a password, particularly with cash cards used in cash points (see *automatic teller machines*, page 20).

Prompt

is a character or message displayed on a screen to indicate that the user is expected to do something, usually to input data into the system. Sometimes a visual prompt is emphasised by a sound.

Screen editing

is the process of changing (editing) stored data or programs using a computer screen. The characters which are the data or programs are altered on the screen by adding, removing or changing individual characters or groups of characters.

Smart card

is a plastic card in the same format (the same size and shape) as a credit card which has a microprocessor and memory built into it. It has much greater memory than the magnetic stripe on a normal plastic card.

Light pen

is an input device, which looks like a pen with a wire connecting it to the computer. The light pen is used to point at, and thus indicate, a position on the screen. Software is used to calculate this position and perform an appropriate action. One application is the use of the pen to draw on the screen rather like an artist drawing on paper.

Touch sensitive keyboard

including: concept keyboard

is a type of keyboard in which the 'keys' are sensitive areas of a plastic surface. These keyboards are generally used in special situations, for example where there is a risk of dirt or liquids getting into a conventional keyboard. Overlays are put on the keyboard to indicate the areas and their meaning, and software interprets this for the computer. One particular kind of touch sensitive keyboard is called a *concept keyboard.* This has programmable areas to input information to the computer. It is often used with young or disabled learners.

Touchpad

also known as: touch switch, pressure pad, pressure switch

is one of a number of names for *touch* or *pressure* operated sensor *pads* or *switches*, used as input devices for some applications. They can be used in conjunction with special software to enable people with severe physical disabilities to select items displayed on a screen by touching (or pressing) the pad when the item needed is highlighted. See also *touch sensitive keyboard,* above.

Touchscreen

is a special screen that is able to detect the position on the screen which a user's finger is touching or pointing at. One way of doing this is by having two sets of fine wires on the screen (one set across and the other down) which sense the finger position. Another way is to have vertical and horizontal patterns of infra red light beams which are interrupted when a finger (or pointer) is close to the screen. With both these methods, the software can calculate what position has been touched.

User friendly

describes a system, either hardware or software, which is kind to its users. Since the user interface largely determines what a user experiences, it is the software system which is generally being described. However, some aspects of hardware, such as the feel of a keyboard, can improve or spoil user friendliness.

User transparent

sometimes: transparency

describes actions by a computer system, hardware or software, which are not obvious to the user. Nearly all hardware actions, other than those affecting the screen, are transparent, and most operating system actions take place without the user being aware of them. Well designed user interfaces achieve high levels of *transparency*.

Wizard

is a feature of some applications packages, which helps users to perform a task. By asking the user some questions, a wizard provides help in making best use of the available facilities. For example, a table wizard might help to create tables by offering a number of possible types, or a letter wizard might show how you could set out a letter for a particular situation.

A16　User Documentation

Other terms related to documentation will be found in
C2 Systems Documentation, and C8 Program
Documentation. As User Documentation is concerned with
making the computer easy to use, terms in section A15 User
Interface may also be of interest.

Software Documentation

When a computer software package is bought, whether it is a computer game, a spreadsheet or a programming language, user documentation will also be received. This may be anything from an instruction leaflet to a series of manuals. This 'user documentation' is designed to introduce the package and to tell the user how to use the software to its best advantage. This documentation may be totally in printed form or it may be seen on the screen when running the package. There may also be files on the accompanying disks called "Readme" or "Help".

There must be an overview of the package describing what it is capable of doing in fairly broad terms but also include some specific uses and features that are important with this package. This may include some sample screen displays and printouts to show the users what to expect.

An early section should be on how to install the software (to make the software available on the user's system). These instructions might well include

how to make extra copies of disks for safety (in case the working disk is damaged)

how to copy on to a hard disk and configure the software (where the user has a choice of options as to how the software is to work and what hardware will be used, such as the type of printer)

how to make hardware adjustments that may be needed. These may be described for the user to do or may require the help of a dealer.

Some of these operations may refer to hardware documentation. For example reference may be needed to printer documentation.

It may be that the software has already been installed, so installation and configuration may not seem to be of interest. However, if the printer is changed, the configuration process will probably need repeating, either by the user or the supplier.

It is important that the novice user has access to tutorial material consisting of written instructions or similar sequences given as an on-screen tutorial. This is designed to speed the user through the simple aspects onto the more advanced usage that may have been in mind when the purchase was made. Equally for the more experienced user there should be some summary sheet or quick reference guide. It is useful to have a reference to the use of specific keys (such as the function keys), perhaps in the form of a **keystrip** (a piece of card or plastic that is fitted onto the keyboard).

One of the first actions of the user should be to register the purchase with the publishing software company so that any upgrade or fault information can be passed on. With more sophisticated packages there might be a telephone help line.

An index to the documentation should help the user to find how to do specific tasks and to find more detailed explanations of error messages.

Hardware Documentation

Any piece of hardware will need some instructions on how to use it. Usually a physical connection will need to be made between items of equipment, for example between a monitor and computer. This will specify details of the connecting leads and where they are to be connected.

Most computers can have 'add on' peripherals, such as scanners or hard drives, to attach to existing systems. Some hardware needs minor physical adjustment before connecting it to a computing system. Some hardware devices are attached via a SCSI (Small Computer Systems Interface) and these devices need a unique device number. These could be set by use of jumpers. Printers commonly have switches which are controlled *either* by software *or* by hardware. **DIP switches** (see Figure A16.2 for an example) are commonly used to specify the details of paper to be used, the characters to be printed and the type and speed of communication between computer and printer. These details may alternatively be specified by a special sequence of key presses on the device. Printers also may need to have paper feed mechanisms fitted.

With a new computer system the user documentation will also give the options that are controlled by software. These might include the type of monitor to be used, the type of printer and the speed of response of the mouse. Instructions on using the mouse, general care of the computer and use of disk drives are usually included. These will include how to format and copy disks and precautions that should be taken to prevent accidental damage and loss of data. Documentation may contain details on how your hardware may be customised for improving performance in a variety of circumstances. There is often a section on troubleshooting faults should your system not respond as it should, for example what to do if the printer produces gibberish or the screen remains blank.

More technical detail is usually available (at extra cost) from the manufacturer or a third party. The quality of such literature varies in its accuracy and clarity.

Keystrip

is a piece of card or plastic used with a keyboard. It labels the operations performed by function keys within specific programs. For example, in a word processor the function key F4 might have Search/Replace above it (see Figure A16.1).

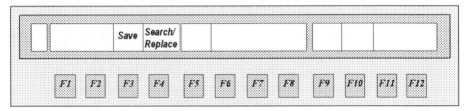

Figure A16.1: A keystrip

Tutorial

provides the user with a guided tour through the software. It is a sequence of tasks to be carried out. This will help the user to find out how to use the software by experimenting with it and seeing the results.

User documentation

gives the user any information necessary for the successful running of a piece of software or hardware. This does not generally include many technical details which will usually be found in *maintenance documentation* (see page 172)

README file

is a file which is provided on the medium with the software. It contains the latest details of using or loading the software.

HELP system

is a means of providing helpful messages to guide a user when using a software package. It will give indications of how to answer prompts from the software and how to perform relevant operations.

DIP switch

is one of a set of small slide operated switches mounted together in a bank (Figure A16.2). These are used to set options on hardware, such as printers.

Figure A16.2: *Bank of eight DIP switches*

Jumper

is a detachable flexible-wire connection between suitable socket points on a circuit board. Sometimes a rigid version may be found on printers and other peripherals, possibly arranged in banks like *DIP switches* (see above), for which they are an alternative.

Install

is to transfer software onto the medium from which it is to be run; normally a hard drive, but could be onto a floppy disk or a network.

Deinstall

including: key disk

is to remove software from a medium, the process is the reverse of *install*. This should remove all traces of the software and release the space from the storage medium. If the license is to install a limited number of copies, then deinstallation recredits the disk (normally called the *key disk*, see below).

Control panel

is a small display/keyboard that enables the user to set device options. On a printer this may be used to set the print style or change the paper source.

Key disk

is a disk used to install software which contains credits that are reduced by one on each installation. It may also be a disk that is required every time a program is run to reduce the possibility of software piracy. See also *software copyright*, page 97.

Dongle

is a piece of hardware used to reduce the possibility of software piracy. It usually plugs into a standard interface on a computer. Without the correct dongle the protected software will not run.

A17　Computer Personnel

Further definitions related to the area of human-computer interaction are found in section A15 User Interface.

Computer systems are the concern of people and human-computer interaction is extensive.

It is people who ask for systems, specify systems, design and build systems. They develop and enhance existing systems, implement systems, manage and use systems. People – as described through their personal information – are often both the direct source and the subject of the computer's database. The demand, by people, for information is the main reason why computers are needed.

In many organisations, the 1990s have seen an increase in both the number and the types of task which computers have been required to perform. To enable this expansion of use to be managed in a controlled and professional manner, not only have computer-related job descriptions and responsibilities changed but many jobs on the user side of the interface have similarly been affected.

This section gives an indication of the types of job related to computer use and offers a brief description of some of those jobs. A more detailed description of the wide range of IT (information technology) jobs, and the skill levels involved, can be obtained by examining the British Computer Society's **Industry Structure Model**.

Recently, some large organisations have changed their operational methods and, instead of employing teams of IT specialists themselves, have signed contracts with outside firms who agree to supply these specialist staff as and when required. This is known as **outsourcing**.

Computer support personnel

are those involved in the day-to-day running of an organisation's computing installation.

Computer operator

is the person who operates the computer and, where appropriate, responds to requests from the operating system and from remote users in a time-sharing system.

Data processing manager

is the person responsible for the overall running of a data processing department.

Database administrator

is the person in an organisation responsible for the structure and control of the data in the organisation's database. See also *database management system*, page 26.

Decision support specialist

is responsible for organising database interrogation procedures to allow business managers to access management information in appropriate formats.

Network controller

also known as: network manager
is the person responsible for the smooth running of a network. This will generally include communications (software and hardware), access (user identifications and passwords) and shared resources such as common data storage. (Compare with *network controller - types of computer.* page 104.)

Data preparation staff

are those responsible for organising and entering data into the computer system.

Hybrid manager

combines business understanding, IT technical competence and organisational knowledge and skills. Typically, IT competence will be gained after the acquisition of the business and organisational components.

Programmer

including: systems programmer, applications programmer, information systems engineer, coder
is the person responsible for writing and testing computer programs. Those involved in the writing of operating systems, general utilities (such as sort routines) and specialist tools (such as a graphical user interface) are usually called *systems programmers*, while those writing programs for specific user applications are known as *applications programmers*.

Those programmers working on the design and testing of programs are often called *information systems engineers*, while those who are mostly involved in translating statements into machine readable form are called *coders*.

Systems analyst/systems designer

is the person responsible for the analysis of a system to assess its suitability for computerisation. Where computerisation is decided upon, the systems designer will be responsible for building on the analyst's results to create the new computer-based system and will normally work up to the point where programmers can sensibly take over.

Where persons who have been responsible for the analysis then work on the new system design, they are referred to as *analyst/designers*.

Technical support staff

are computer specialists who are concerned with the integrity and functionality of the computer system. They may be hardware rather than software oriented.

Computer service engineer

including: computer engineer, maintenance engineer, service engineer
is the person responsible for the maintenance of the hardware, and is often employed by a specialist contract servicing company.

Software support staff

including: help desk, hot line
are usually employed by software houses or specialist vendors in order to respond to questions relating to the use of particular pieces of software. They are often referred to as a '*help desk*' and may be contacted quickly using the telephone '*hot line*' to give advice on problem solving.

Information systems manager

is the current term for the person who manages the interface between the computer system and the organisation's user community.

Data Protection Officer

is the named person in an organisation who is responsible for seeing that the organisation's registration (under the *UK Data Protection Act 1984*, see page 95) is adhered to.

Outsourcing

is the principle of buying-in information systems services from specialist organisations instead of continuing the traditional practice of retaining company employees to provide them.

Industry Structure Model (ISM)

Designed by the British Computer Society, this sets out, as a series of competences, what is expected of a person performing computer-related task at each stage in a variety of career paths.

Computer systems contain valuable and meaningful data. Its accuracy, currency, integrity and accessibility form the basis of reliable output. Safeguarding this data is vital both to the owner and to the user of the data.

Incorrect data can result in inappropriate output. Actions based on that output can be costly. Damage can be caused to machines controlled by such output and the reputation, health or livelihood of people can be put at risk.

In the United Kingdom, and also in many other countries, there is legislation which covers the use of a variety of data processing activities with severe penalties for breaking these laws. Therefore, safeguarding data makes sense for both economic and legal reasons.

Computer systems in manufacturing, real-time processes and safety critical applications may need to meet certain design standards and their implementation may need to conform to quality assurance standards. Product Liability legislation, particularly in the USA, imposes severe penalties on the producers of poor quality computing products.

There is also legislation covering copyright which enables software producers to protect their investment in software development.

Computer Misuse Act

including: computer abuse
is the 1990 United Kingdom Act of Parliament aimed specifically at 'hackers'. It defines *computer misuse* as the unauthorised use of computer systems and relates both to hardware (using a particular computer without permission) and software (accessing parts of the system without authorisation). It introduced three new offences relating to unauthorised computer access and to unauthorised modification or deletion of data.

Computer abuse is not legally defined, but is generally taken to be the wrongful use of computer systems and software for improper anti-social or illegal purposes, including fraud, the propagation of *viruses* (see below), data terrorism (threats made against computer systems and data) and computer pornography.

Data protection

including: Data Protection Act
is the establishment of safeguards to preserve integrity, privacy and security of data.

Data Protection Act is the 1984 United Kingdom Act of Parliament which sets out requirements for the control of personal data stored on computer systems. The Act covers many aspects of data protection. It also requires that data users attend to such matters as the accuracy and appropriateness of the data they hold. The right of individuals to see – and where necessary to correct – personal data is also covered. Data users covered under the Act are required to supply, to a public register, sufficient details about themselves and the nature, purpose and range of the data they hold. This information should enable any individual to ascertain if personal data relating to them is likely to be held by that data user. If a data user holds personal data about an individual, that individual can require the data user to supply a copy of that data.

Hacking

is the term used to describe attempts (successful or otherwise) to gain unauthorised access to computer systems. This may relate to the unauthorised use of a computer or to unauthorised access to particular programs or data stored on that computer (for example, by persons who exceed the legitimate permissions which they may have to use only part of a total system).

Integrity

describes the consistency of data during and after processing. Data which has not been accidentally or maliciously corrupted is said to have integrity.

Piracy

is the illegal copying of software whether for personal use or re-sale.

Privacy

is the recognition of the private nature of certain data which should only be accessed by, or disclosed to, an authorised person. In considering the maintenance of privacy, systems designers build safeguards into both operational routines (for example, the use of *passwords*, see page 83) and physical areas (for example, the use of *personal identification devices*, see page 83) to allow systems controllers to reduce the risks of unauthorised access.

Security

is the establishment and application of safeguards to protect data, software and computer hardware from accidental or malicious modification, destruction or (in the case of data) unauthorised disclosure.

Encryption

is the encoding of data by a computer system. Its purpose is to add a level of security to the data, both when stored electronically and when being transmitted between computer systems. To provide the correct output, matching encoding and decoding algorithms need to be used.

In conventional systems the same cipher key is used for both the enciphering and deciphering stages and therefore all users must have a copy of the key. Where the number of users is small and the concern is for security of stored data, a single cipher key is usually sufficient. Where transmission, rather than storage, requires extra protection it is possible to have different enciphering and deciphering keys. See *public key cryptography*, page 44, and *data encryption standard*, page 43.

Electronic signature

is a specific code related to a particular operation or data set, which needs to be matched by an input signal, before that operation can be authorised or before that data set can be addressed.

Virus

including: worm,, Trojan, computer hygiene, virus checking, disinfection
is a routine which is designed to alter any other routine if a particular pre-determined set of conditions occurs. The design of viruses often includes an instruction to replicate itself under some other pre-determined set of conditions. Most viruses are specific to some particular host (such as a boot program) but others, once activated, can replicate spontaneously (this type may be called a *worm*) or perform their illegal objective (called a *Trojan* or *Trojan Horse*).

Virus problems may be dealt with by the use of proprietary software designed to detect and remove a wide variety of them (often this software is marketed under the heading of *computer hygiene*). The process of detecting viruses already in the system is usually called *virus checking*.

Some computer hygiene programs may be placed resident in memory and continually monitor executable files for changes in size. If any change is detected, the file is prevented from being run and a user message is given. New data read into the computer is also screened for viruses and appropriate action taken. These actions are known as *disinfection*.

Software copyright

including: software licence, FAST (Federation Against Software Theft), freeware, shareware

It is not always realised that computer software is covered by similar copyright laws to those which apply to books and other publications. The 1988 Copyright, Designs and Patents Act protects 'intellectual property' and establishes the rights of the author. The unauthorised use of any commercial software that has not been properly purchased with a *software licence* is illegal. In practice, this means that copying software bought by someone else is likely to be an offence. Even the use of properly-purchased software on a network can be illegal unless the licence specifically allows this form of multiple use. See also *key disk,* page 89.

FAST (Federation Against Software Theft) is an organisation operating on behalf of software producers; it actively pursues breaches of software copyright. Sometimes, however, software is offered copyright-free; this may be called *freeware* or *shareware.*

Part B:
What Computer Systems Are Made Of

B1   Types of Computer   100

B2   Peripherals   105

B3   Memory   109

B4   Display Devices   125

B5   Printers   133

B6   Networks   143

B7   Communications Devices and Control Devices   153

Computer systems can be assembled out of a variety of different pieces of equipment in a whole variety of different arrangements. This part of the Glossary defines terms which will be encountered when considering how computer systems are arranged, organised and connected to other computer systems. Terms related to the uses of computers are in part A and terms concerned with the internal workings of computers are in Part C.

B1   Types of Computer

This section includes those terms that are descriptive of computers in general.

A computer is an automatic, programmable, digital data processor. Every part of this definition is crucial to our understanding of what the modern computer is, and how it works. **Automatic** means simply that it operates without human intervention, except where this is expressly pre-planned and provided for. This feature alone distinguishes the computer from the simple pocket calculator, where each computation results from a manual key-press. **Programmable** means that the instructions to be followed automatically are held (as a 'program') within the store of the computer. If a repetitive calculation (a 'loop') is necessary, the same instructions can be used and re-used. The instructions are usually held in the same storage area as that used for data – computer programs and the data they operate on can comfortably co-exist in the same sort of storage. Often (usually), the instructions can be replaced with other instructions: either as a part of developing a program to completion, or as a wholesale replacement of one program with another. **Digital** means that the computer operates with quantities that take only distinct values from a known range: often, but not always, these are binary quantities that take only two values, 'on' and 'off'. The power of digital data is that the computer (and the programmer) knows in advance what the data will look like: this is very similar to the human knowledge that all numbers, no matter how large, can be expressed as a combination of the ten digits 0, 1, 2, 3, ... 9. In principle, humans can add together (or multiply, divide – whatever) *any* two numbers. The 'hundreds, tens and units' method can easily be extended to numbers as large as we please. Notice that, because programs and data can occupy the same storage in the computer, programs are also expressed digitally. Although digital processing is now universal, computers did not always work this way – see *analog computer* below.

Finally, **data processor** simply expresses what a computer *does* – it operates on digital data, and produces some actions as a result.

Types of computer

including: mainframe, mini-computer, microcomputer, Lisa, Macintosh, PC, Personal Computer, personal digital assistant (PDA), home computer, portable computer, palmtop computer, laptop computer, notebook computer, multimedia computer, super-computer

Newer computers tend to be smaller than those they replace. Names are needed to distinguish each new type of computer. Originally 'computer' meant something that filled a room, needed air-conditioning and several operators to run it. When the same level of computing power became available in a much smaller package, the rather ill-defined term *mini-computer* was introduced to describe the newcomer, while *mainframe* was reserved for the original monster.

The most significant development of the late 1970s was the introduction of a type of computer small enough and cheap enough to be bought by individuals. Apple Computers led the way commercially with their range of computers which evolved through the *Lisa*, offering the first convenient *graphical user interface* (see page 71), to the *Macintosh*. Later still, when IBM introduced the *Personal Computer* (or *PC*), a general name was needed for these types of computer. *Microcomputer* (or simply *micro*) became the general name, with 'PC' reserved for the IBM small business machines and *home computer* for the domestic hobbyist or games-playing machines.

Portable computers were the next development: *laptop computers* run off battery power and are suited for use while travelling, or at business meetings. A *notebook computer* (sometimes called a *palmtop computer*) is one that is very compact, and is designed to be carried in a pocket – because it is useful in situations where a mains-powered computer is not appropriate; a notebook computer usually includes software to transfer data to a PC or a larger machine. The current trend is for smaller and even more portable computers: the *personal digital assistant* (*PDA*) is a pocket-sized device without a keyboard (it is accessed through a pen-like stylus moving over the display, and the software recognises handwriting) but has failed to take the market by storm. The future in this area is extremely unpredictable.

A computer, often a PC, which has facilities for processing data as text, graphics, video moving images and sound, and can interface with a range of input and output devices for these different forms of data, is called a *multimedia computer.*

A *super-computer* is a very large machine which processes hundreds of millions of instructions per second. It is likely to have many parallel processors to achieve this. Data is processed simultaneously (in parallel) as well as sequentially to complete the tasks very quickly.

These names are all relative to one another, and are ill-defined: most personal computers now are more powerful than the earlier mainframes.

Analog computer

including: hybrid computer

Originally the word computer meant simply something that calculated (once, it even meant a *person* who performs calculations.). When modern computing began, as well as the digital computer described in the introduction, there were devices known as analog computers. Instead of operating on digital data, these used continuously varying quantities, such as voltages, or positions, to represent numbers, and combined these electrically or mechanically as a way of 'processing'. This term is now only of historic interest. Inevitably, some computers, known as *hybrid computers* used both analog and digital technology in combination.

Computer

is an automatic, programmable, digital data processor. This definition is expanded and explained in the introduction to this section; the definition also excludes the *analog computer* (see above).

Computer generations

including: first, second, third, fourth and fifth generation computers,
EDSAC, ENIAC, EDVAC, Atlas, Univac I, LEO (Lyons Electronic Office),
ICL 1900, IBM 360

are a convenient way of distinguishing major advances in computer technology. The first three generations have well-accepted meanings, but the later generations tend to be used by manufacturers to stress the more modern features of a particular machine.

First generation computers were the earliest, and used valves, mercury delay lines, electrostatic memories and had very limited storage. Important first-generation computers include the experimental EDSAC, EDVAC and ENIAC (which lacked stored-program facilities, and would now fail our definition of computer.) and the production scientific computers DEUCE and Pegasus. Commercial machines were LEO (Lyons Electronic Office) and Univac I. These machines were all large, typically filling one or more rooms, and consumed large amounts of power.

Second generation computers arrived when the transistor replaced the valve as the basic component. They were consequently much more reliable, and consumed less power. They were cheaper, but still out of reach for most businesses and certainly for individuals. One of the most significant machines was *Atlas*.

Third generation computers saw the transistor replaced by the integrated circuit (the 'silicon chip'). They were again cheaper, and consumed less power and became even more reliable. One consequence of new design methods was the ability to produce whole families of similar, but differently-powered, computers – the ICL 1900 series, or the IBM 360 family, for example.

Fourth generation computers are those commonly encountered today. There is no single technological advance that distinguishes fourth generation computers from the third generation, except possibly the much greater use of *large-scale integration* (see page 312) of components on silicon chips, which resulted in increasing similarity of machine design. A dramatic fall in the cost of internal memory, and increases in the speed and capacity of external storage, led to new applications and new methods of programming. In addition there was a growing realisation that standardisation of software, particularly operating systems, is necessary.

Fifth generation computers are (still) something between an experimental prototype and an advertising agency's slogan. Many new computing concepts, that seemed to be significant advances on the previous generation, attracted this label: the use of formal mathematical logic in programming, for example, or the move away from a 'traditional' *Von Neumann* architecture (see page 305); increased use of *distributed processing* (see page 150), *parallel processing* (see page 298) and so on. New methods of interacting with a computer – speech, touch – also came to be known as 'fifth generation'. The term should be used with caution, until the sixth generation arrives, and we fully understand what was in the fifth.

Computer system

including: configuration
is the complete collection of components (hardware, software, peripherals, power supplies, communications links) making up a single computer installation. The particular choice of components is known as the *configuration* – different systems may have the same configuration or not.

Front-end processor

is a computer dedicated to managing communications devices or other computers linked to a more powerful computer, generally a *mainframe* (see above). The front-end processor receives messages and commands from the communications devices, and organises these before passing them on to the larger computer for processing.

Hardware

is the physical part of a computer system – the processor(s), storage, peripherals, etc., as opposed to the *software* (see page 168) and the data in the storage.

Multiprocessor system

is a computer system with several *processors* (see page 291). These will work co-operatively, handling specific tasks (managing the screen display, doing arithmetic computation, handling peripherals) or simply sharing out the processing to enable tasks to proceed in parallel where possible.

Network controller

is a computer dedicated to organising a computer network. It handles the communications between users and the shared resources, such as disks and printers. Some network topologies, such as the *star network* (see page 147), where the central computer is the network controller, can only operate with a controller; other arrangements may not use one. See also *server*, page 151.

Word processor

is a computer dedicated to, or primarily for, word processing. Some have displays which are the proportions of conventional paper sizes; some offer black text on a white, or coloured, background; most provide an extended keyboard with function keys for the software provided with the computer. Nearly all these facilities are now available as standard on general-purpose computers.

B2   *Peripherals*

Peripherals are devices that can be attached to a computer system to do specialised jobs and which are frequently necessary for the effective use of a computer system. They are not necessarily provided as part of the computer. The range of devices is varied and many peripherals have been covered in other sections:

> *Additional memory, and terms relating to it, will be found in B3;*
>
> *Display devices and related terms will be found in B4;*
>
> *Printing devices and related terms will be found in B5;*
>
> *User interfaces often rely upon extra equipment being attached and details of such equipment will be found in A15;*
>
> *Sound, communications and control each have their own peripherals and details will be found in A11 (for sound), A4, B7 and C17 (for communications) and A9 and B7 (for control)*

This section is concerned with those peripherals which do not find a place in the sections listed above.

There is a vast range of peripherals available but each performs one or both of the functions of **input** or **output**. At one time all memory, apart from immediate access memory, and all input and output devices were seen as 'peripheral'. This has changed, especially in microcomputer systems, and things that used to be seen as special input devices, such as a mouse, are now a fundamental part of the system.

Peripheral device

is the term used to describe an input, output, or backing storage device which can be connected to the central processing unit.

Input/Output device (I/O device)

is a peripheral unit which can be used both as an input device, or as an output device. In some instances, 'input output device' may be two separate devices housed in the same cabinet.

Input device

is a peripheral unit that can accept data, presented in the appropriate machine-readable form, decode it and transmit it as electrical pulses to the central processing unit.

Document reader

is an input device that reads marks or characters made in predetermined positions on special forms.

Machine readable

including: mark sense reader, optical mark reader (OMR), optical character recognition (OCR), magnetic ink character recognition (MICR), bar code reader/scanner, wand

describes data that can be input to a computer without the need for any preparation. This may be a magnetic pattern stored on a credit card or travel ticket, or printing on paper which is also visible to humans. There is a variety of ways of reading printing into the computer, but in most cases there will be the need to have software to analyse what has been read in order to recognise it – for example, after a page of typed text has been read in using a *scanner* (see page 30), it requires complex processing before the image can be turned into codes for the individual characters.

A *mark sense reader* is an input device that reads special forms (or cards), by detecting the marks made in predetermined positions. The marks may be put on the form by hand or may be printed in some way.

An *Optical Mark Reader* (*OMR*) is an input device that reads marks made in predetermined positions on special forms (or cards) by a light-sensing method; for example, the numbers recorded on a National Lottery entry form.

Optical Character Recognition (*OCR*) is machine recognition of printed characters by light-sensing methods. For example, the reading of typed post codes when mail is automatically sorted or the machine-readable section of a European Community passport.

Magnetic Ink Character Recognition (*MICR*) is machine recognition of stylised characters printed in magnetic ink. The commonest application is the data printed on a bank (or building society) cheque: the cheque number, the branch number and the account number. These characters are both machine and human readable.

Bar code reader or *bar code scanner* is an input device used to read information in *bar code* form (see page 3). Sometimes the reader is built into equipment such as a supermarket checkout terminal, where it is usually referred to as a scanner. This form of reader shines laser light beams onto the object being scanned and interprets the patterns reflected by the bar code. An alternative form is a hand-held device, which is usually called a *wand*; this also works by sensing light reflected by the bar code.

Key-to-disk system
including: key-to-tape system
is an input device for accepting data from a keyboard and writing it straight onto magnetic disk. This method of data input for large computer systems has mostly been replaced by entry into microcomputers acting as terminals to the system or by automatic data capture systems, for example, hand-held key-pads for meter readers. Where the data is written to tape it is called a *key-to-tape system*.

Output device
is a peripheral unit that translates signals from the computer into a human-readable form or into a form suitable for re-processing by the computer at a later stage.

Computer Output on Microfilm (COM)
is a technique for producing computer output directly on microfilm, for example the creation of computer-generated microfiches. This provides a very economical method of storing archive copies of documents and diagrams as well as making them generally available in microfiche form.

Original Equipment Manufacturer (OEM)
including: badging
is a firm which makes basic computer hardware for other manufacturers to build into their products. For example, a manufacturer using a microprocessor as a control device in a washing machine, or a computer manufacturer fitting another manufacturer's disk drive mechanisms into their computer. Many components of computer systems are made by only a small number of manufacturers, and are then built in to systems which are sold by other manufacturers under their own brand name: this practice is known as *badging*.

Plug compatible

including: plug and go

is used to describe any peripheral equipment, made by a manufacturer other than the computer maker, which is intended to be connected to the computer and will work successfully without any adaptation being needed. This has happened successfully only rarely in the past, and a group of hardware and software companies have co-operated to define a set of standards (known as ***plug and go***) to make this more effective.

Timing information

including: index mark, clock mark, clock track

is required because mechanical devices cannot operate with the precision needed by computers. So, for example, an ***index mark*** in the form of an *index hole* (see page 113) is found on some floppy disks to provide a fixed reference point for reading and writing data. Another example is the ***clock marks*** making up the ***clock track*** which synchronise the reading of the items on a mark-sense document.

Figure B2.1: *Clock Track on a machine readable document*

Operator's console

is the *terminal* (see page 150) used by the computer operator to control the operation of a mainframe or mini-computer.

B3   *Memory*

Memory is the name given to that part of a computer system in which data is held. This data is made up of files, either program files or data files. Computer memory serves two purposes. The first is to hold programs or data that the processor needs immediately; for this reason it is sometimes called **immediate access memory**. The second is to hold data that may be needed at some time; it is often called **backing store**. Immediate access memory must be able to be read (and be written to) very quickly, since most computer instructions require that data is moved around in the immediate access memory. Backup memory can have distinctly slower reading and writing times. Immediate access memory is usually about 1000 times as fast as backing store. The immediate access memory is located very close to the processor, so that signals take the shortest possible time in coming from and going to the processor; but backing store can be in separate units connected to the processor by cables.

Memory and storage have meanings that overlap and are often used as interchangeable words; but memory suggests data is immediately available whereas storage suggests that data has to be retrieved. Sometimes memory is described as **primary**, for the immediate access memory; **secondary**, for the principal backing store; and **auxiliary,** for other forms of backing store. A variety of other names are used for immediate access memory, such as IAS, main memory, the memory, the store and for backing store, such as backup memory, peripheral memory, off-line storage.

Throughout the development of computers there has been a continual search for ways of improving memory technology. The search has been for reliable, compact storage devices with low energy consumption. Whenever a suitable new device has been developed, ways of cheap mass-production have been found.

Because of the different requirements for the two functions of memory, it is usual for completely different kinds of technology to be used in a particular computer system. For immediate access memory, most present-day computers use some form of random access memory integrated circuits, in which very large amounts of data can be stored in a single plastic encapsulated chip. For backing store most use some form of magnetic storage, such as disks or tapes, and may also have read-only storage, such as CD-ROM.

Immediate access memory is sometimes in two parts. One part, called **cache** memory, is made up of a small capacity but exceedingly fast memory and is located next to the processor. The other part is much larger, and a copy of some of its contents is put into the cache memory in readiness for instant use. The choice of size for the main memory of a computer is partly determined by the addressing methods used and the cost of memory components. It is usual for computers to be sold with the potential for later memory expansion.

Backing store consists of the medium (the material on which the data is stored) and any associated mechanisms. Most computers use magnetic backing store (tapes or disks), while some use integrated circuit semiconductor memory, and optical systems are increasingly being used. As far as the user is concerned, the medium may be removable; for example, tapes, floppy disks and optical disks, or fixed; for example, hard disks. The advantage of using removable media is that an expensive mechanism can be used for a variety of purposes with cheap media. Fixed disks provide faster access and greater capacity than removable disks and are used to store programs and data that are frequently needed. Most computer systems now have both fixed and removable disks. A large computer system will have fixed disks, removable disks, tape storage and, possibly, optical storage. A personal computer will have at least a hard fixed disk and a floppy disk unit and, possibly, an optical disk unit.

Memory may be **volatile** or **permanent**. Volatile memory loses its data when there is no power supply to it, whereas permanent memory does not require power. All magnetic and optical media provide permanent memory as do some forms of integrated circuit memory. However the most widely used form of integrated circuit memory for immediate access store is volatile; this means that, when the computer is switched on, programs and data have to be loaded from backing store. If power is cut off, for some reason, then all data in memory will be lost.

Memory is often described by the type of *access* that is possible. For example, all the storage locations in immediate access memory can be directly accessed and the access time for all locations is the same; this is described as **random access memory**. In contrast, the data stored on a tape can only be reached by going through the tape, in sequence, until the right place is found; this is described as **serial access memory**. Storage on a disk is in concentric rings and is a collection of small sequential lengths of storage. Since disk storage can be so quickly accessed, it is generally thought of as direct (random) access storage.

Some forms of memory can only be read (**read-only**) and normally cannot be written to except during manufacture. Some semiconductor memory chips are manufactured as a blank memory array that can have data 'programmed' into it at a later time. One advantage is that some of these programmable memory chips can have the data erased and rewritten if necessary. Uses for programmable chips include storing programs for controlling traffic lights or lifts, and computer games programs. Most current optical disk technology is read-only, of which compact disk read-only memory (CD-ROM) is one example. Experience of technical advances suggests that it is only a matter of time before read-write optical devices become generally available at low cost. Some storage devices use a laser system to etch data onto a blank disk; the recorded data can then be read as often as needed but cannot be rewritten. They are called a write-once, read-many (**WORM**) devices.

Storage

also known as: memory

is a general term covering all units of computer equipment used to store data (and programs).

Store

also known as: memory

including: store location, (memory) cell, address (store), main store, immediate access store (IAS), primary store

The store, or memory, is the part of a computer system where data and instructions are held for use by the central processor and where the central processor puts results it generates. The computer store is made up of a large number of identifiable units, called *(store) locations*. Each store location has a unique label, called a *(store) address*, which is recognisable and used by the central processor. Those store locations that can be addressed directly by the central processor are called the *main store, immediate access store (IAS)* or *primary store*. A store location, sometimes called a *(memory) cell*, is capable of holding a single item of data, a *byte* (see page 269).

Backing store

also known as: secondary store, mass storage

including: magnetic disk storage, magnetic tape storage, optical disk storage, magneto-optical storage

is a means of storing large amounts of data outside the *immediate access store* (see above). A computer system will have at least one form of backing store. Most backing store uses magnetic storage, but increasing use is being made of optical storage systems. Backing store is sometimes referred to as *secondary store* or *mass storage.*

Magnetic disk storage is backing store in which flat rotatable circular plates, coated with a magnetic material, are used for storing digital data. The data is written to and read from a set of concentric circular *tracks* (see *magnetic disk*, below).

Magnetic tape storage is backing store which uses plastic tape coated on one side with magnetic material. Digital information is stored on the tape as a set of parallel *tracks* (see *magnetic tape*, below), which are written or read simultaneously.

Optical disk storage is backing store which uses plastic disks on which the data is stored as patterns on the surface. One method uses hollows etched into the surface of the disk for pre-recorded data in the form of *CD-ROMs* (see below). Other methods, such as *Phase Change Optical Disks* (see below) provide read/write optical storage.

Magneto-optical storage is backing store which uses plastic disks on which data is stored by a combination of optical and magnetic methods.

Cache memory

also known as: the cache

including: disk cache

is a part of the main store, between the central processor and the rest of the main store. It has extremely fast access, so sections of a program and its associated data are copied there to take advantage of its short fetch cycle. The use of cache memory can greatly reduce processing time. It is sometimes called the *cache.*

Figure B3.1: *Cache memory*

A way of speeding up the transfer of large amounts of data from disks is to use a *disk cache*, which is a section of memory for holding data that has been read from disk storage. See also *buffering*, page 298.

Disk drive

also known as: magnetic disk drive
including hard disk drive, Winchester drive, fixed head disk unit, floppy disk drive, CD-ROM drive, CD-ROM jukebox
is the unit made up of the mechanism that rotates the disks between the *read/write heads* (see below), and the mechanism that controls the heads. Most disk drives have one set of read/write heads for each surface and have to be moved to the required track. A disk unit with one set of heads for each disk track is called a *fixed head disk unit*. This arrangement gives much faster access to data on the disk(s) but at increased cost.

A *hard disk drive* uses rigid magnetic disk(s) enclosed in a sealed container. It has the advantage of allowing high recording density because the recording heads can be very close to the magnetic material on the disk. A small hard disk drive, sometimes known as a *Winchester disk (drive)*, is widely used in microcomputer systems as the principal back-up store in addition to one or more floppy disk drives.

Floppy disk drives use flexible disks which can be removed from their drives by the user, unlike hard disks which are permanently mounted. See *magnetic disk*, below.

A *CD-ROM drive* (sometimes called a CD-ROM player) is very similar to an audio compact disk player and is used to read CD-ROM disks. A *CD-ROM jukebox* is a CD-ROM drive with a mechanism for automatically changing the current disk for another selected disk; it is similar to the old-fashioned jukebox for playing gramophone records.

Magnetic disk

also known as: computer disk, disk
including hard disk, floppy disk, disk pack, exchangeable disk pack, diskette, index hole, track (disk), cylinder
is a circular disk, usually made of plastic, coated with a layer of magnetic material on which data can be stored by magnetically setting the arrangement of the magnetic material. This is done by electro-magnetic *read/write heads* (see below). Disks may have data stored on one side only (single sided) or on both sides (double sided). The disk may be rigid (a *hard disk*), or flexible (a *floppy disk*). Where a disk drive has multiple disks (a *disk pack*) these are generally rigid, hard disks, on a common spindle with read/write heads for each disk. If the disk pack is removable so that it can be exchanged for another complete pack, it is called an *exchangeable disk pack*.

A floppy disk (sometimes called a *diskette*) has to be protected by an outer covering which prevents the magnetic coating from being damaged and keeps out dirt. Floppy disks are made to agreed standard designs, which can be used on any drive for the same size of disk. The commonest size is 3½ inch, but the earlier 5¼ inch standard is still significantly used.

Floppy disks need to have some way of showing where the tracks start. In 5¼ inch disks this is done by an *index hole*. This is a small hole near the central hole, which lines up with a gap in the casing once every revolution. In 3½ inch disks, it is only possible to fit the disk onto the drive in one position. Floppy disks provide one of the most common ways of passing data and programs from one computer user to another.

The general layout of recording surfaces on a disk and on a multi-surface disk pack is shown in Figure B3.2.

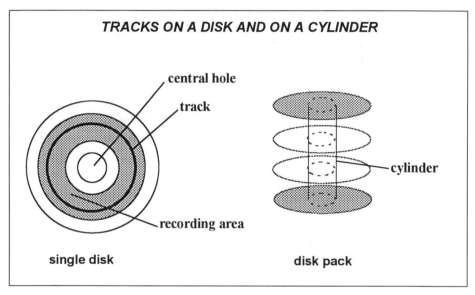

TRACKS ON A DISK AND ON A CYLINDER

central hole

track

cylinder

recording area

single disk   disk pack

Figure B3.2: Track and cylinder

Data is stored on disks in concentric rings, called **tracks**. In a disk pack, a set of tracks one above the other, for example, the tenth track on each disk, is called a **cylinder**. It is normal to store data which needs to be kept together, on a cylinder rather than on one disk, because the read/write heads will not need to move to access the data.

Disk format

including: (disk) formatting, sector, hard-sectored disk, soft-sectored disk, disk verification is the arrangement and organisation of the *tracks* (see above) on a disk. Each track is divided into a number of equal-length portions, called *sectors,* (see Figure *B3.3*). A sector is the smallest addressable portion of a track and is the smallest unit of data that is written to or read from a disk. Each sector on each track will hold the same amount of data, even though outer tracks are longer than inner tracks, so the *packing density* (see below) depends upon the distance of the track from the centre of the disk.

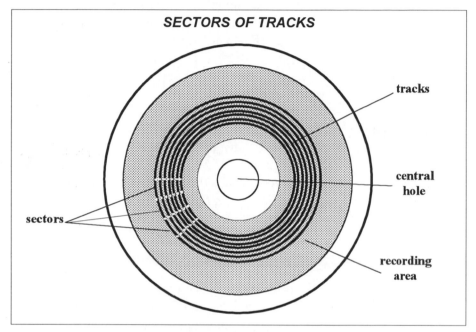

SECTORS OF TRACKS

Figure B3.3: Tracks and sectors

If the sectors are partially or wholly created when the disk is made, the disk is called a *hard-sectored disk*. If the sectors are created by software on an unformatted disk, the disk is called a *soft-sectored disk.* Floppy disks may be either hard- or soft-sectored.

The initial preparation of a blank disk for subsequent writing and reading by adding control information such as track and sector number is called *(disk) formatting*. When a disk is formatted, it is also *verified*; it is checked to ensure that all the tracks and sectors are fit for recording data. Formatting a disk that contains data will erase all the data on it. Floppy disks for personal computers need to be appropriately formatted for the machine on which they are to be used, although some machines may be able to read disks in a variety of formats. It is possible to buy floppy disks which are already formatted.

Disk array

including: RAID (Redundant Array of Inexpensive Disks)
is set of hard disk units used as if they are a single mass storage device. By
using two disks to hold the same data, a disk drive fault will be unlikely to
have any effect on the operation of the whole system. By writing some of the
data to each of a number of disks, storage and retrieval of data can be
speeded up. This method of organising backing store for large computer
systems is known as *RAID*, which stands for *Redundant Array of
Inexpensive* (or *Independent*) *Disks*. RAID systems provide a low-cost
method of ensuring that losses of data are nearly impossible.

Read/write head

including: head crash, park, seek time, disk access time, latency
is the set of electro-magnets and necessary circuitry used to magnetise the
magnetic material used for storage. Tape units have fixed heads and the tape
moves past them. Most disk units have the set of heads on an arm which
moves them from track to track, but fixed head disk units have a set of heads
for each track, which greatly reduces the time taken to access data on the
disk. Double sided disks require a set of heads for each side. The time taken
to get data from a disk, the *disk access time*, includes the time taken to move
the heads to the correct track, called the *seek time*, and the time taken for the
disk to rotate to the correct part of the track, sometimes called *latency*.
However, some people use latency to mean the total waiting time.

    Head crash is when the read/write heads hit the surface of a disk. This can
cause serious damage to the mechanisms and loss of data. To avoid this
happening with personal computers, for example when a machine is moved,
the read/write heads are often automatically put in a safe position, *parked,*
whenever they are not being used to access the disk. Following the proper
procedures of closing all files before ending a session of work will ensure
that the disk is properly parked. Some early personal computers require the
user to give the command for parking the disk.

Magnetic tape drive

also known as: tape drive
is the mechanism that winds the tape between the spools across the
read/write heads. Tape drives are capable of sensing the presence of stored
data on the tape. Tape drives for cassettes are similar to those in domestic
audio and video tape recorders.

Magnetic tape

including: (tape) spool, (tape) reel, (tape) cartridge, (tape) cassette, serial access storage, track (tape), frame, inter-block gap

is a storage medium consisting of a flexible plastic tape covered with magnetic material on one side, and kept on spools. The tape is similar to the tape used in domestic video systems, but of a higher quality since computer tapes need to be accelerated and decelerated very rapidly. The tape may be held on **reels** (or **spools**), requiring an operator to change the reels and thread the tape, or in **cartridges** or in **cassettes** (similar to the domestic video cassettes). This form of storage medium provides **serial access storage**. There are a number of methods of data storage on tape and a number of standard tape widths.

In older systems, many of which are still in use, the data is stored on the tape in parallel **tracks** using either a 7-track or a 9-track system on ½ - inch. A single character is represented by a line of magnetised spots, a **frame**, across the tape; these represent the bits for that character in an appropriate code, such as *EBCDIC* (see page 267).

Figure B3.4: Magnetic tape (½ - inch).

Data is written to the tape in blocks, with a gap between each block, called an **inter-block gap.** The gap is needed for the tape to accelerate to the correct speed for reading or writing or to stop after reading or writing. Since the data is stored sequentially, finding an item of data will require that all the tape up to the data item is wound past the read/write heads until the required item is found. Figure B3.4 shows a diagrammatic representation of data on this form of magnetic tape; the data is stored as discrete areas of magnetism along each track.

More recent systems use the same technology as video recorders, where the data blocks are written on diagonal tracks (Figure B3.5) across the tape by a rotating head. This gives very high density and greater read/write speeds than the earlier tape systems.

Figure B3.5: Blocks in diagonal tracks.

Other tape formats include blocks arranged side by side on multiple tracks (Figure B3.6) and blocks one after another in a 'serpentine' arrangement with alternate tracks written in opposite directions (Figure B3.7).

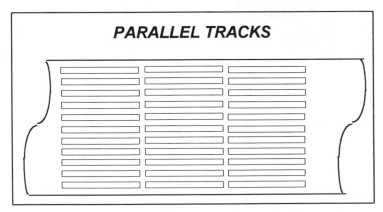

Figure B3.6: Blocks in parallel tracks.

Figure B3.7: Blocks in serpentine tracks.

Large amounts of data can be stored on a single tape. Tapes are used as backup or archive storage and are very useful for storing data which is required only on planned occasions, or when the majority of records will be accessed in any processing, for example, data which is updated monthly or quarterly. Applications which have very large storage requirements are increasingly using high packing density tapes for on-line purposes.

Tape streamer

is a small tape drive unit, usually using tape cassettes, with very large storage capacity. They are frequently used to make backup copies of data for security purposes.

Packing density

including: bits per inch (bpi), disk density, density

is a measure of the quantity of data that can be held per unit length of track on a storage medium. It is usually measured in *bits per inch* (*bpi*) and is the number of binary digits (or bits) stored in one inch (2.54cm) along each track.

Terms such as single density and double density (DD), quad density (QD) and high density (HD) are used to describe the packing density of magnetic disks (*disk density*). The interpretation of these terms is not uniform, since the size of the disk, the age of the drive and the sophistication of the operating system cause differences in meaning.

Semiconductor memory

also known as: integrated circuit memory
including MOS, CMOS
is a form of memory which uses integrated circuit semiconductor chips. The storage capacity of this form of memory is very high, the time taken to read a data item is very short and the access is direct. There are a number of different forms of semiconductor storage, the more common ones use **MOS** (**metal-oxide-semiconductor**) or **CMOS** (**complementary MOS**) technology. The advantage of CMOS types is that they require little power to retain their contents; powered by small batteries they can be used as *non-volatile memory* while the computer is switched off. (See *volatile memory*, below.) Most current computer designs use semiconductor memory for immediate access storage.

RAM (Random Access Memory)

including: static RAM, dynamic RAM (DRAM), memory refresh
is memory that has the same access time for all locations. Each location holds one *byte* (see page 269) and is directly addressable. RAM may be either **static**, which holds its memory so long as there is a power supply, or **dynamic**, which has to be **refreshed** by reading and rewriting the contents very frequently (about every 2 milliseconds). Dynamic RAM (**DRAM**) is more widely used than static RAM because it needs less power. Both dynamic and static RAM are *volatile* (see *volatile memory*, below). See also *semiconductor memory*, above.

RAM disk

also known as: silicon disk
is memory which is addressed as if it were a very fast random access disk. It behaves as an extremely fast backing store for the user but is usually volatile and has to be loaded from backing store. It is normally an area of main memory reserved for this use.

ROM (Read-Only Memory)

including: PROM (Programmable Read-Only Memory), EPROM (Erasable PROM), EAROM (Electrically Alterable Read-Only Memory), EEPROM (Electrically Erasable PROgrammable Memory), flash PROM, cartridge
is memory for which the contents may be read but cannot be written to by the computer system. Read-only memory is used for both data and programs. There are optical ROM systems (see *CD-ROM*, below), and semiconductor (integrated circuit) ROM systems (see *semiconductor memory*, above).

The term **ROM** is frequently used to mean the (integrated circuit) read-only memory used to hold programs and associated data for building into computers. Software in ROM is fixed during manufacture, but there are other ways of putting programs and data into ROM.

PROM (Programmable Read-Only Memory) is a type of ROM which is manufactured as an empty storage array and is later permanently programmed by the user.

EPROM (Erasable PROM) is a type of PROM whose data can be erased by a special process (e.g. by exposure to ultraviolet radiation) so new data can be written as if it were a new PROM.

EAROM (Electrically Alterable Read-Only Memory) and **EEPROM (Electrically Erasable Programmable Read-Only Memory)**, sometimes called **flash PROM**, are other similar types of read-only memory.

Some small computers and games computers use software on (integrated circuit) ROM which is packaged in plug-in modules called **cartridges.** This is a convenient way of preventing the software from being copied.

Optical storage
including: CD-ROM (Compact Disk Read-Only Memory), videodisk, laser disk, EB disk (Electronic Book disk), WORM (Write-Once, Read-Many), multisession CD, Photo-CD

uses laser technology to etch the surface of a storage medium to form minute patterns which represent the data. The scattering effect on a narrow laser beam is used to read the data which may be digital or analog. At present, the process of making optical disks requires costly equipment, but this may change. The digital technology is the same as that used in audio compact disks (CDs).

CD-ROM (Compact Disk Read-Only Memory), which uses the same size of disk as audio CDs, is a read-only form of backing store used to hold large amounts of data. CD-ROM disks are pressed from a master disk in the same way that audio CDs are made. A **videodisk**, sometimes called a **laser disk**, is an equivalent analog form, which uses large disks like long playing gramophone records, for which the domestic equipment is quite rare. A recent development is the **EB disk (Electronic Book disk)**, which uses a 3 inch disk. The data on CD-ROM may include programs as well as sound, graphics or text data. CD-ROM with a computer capable of manipulating, storing and outputting high quality sound and graphics is a multimedia system. See *multimedia computer*, page 100.

WORM (***Write-Once, Read-Many***) is an optical (compact) disk system, which allows the user to write data on the next available portion of the disk. A portion of the disk can only have data written on it once, but this data can be read as often as required. Some worms allow the overwriting of data so as to spoil or erase it. ***Multisession-CD***, which is designed to capture and store materials created during separate work sessions, is one example of a worm; another form is ***Photo-CD***, which stores conventional camera images on optical disk.

Magneto-Optical Disk is a re-writable optical disk which uses magnetic and optical techniques. Writing uses a laser beam to heat a small part of the surface of the disk and, at the same time, a magnetic field arranges the magnetic material in this heated area in one of two ways. Reading uses the effect that the magnetic field on the surface of the disk has on a weak laser beam.

Phase Change Optical Disk is a re-writable optical disk which uses a laser to read and write data. It uses three strengths of laser signal. The weakest signal is used to read data; the other two signals are used to write data, by making parts of the material of the disk surface reflective or non-reflective to the weakest signal.

Content-addressable storage

also known as: associative storage

is a physically separate module of storage, designed to allow access to a location by its contents rather than by an address label. The normal address *decoder* logic (see page 342) is replaced by logic which compares the contents of part of each store with the address item. The remainder of each store contains indications of where the required data is stored.

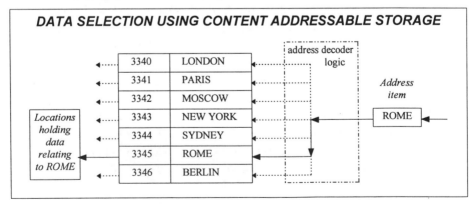

Figure B3.8: *Content-addressable storage*

Block

including: bucket

is the name for the smallest unit of data which is transferred between backing store and main store in one operation. In large computer systems, a ***bucket*** defines a unit of storage in random access memory. A bucket will contain a (variable) number of blocks. Access to the data is by reference to the bucket it is in.

Memory map

including: disk map, file allocation table (FAT)

describes the way storage is organised in a computer. For example, sections of memory may be allocated to the screen display, program code, variables. The memory map for disk storage is called a ***disk map.*** It describes how the information held on the disk is organised, and is kept on the disk. It may be held as a *bit map* (see page 298). Details of where files are stored in backing store is kept in a ***file allocation table (FAT)***, which is a file kept on the backing store. See also *directory*, page 82.

Scratch pad

also called: work(ing) store
including: scratch file, scrap file, work(ing) file, scratch tape

is a section of immediate access store reserved as a temporary working area for use by an application. It is also called a ***work store*** or ***working store***. An area of file space on backing store assigned for this purpose is called a ***scratch file, scrap file, work file*** or ***working file.*** If tape is used, it is called a ***scratch tape***. See also *clipboard*, page 8.

Virtual storage

also known as: virtual memory

is a means of apparently extending main storage, by allowing the programmer to access backing storage in the same way as immediate access store. Often personal computers provide this facility, using an area of disk as if it were main memory, without the user being aware of it. This has an advantage when running large programs but the processing speed will be slow.

Volatile memory

including: permanent memory, non-volatile memory

is a form of storage which holds data only while power is supplied. This is in contrast to **non-volatile memory**, which keeps its contents even when the system is switched off. All currently used forms of magnetic storage and optical disk storage are non-volatile, but most other forms of storage are volatile. **Permanent memory** retains its contents regardless of power supply and cannot be erased or altered; many forms of read-only memory (ROM) are permanent.

Write protection

including: blocking ring, write-inhibit ring, write-permit ring, request verification

is the prevention of unintentionally overwriting data on backing store. This can be achieved *either* by hardware features *or* by provisions in software.

Hardware write protection is built into floppy disk drives and floppy disk cases; for the older, 5¼ inch disks a cut-away portion of the case has to be covered over with an adhesive patch, while for 3½ inch disks there is a sliding cover for a hole in the case. There are no similar standards for large disk units; each manufacturer provides their own system. There is no hardware write protection for small hard disks in personal computers. Tape units have removable **blocking rings** behind the tape spools which act either as **write-inhibit** or as **write-permit rings** depending on the system used; cassettes or cartridges have sliding tabs.

Software methods include double checking a request (**request verification**) if it will over-write or delete a file, checking the characteristics of file names to see if they are protected and asking for passwords before overwriting or deleting any data.

B4　Display Devices

Human beings possess a very high resolution, multicolour and fast moving vision system. Thus it is understandable why so much technical effort has gone into producing displays from computer systems that can exploit the facilities of the human eye.

Much of the current display technology uses the cathode ray (television) tube. The tube looks like a large electric light bulb with a flat end. The user only sees the flat end. The electronics of the system makes the end glow with patterns of dots. It is the number and nature of these dots that determines the quality of the picture that the user sees.

For such applications as word processing then perhaps a monochrome (one colour) display is all that is needed but at the present state of development the software that would be used to produce the word processed document would no doubt require a colour display. We are now at the stage where colour display is considered to be the norm.

All the colours of the rainbow can be made by mixing various amounts of red, green and blue light. A colour display screen is coated with substances that glow when they are hit by electric particles (electrons).

The coating is arranged in horizontal lines of **triads**. A triad is a cluster of three dots that will glow; one will glow red, one green and one blue. The electronics of the whole system will excite different members of the triad to a greater or lesser amount, so as to produce a glowing dot (a **pixel**) of the required colour and brightness. It is an arrangement of a large number of these pixels that produces the final picture. The screen picture needs to be able to change quickly, anything from just simple text editing to a fast moving graphics image. This ability to change is achieved because the picture is redrawn many times a second (in the range of 25 to 72 times) even if it is not actually changing. This screen **refresh** process is done by the electron beam making a horizontal sweep over each line of triads. It is technically easier, and thus cheaper, for the screen refresh to be done in two passes; every other line of triads is refreshed on a first pass then the other lines are refreshed at the second pass; this is called **interlace** scanning. Interlace scanning is the method normally used in domestic television but a system that refreshes all the lines of triads in sequence, called **non-interlaced** scanning, is used in a number of designs for computer display screens.

The electronics that pass the information from the computer to the screen device are generally specific to the type of screen device. These electronics have to be installed by fitting a specific electronics board, called a **display**

adapter, into the computer. For example, when a system has a VGA display this means a VGA screen device and a matching VGA display adapter in the computer.

The development of laptop computers has required high performance flat screen display systems. This has been achieved by major enhancements to liquid crystal technology, which was originally developed for pocket calculators. In its basic form, liquid crystal display consists of a thin layer, a film, of fluid sandwiched between two sheets of glass or plastic. Complex wiring is used to apply voltages to different small areas of the film of liquid. The applied voltage alters the ability of the liquid to reflect or transmit light. Thus a pixel display is built up of light and dark dots of varying intensity. One way of producing colour is to have three layers of different types of liquid, with different colour characteristics, where each layer has its own associated wiring. Some systems rely on reflected light and cannot be used in poor lighting conditions. Back lighting systems, where the liquid films transmit light from a light source behind the screen, give a more easily viewed display than reflective systems.

Monitor

including: monochrome monitor, colour monitor, scan rate, multiscan monitor

is the term generally used for any device that displays information using a cathode ray tube. Although this definition could include a standard television set, a monitor normally does not have the receiving part of a television set. All monitor displays are made up of illuminated dots on the screen. Monitors may be monochrome or colour.

A *monochrome monitor* gives a display of varying intensity of a single colour, for example white, green or orange on a dark (black) background.

A *colour monitor* gives a display with a range of colours determined by the colour circuitry in the monitor and the computer.

Monitors may have a fixed or variable *scan rate*, that is how often the image is redrawn or refreshed (see *screen refresh*, below). Monitors that can operate at different scan rates are called *multiscan monitors* or *multisync monitors*; they can adjust to different scan rates set by a *video adapter* (see below). Multiscan monitors first appeared in 1985 and are essential for modern high definition display systems, such as *SVGA* and *EGA* (see below).

Video adapter

also known as: display adapter, graphics adapter
is the circuitry which generates the signals needed for a video output device to display computer data. The data may be text only or text and graphics. The circuits are contained on a circuit board which is installed in the computer with output via a cable to the display unit (the monitor). A variety of adapters have been devised and sold. Most are associated with one computer manufacturer and require the use of a particular design of *monitor* (see above). There is a range of *standard adapters for IBM PCs* (and IBM compatibles), some of which are described in *Table B4.1* (page 130). In addition, there are video adapters from other manufacturers which can be installed in PCs. Computers which are not IBM compatible frequently use their own video adapters with different standards.

Frame

including: interlace
is used to describe a screenful of information treated as a single unit. An example is a response frame for the input of data in a screen input data capture system.

In electronics, a frame is one complete screen picture. In a standard television set, this consists of 625 separate lines; a new frame is transmitted every 1/25 of a second, as two *interlaced* fields: the first field is the odd-numbered lines and the second is the even-numbered lines.

PAL (Phase Alternating Line)

is the UK standard method of encoding colour information in a television signal. If a domestic television set is used as a display device via the ordinary aerial socket, the computer must contain a PAL encoder for colour.

Palette

is the range of display colours available in the computer system. Any particular display system may not be able to support the total number of colours, hence a selection is made from the possible palette. The user may be allowed to change this selection.

Pixel

is a contraction of 'picture-element'. As used in graphics, it is the smallest element of a display. A pixel will have one or more attributes of colour, intensity (or brightness) and flashing.

Pixel graphics

is where a picture is constructed of a rectangular array of dots. Each dot may be any of the colours available to the computer but it is not possible for a dot to be split into smaller pieces. This means that it is impossible to have detail smaller than the size of the *pixels* (see above).

Raster graphics

including: raster, scan, interlaced scan, non-interlaced scan, scan frequency, screen resolution, dot pitch, low-resolution graphics, High-Resolution Graphics (HRG)

is a method of producing an image on a display screen. The image is drawn on a cathode ray tube (a CRT) by illuminating *pixels* (see above) as horizontal lines of dots covering the whole screen, this is called the *raster*. An electron beam sweeps over these lines of pixels, drawing the display many times a second, in the same way that a picture is drawn on a television set (see *frame*, above).

Sweeping over the lines of the raster display is called *scanning*. The scan may be done by drawing alternate lines (line 1 followed by line 3, and so on) on a first pass and then the rest of the lines on a second pass. This is called an *interlaced scan*, and is the method used in television sets. Alternatively the scan may draw each line successively (line 1 followed by line 2, and so on), called a *non-interlaced scan*. How often the screen is scanned is called the *scan frequency*.

The quality of a raster display depends upon the *screen resolution*, which is usually quoted as the number of pixels in a row × the number of rows (horizontal × vertical), and the *dot pitch*, which is the size of a dot (pixel) on the screen. Values of between 0.28mm and 0.38mm for the dot pitch are considered acceptable; this is between 100 and 70 dots per inch. To provide an acceptable image on a large screen, the pixel resolution has to be increased to give the same dot pitch as on a smaller screen. In general, raster graphics will produce untidy display of any line which is neither vertical nor horizontal. If high quality screen display of line drawings is required, then *vector graphics* (see below) is the appropriate system.

A number of general descriptions of display resolution are used:

Low-resolution graphics is generally applied to graphical display units where simple pictures can be built up by plotting large blocks of colour or by using special graphics characters. It is used for *teletext* images (see page 23).

High-Resolution Graphics (HRG) is generally applied to graphical display units capable of plotting around 300 or more pixels in the width of a *monitor* screen (see above).

Graphical Display Unit (GDU)

is an output device, incorporating a cathode ray tube (CRT), on which both line drawings and text can be displayed. The term has become used for display systems specifically for high quality graphics work. A graphical display unit is often used in conjunction with a light-pen to input or re-position data. High quality graphical display units normally use *vector graphics* (see below).

Vector graphics

is a screen display method using a cathode ray tube (CRT) in which each line of a drawing is drawn on the screen individually. A line can be drawn in any direction (although there is a minimum width of a line) and so the display is a more accurate presentation of the picture with no jagged edges. The resolution of vector graphics screens is usually very high so that the size of pixels is small, which gives the high quality display. Vector graphics is an expensive technique to implement with the result that most displays use *raster graphics* (see above).

Font

is the set of printing or display characters in a particular type, style and size. The characters may take the form of pictures.

Liquid Crystal Display (LCD)

is a display technique that uses the phenomenon that certain liquids alter their ability to reflect or transmit light if a voltage is applied to them. Originally used for pocket calculators it is now common for laptop computers.

Light Emitting Diode (LED)

is a display that uses the property of some semiconductor diodes to emit light when a voltage is applied to them. Their power consumption is negligible and they give off no heat. They are commonly used as indicator lights on devices such as disk drives. They are also useful for monitoring the logic state of lines in control applications.

RGB (Red Green Blue)

describes a method of connecting a computer to a (colour) display monitor in which the colour information is transmitted as three separate signals. RGB signals do not need to be decoded, as does a *PAL* signal (see above). Thus, definition is generally better using an RGB connection.

IBM PC-COMPATIBLE VIDEO GRAPHICS ADAPTERS

NAME	DESCRIPTION	RESOLUTION	character size	COLOUR PROVISION
		text: (rows × characters) graphics: (pixels: width × height)		
Monochrome Display Adapter (MDA) Released 1981	text but no graphics: (for monochrome monitors)	text: 25 rows of 80 characters graphics: not available		monochrome only
Hercules graphics adapter Released 1982	text and graphics (for monochrome monitors)	text: 32 rows of 80 characters graphics: 720 × 320 pixels	10×9	monochrome only
Colour Graphics Adapter (CGA) Released 1981	colour text **two** colour graphics modes: (MDA compatible)	text: 25 rows of 80 characters graphics: 640 × 200 pixels graphics: 320 × 200 pixels	8×8	16 foreground + 8 background two colours four colours
Enhanced Graphics Adapter (EGA) Released 1984	improved version of CGA text and graphics bit mapped	graphics: 640 × 350 pixels		16 colours
Video Graphics Array (VGA) Released 1987	improved version of EGA text and graphics bit mapped	graphics: 640 × 480 pixels		256 colours

Super Video Graphics Array (SVGA) Released 1988	Analog display system: needs multiscan monitor	graphics: 800 × 600 pixels	16 colours infinite range of shades of grey
Extended Graphics Array (XGA) Released 1991	Analog display system: needs multiscan monitor	graphics: 1024 × 768 pixels	256 colour text theoretically infinite range of colours; in practice usually limited to 262,144 ($= 2^{18}$)

Notes:

The quality of screen image depends upon the screen **dot pitch** rather than just on the numbers of pixels. On a 14-inch screen with 1024 × 768 pixels the dot pitch is 0.28mm (approx. 90 dots/inch); to achieve similar quality of image on a 17-inch screen requires a resolution of 1280 × 1024 pixels (dot pitch 0.26mm, approx. 98 dots/inch).

The vertical and horizontal resolutions are not the same for all the above specifications.

The above specifications were all promoted by IBM. After 1991, a number of other manufacturers developed adapters with different screen proportions and higher resolutions such as 1280 × 1024 pixels.

See also *pixel* and *monitor* (above) and *bit map* (page 298).

Table B4.1: *Graphics adapters*

Screen refresh

including: refresh rate, Vertical Refresh Rate (VRR)

is the process of continuously energising the glowing substances on a cathode ray tube device to keep the display visible. The screen is refreshed between 25 to 72 times per second (known as the ***refresh rate***) depending on the display system used. The technique allows the easy display of changing images.

Vertical Refresh Rate (*VRR*) is related to the horizontal sweeps that the electron beam makes in a cathode ray tube (CRT) display. Once an image has been entirely repainted by horizontal sweeps then it has been vertically refreshed. A low vertical refresh rate tends to produce flicker. A *VGA* monitor has a vertical refresh rate of 60 - 70 scans per second and the standard for *SVGA* monitors is 72 scans per second. See also the table of *video graphics adapters for IBM PCs,* Table B4.1, page 130.

Video RAM (VRAM)

is a separate high-speed memory into which the processor writes the screen data, which is then read to the screen for display. This avoids the use of any main memory to hold screen data.

B5   *Printers*

A printer is connected to a computer for the single purpose of transferring the information from the computer to paper. The version printed out on paper is often referred to as hard copy. There are many types of printer that can be connected to a computer system varying in quality, cost and use. Broadly speaking the printers divide themselves up into three groups: **character printers, dot matrix and ink jet printers** and **laser printers**.

Character printers, which print a single character at a time, were really a development from typewriters, often with all the characters on a single element (a golf-ball or a daisy-wheel). They were mechanical in action and, as a result, printed slowly and tended to be extremely noisy. However, they produced good quality printing and so were often used by businesses. Today they are hardly used as there are now other printers that can work faster, produce quality printing, do it quietly and are more flexible.

Dot matrix printers rely upon a print head moving in straight lines across the paper. Inside the print head is a vertical line of pins each of which can print a dot on the paper. By making the pins hit the paper at the right moment it is possible to print a pattern of dots that looks like any character that is wanted. For example:

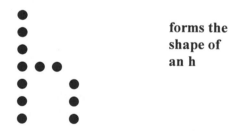

**forms the
shape of
an h**

The advantage of the dot matrix printer is that it is possible to produce any character or shape that is required simply by arranging for the appropriate pins to be 'fired' at the right moment - this makes it useful for printing out a copy of a piece of computer graphics (i.e. some form of picture or design). It can also be made to produce effects such as different styles of letter, different sizes of letter and even produce output resembling a document produced by a publisher. Other advantages are that such printers are relatively cheap, they will work with almost any quality of paper and some of them can even print in colour by using a special ribbon containing the four colours black, red, blue and yellow. They are generally able to print on either continuous paper or single sheets.

Ink jet printers (sometimes called *bubble jet*) create the printed image by forcing droplets of ink from a cartridge through a fine nozzle onto the paper, forming the characters by patterns of ink droplets similar to a dot matrix printer. The print quality of most ink jet printers is much better than dot matrix printers, however they do suffer the problem of saturating the paper with ink, which causes the paper to crinkle —special paper for ink jet printers removes this problem, but at a cost. It is possible to print in colour with them, the better printers having four separate cartridges for cyan, magenta, yellow and black (sometimes referred to as CMYK, the K standing for Key or black). These printers have the advantages of being compact, many of them are classed as portable, and they produce print quality rivalling that produced by a laser printer (but not as quickly.).

Laser printers essentially use the Xerographic technology of the modern photocopier. An image is produced on a special drum that then attracts the toner (a black fine plastic powder) where the lines/areas of the image are, the paper then presses against the drum transferring the toner image to the paper. The paper then goes through a heater which melts the toner onto the paper before it emerges from the machine. The only difference between a laser printer and a photocopier is in the way the image is formed on the drum. A printer uses a laser light source to write the image onto the drum from the image in the printer's memory. This requires that a laser has to have a fairly large amount of memory in order to print a page — at least 1 Mb, but preferably more. Colour laser printers do exist, but they are very, very expensive.

The main advantages of a laser printer over almost any other printer are:
    i) the quality of printing (though this does vary from one machine to another)
    ii) the speed of printing (from about 4 pages per minute up to 16 pages per minute for small machines)
The main disadvantages of a laser printer are:
    i) can only print complete pages as opposed to individual lines·
    ii) the size of the machine
    iii) the relatively high running costs (toner cartridges, paper, etc)

In summary, deciding upon a printer is not easy as all printers today can print anything that your computer can produce. Probably cost and quality of print are the two main areas to focus upon - and noise, if you are likely to be printing a lot or late at night.

Printer

including: print head

is an output device producing characters or graphic symbols on paper. There are many methods of printing and of organising the operation of a printer. Many forms of smaller printers use a moving ***print head*** which travels backwards and forwards across the paper and carries the printing mechanism. For a summary of information about printers see *PRINTERS Types and Characteristics, Table B5.1,* page 140.

Character printer

including: daisy wheel printer, golf ball printer, bi-directional printer, logic-seeking

is one which prints the characters one at a time.

A ***daisy wheel printer*** is a character printer where the characters are arranged near the ends of the spokes on a rimless wheel (like the petals of a daisy), the wheel turning to give the character. A hammer is used to strike the character petal onto a ribbon against the paper. The daisy wheel is manually interchangeable to enable alternative character sets to be used.

A ***golf ball printer*** is a character printer using a moving spherical print head as in many electric typewriters. The golf ball twists to set the character and then strikes a ribbon against the paper. The head is easily removable enabling many different character sets to be used.

Both daisy wheel and golf ball printers have a moving a print head, which holds the daisy wheel or golf ball and their mechanisms, and can travel from side to side across the paper.

A ***bi-directional printer*** is a character printer where the right-to-left return movement of the print head is used to print a second line, thus increasing printing speed.

Logic-seeking is the ability of a character printer to organise its own operation to cope efficiently with blank, short or right-justified lines. Such a printer does not always alternate its direction of printing.

Impact printer

is a term applied to any printer which creates marks on the page by striking an inked ribbon (or carbon paper) against the page. The object that strikes the ribbon may form complete characters at one strike, as in a typewriter, or may form a pattern of dots, as in a pin dot matrix printer.

Dot matrix printer
including: pin printer, thermal printer
is a printer which forms characters or graphics images out of ink dots in a rectangular matrix of printing positions. The image is made up of dots in the same sort of way that a screen image is generated using *pixel graphics* (see page 128).

The term is frequently used for ***pin printers***, which were the first kind of printer to build up characters by printing patterns of dots. The dots are printed by pins striking a ribbon against the paper. A vertical line of pins is mounted in a print head which travels backwards and forwards across the paper.

A ***thermal printer*** uses wires arranged like the pins of a dot matrix printer which are heated to form dots on heat-sensitive paper. Thermal printers are very quiet but do not produce good quality printing.

Ink jet printer
also known as: bubble jet printer
including: ink cartridge, print cartridge, CMYK
is one which uses a fine jet of quick-drying ink to produce the printing. What is printed may be text or graphics. A monochrome ink jet printer will print characters in black and diagrams in shades of grey. Colour versions use four colours, cyan, magenta, yellow and black (sometimes referred to as *CMYK*, the K standing for Key or black). The ink is held in small containers, called ***ink cartridges*** or ***print cartridges,*** from which the ink is directly jetted onto the paper. These cartridges are mounted in a print head which travels backwards and forwards across the paper.

Page printer
is one which forms and prints a whole page in one operation, for example a *laser printer* (see below).

Laser printer
is a page printer which uses a laser to 'write' the image to be printed onto a light-sensitive drum. The drum then uses electrostatics (as in a photocopier) to attract toner, a black fine plastic powder, to coat the image with powder. Paper is then pressed against the drum transferring the toner to the paper. The paper is then heated to melt the toner onto the paper.

Line printer

including: barrel printer, chain printer, print hammer

is one that prints a complete line of characters at one time, and hence is generally faster than a character printer. The printers described below are large machines capable of printing at very high speeds and are generally only used with mainframe computers.

In a *barrel printer* the complete character set is provided at each printing position, embossed on the surface of a horizontal barrel or cylinder, and each printing position has a *print hammer*, which is used to press the paper against a ribbon to print a character. The barrel turns and as the correct character for a position occurs, its print hammer strikes the paper against a ribbon and onto the character, causing the character to be printed.

In a *chain printer* the characters are carried on a continuous chain between a set of print hammers and the paper. The chain moves along the print line and as the required character appears at a print position the print hammer strikes the paper against a ribbon and onto the character.

Unless these printers are well maintained the quality can be poor with the characters badly aligned.

Font

including: printer driver, font cartridge

is the set of printing or display characters in a particular type, style and size. Printers may offer a choice of fonts, either by exchanging the printer head (daisy wheel or golf ball) or by software control as with dot matrix, ink jet or laser printers. The font options, which can be selected by the user, may be stored in the computer and accessed through *printer drivers*, which are part of the system software that formats data for printing, or stored in read only memory (ROM) *font cartridges* installed in the printer.

Page description language

including: Postscript

is a kind of computer language used to pass instructions to printers for setting up the data to be printed.

Postscript is a page description language used by some laser printers. The computer would code its printout requirements, for example the size, direction and style of a piece of text or the format for a diagram. These would then be interpreted by the postscript translator, which is in the printer, into the corresponding image of dots ready for printing.

Print quality

including: correspondence (or letter) quality, Near Letter Quality (NLQ), draft quality

is a description of how well formed the characters are when printed. The descriptions are in terms of the standards expected of printed output for different purposes.

Correspondence quality, also known as *letter quality,* is the quality of print obtained from daisy wheel printers, which is similar to the quality of a traditional typewriter, or from ink jet and laser printers.

Near Letter Quality (NLQ) is the best available quality on a dot matrix printer, which used to be considered acceptable for correspondence, but with the availability of low cost ink jet printers few people now find this good enough.

Draft quality is a quality of printing whose characters are not well shaped, but can be printed quickly. Often this is the standard print available from dot matrix printers.

Graph plotter

also known as: plotter

including: digital plotter, incremental plotter, flat-bed plotter

is an output device which draws lines on paper by moving a pen in a holder relative to the paper on which the drawing is being made. In some designs the paper is on a roller and both the pen and the roller move; in others the paper is fixed on a flat surface, a *flat-bed plotter*, and all the movements are made by the pen.

A *digital plotter* receives digital input specifying the co-ordinates of the points to be plotted, together with information about how the point to be plotted is joined to the current point.

An *incremental plotter* receives input data specifying increments to its current position, rather than data specifying co-ordinates.

Paper feed mechanism

including: friction feed, tractor feed, (cut) sheet feeder

is the means of making the paper move through the printing process. Many printers require that the paper is moved after a line (or sometimes half a line) has been printed.

Friction feed is a mechanism for advancing paper by gripping it between rollers.

Tractor feed is a mechanism for advancing paper by the use of perforations down the side of the paper and a toothed wheel (a sprocket).

Cut sheet feeder (also known as *sheet feeder*) allows ordinary separate sheets of paper to be automatically fed in for printing. Where a sheet feeder is not provided as part of the printer, it may be available as an accessory.

Media

is the collective name for materials (tape, disk, paper, cards, etc.) used to hold data.

Hard copy

also known as: printout
is computer output printed on paper.

Continuous stationery

including: fan-fold paper, multipart stationery
is printer paper which is perforated to make pages and folded in alternate directions at each set of perforations to form a stack, *fan-fold paper*. It normally has a tear-off margin on both sides with holes for a tractor feed mechanism to use. It can be a series of pre-printed forms. For some applications it may consist of several sheets together, either with carbon paper in between or made of pressure-sensitive paper, (termed *multipart stationery*) so that several copies are printed at the same time using an impact printer. See also *pre-printed stationery*, below.

Pre-printed stationery

has certain fixed information already printed on each sheet so that the computer can fill in the gaps. This increases the speed of printing and improves the presentation. The paper may be cut sheets or continuous stationery. Common examples are customer accounts for gas and electricity, and computer printed cheques.

Bursting

is the separating of *continuous stationery* (see above) into individual sheets by tearing the paper along the perforations.

Decollate

is to separate the sheets of *multipart continuous stationery* (see above) which has been produced as output from a printer.

PRINTER TYPES AND CHARACTERISTICS

CHARACTER PRINTERS	MATRIX PRINTER	PAGE PRINTER
line printers (barrel, chain), golf ball, daisy wheel	*pin dot matrix printers, ink jet printers*	*laser printers*
impact on a ribbon or carbon paper is used to form the characters	use *pins* (impact or thermal) or *ink jet* to print the image	use photocopier principles
print individual characters, text only	can print text and graphics	can print text and graphics
characters are printed as complete characters in a single action	text and images made up of dots in a matrix pattern (similar to a screen image)	print a complete page at a time
line printers etc. – poor print quality; *daisy wheel* etc. – very good print quality	print quality depends on the resolution (dots per inch)	capable of very high resolution
usually only a single (limited) font available at a time	wide range of fonts available through software	wide range of fonts available through software
restricted line spacing, (often only full lines)	flexible line spacing	can print anywhere on the page print area (possibly excluding margins)
unlimited page length, fixed maximum width	unlimited page length, fixed maximum width	fixed maximum page length and width
can print multi-part stationery	*pin printers* –can print multi-part stationery; *ink jet printers* – cannot print multi-part stationery	cannot print conventional multi-part stationery
usually only single colour, fixed intensity	can print in colour, *ink jet* can print a range of shades	can print colour, can print a range of shades
line printers can print at high speeds	slow to medium speed printing	can print at high speeds

Table B5.1: Printers

Printer type	Description	Application range (approx.)	Current speed range (approx.)	Resolution
daisy wheel /golf ball	Replacement for typewriter-style printers: generally compact machines: wide range of speeds and quality. / *Line printers* use a print hammer for each print position to strike the paper and ribbon/carbon paper against embossed type on barrels or chain loops when the right character is in position: daisy wheel and golf ball printers print a character and then move to the next print position and have easily changeable fonts.	small office machines to large scale data processing	5 cps to 35 cps	some proportional spacing
line printers	Obsolescent technology but some *line printers* are still in use in large scale data processing contexts	small office machines to large scale data processing	200 - 2000 lines per minute	
pin (*impact*)	Print mechanisms move backwards and forwards over the paper, which advances after each pass by the print mechanism. Print quality is determined by the number of pins or ink bubble size and the minimum size of head and paper movements.	personal printers to network printers on small networks	25 cps to 250 cps	
ink jet (or bubble jet)		personal printers to network printers on small networks	4 mins per page to 8+ ppm	300 to 600 dots per inch
laser	Image of the page is 'written' by lasers onto a special drum as an electrostatic charge: the drum attracts toner particles which are transferred to the page and heated to set the image. / Have almost completely replaced the older *line printers* for large volume printing. Sizes range from desk-top to very large, floor standing machines.	personal printers to large scale data processing	4 ppm to 40+ ppm (up to 2500+ lines per minute)	300 to 600 dots per inch

Printer buffer

is a store, usually in the printer but can be in a separate box between the computer and printer, which receives the information for printing and stores it until it is printed. It is able to receive the information at a much higher speed than the printer can print, thereby freeing the computer from the printing task a little quicker.

DIP switch

is a switch (often set out in groups of 4 or 8) on a printer that controls various aspects of the printer and how it should behave. They may control what language alphabet to use, what quality of print to print in, the size of print, etc. They may be located inside the printer, since once set they are not often altered. (DIP stands for Dual In-line Package.)

B6　Networks

Other terms and concepts related to networks and communications are to be found in A4 Communications, B7 Communications Devices and Control Devices and C17 Communications Technology.

Connecting pieces of communications and information equipment together in a network is not a new concept. The early telegraph systems, especially in America where the distances are so great, provided the stimulus for telegram services and the later development of telex communications, in which text information could be sent between any telex machines on the world-wide telex network using telephone lines. Passing messages internationally has been possible ever since the development of international cable links which began in the 19th century. For over 70 years the world's newspapers depended upon organisations that gathered news around the world and delivered it to their client newspapers through the telex network. These services are still provided by some of the same organisations but in addition there is now E-mail and other services linking computers around the world.

In a computer network a number of computers are connected together in order to exchange information. For example, an organisation having offices spread over a wide geographical area might install a network to enable employees to examine information held on computers in other offices many miles away.

The connections between computers may be wires, fibre optic cables, microwave links, communication via satellite or any combination of these. The interconnected collection of computers form the network. The computers may be large powerful machines, small personal computers or terminals. They will all be capable of running on their own but with the added advantage of being able to communicate with each other.

In a traditional network, users must explicitly log on (that is, identify themselves to the network) and explicitly move information around on the network by issuing the appropriate instructions. A **distributed system** is normally thought of as a network in which the existence of the other machines is not obvious to the user. Programs and data held on other machines can be used as though they were held locally on the user's computer.

A distinction is usually made between networks of computers that are all situated relatively close to each other - for example in the same building or cluster of buildings - known as a **Local Area Network** (a LAN) and those in which the computers are geographically remote, known as a **Wide Area Network** (a WAN).

A network offers the possibility of sharing work between the different resources available. For example, if one computer has a heavy load of processing, some of the work can be moved to another machine on the network. A network makes all the resources of the network (programs, data and equipment, such as printers and disk drives) available to the whole network without regard to the physical location of either the resource or the user.

Reliability is another advantage of networking. The effect of hardware failures can be reduced by switching work from a failed device to one that is still functioning. This can be particularly valuable in systems such as banking where it is important that the system can continue operating even if there are some hardware failures.

Networks of small computers can be a cheaper way of providing computer power than a single large machine. If a network of small machines has access to outside facilities, whose use may need to be purchased, such as a large specialist database like Prestel, the potential of the network is greatly enhanced. Linking a network to other networks, which are themselves linked to yet further networks, makes it theoretically possible to have the whole of world knowledge available to any computer on such a network.

The INTERNET is an implementation of this concept. It works because there are thousands of networks each connected to other networks in such a way that it is possible for messages (data) to be sent from a computer on one of the networks to any computer on any other network, provided that both networks have access to the Internet. How such data travels through this 'network of networks' is illustrated in *Figure A4.2: The life story of an E-mail message*, page 21.

Network

including: distributed network

is a linked set of computer systems capable of sharing computer power and resources such as printers, large disk drives, CD-ROM and other databases. Sometimes network is used to mean the arrangement of links between the equipment that form the network. See *network topology*, below.

In a ***distributed network*** the sharing of resources is arranged by the (network) operating system without any action being required by the user.

Local Area Network (LAN)

is a network in which the computer systems are all situated relatively close to each other, for example in the same building or cluster of buildings, such as a school. Since the distances involved are small, direct physical connection is possible. The network connections are normally wire cables, such as coaxial cable, but fibre optic cable is being increasingly used.

Wide Area Network (WAN)

is a network in which the computers are geographically remote. Wide area networks make use of a range of connection methods including communication satellites.

Network topology

including: bus network, ring (sometimes called loop) network, star network, FDDI (fibre distributed data interface) backbone
is the theoretical arrangement of components of a network. The actual arrangement will almost certainly be determined by the buildings or other locations for the parts of the network. The network descriptions indicate how the devices on the network, the computers, printers, servers, etc., are connected to each other. Since networks communicate serially, the actual connections will be capable of *serial data transmission* (see page 316).
A *bus network* has each of the devices connected directly to a main
    communications line, called a bus, along which signals are sent. The bus
    will frequently be a twin cable of some kind, for example coaxial cable.

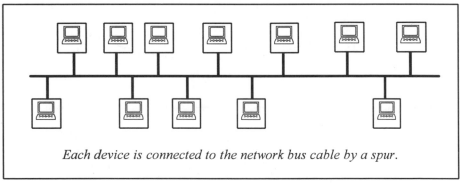

Each device is connected to the network bus cable by a spur.

Figure B6.1: *A bus network with spurs*

Each device has the network cable going into its network interface and out to the network interface of the next device.

Figure B6.2: *A bus network*

A ***ring network*** (sometimes called a ***loop network***) has each of the devices on the network connected to a ring (or loop) communications line around which signals are sent. The devices may be connected to the ring by spurs, as in Figure B6.3 or the connections may pass through the *network interface* (see *interface*, page 300 and *interface card*, page 308) in each device, as in Figure B6.4; in this case, provision has to be made for the system to continue to work if one of the devices is switched off or fails to function properly.

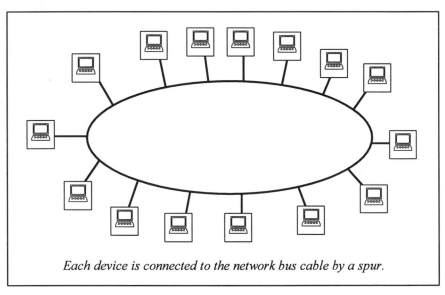

Each device is connected to the network bus cable by a spur.

Figure B6.3: *A ring network with spurs*

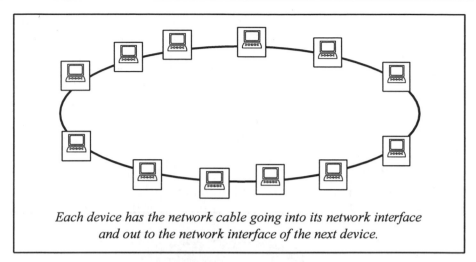

Each device has the network cable going into its network interface and out to the network interface of the next device.

Figure B6.4: *A ring network*

A ***star network*** has all the network devices connected to one central computer which is often used as the *file server* machine (see below). The centre of the network, often called the ***hub*** or ***nexus***, is a computer which has separate connections to each computer or terminal.

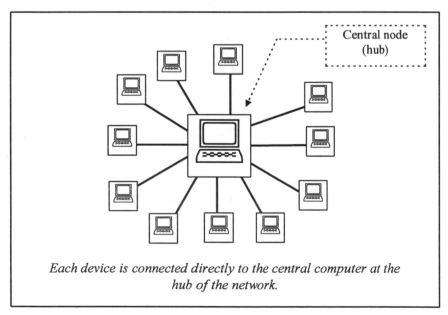

Central node (hub)

Each device is connected directly to the central computer at the hub of the network.

Figure B6.5: *A star network*

A ***FDDI backbone*** is a high-speed communication link used to provide the basis for a network consisting of small sub-networks. The connections are fibre optic cable. ***FDDI (fibre distributed data interface)*** is an ANSI defined standard for high speed fibre optic cable communications with transmission speeds of 100 Mbps.

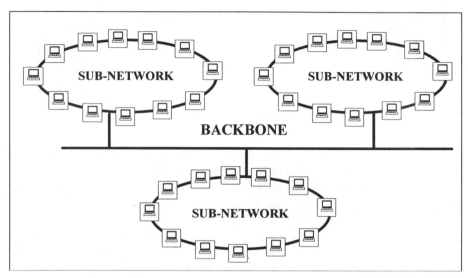

Figure B6.6: *A backbone with three sub-networks*

Cluster

including: cluster controller

is a group of computers in the same physical area, possibly on a network. A ***cluster controller*** is the computer acting as controller for the cluster. See also *network controller*, page 104.

Token ring network

including: token, Cambridge ring

is a *ring network* (see above) in which information is sent around the ring as variable-sized packets of data. In addition to the data, a packet will contain the address of the sender and the destination address. The ***token***, which is a signal that passes round the network, can be thought of as a carrier for the packet. For a packet to travel round the ring it has to be attached to a token. This is a method of avoiding data packets colliding on the ring and creating unreadable signals. In principle, the packet travels round the ring attached to the token until it is taken off at the destination address or it returns unread to the sender, where it is taken off as unread. The token then becomes free and continues round the ring ready to have another package to be attached to it by one of the network devices. The token continually circulates around the ring picking up, carrying and dropping packets off at their destinations. Generally there is only one token.

A *Cambridge ring* is a token ring network which has a number of tokens travelling around the network passing each device at equal time internals. A network device wishing to send a packet simply attaches it to the first available free token. The data transmission capacity of a Cambridge ring is much greater than a simple token ring network.

The network topology for token ring networks is shown in Figure B6.4, page 147.

Network number

including: station number

is the unique number assigned to a network when it is set up. All computers on the network have their own *station number* within the network, which is assigned through software. In addition, the *network interface* (see *interface*, page 300 and *interface card*, page 308) fitted in the computer has a unique number permanently stored in it. Communication between networks requires these unique numbers to ensure that messages get to the correct station in the correct network, since it is now possible for any network to communicate with any other network.

Econet

is an obsolete local area networking system designed to provide cheap computer networking for BBC and some Acorn microcomputers. Both the hardware (the cabling and computer interfaces) and the software (the *network operating system*, page 152) were non-standard and only worked with those computers. It has been used in a large number of British schools.

Ethernet

is a popular general-purpose *local area network* (see above). The network can be used by different types of computer system, even at the same time. Network interfaces are available from many manufacturers. It uses either wire connections (coaxial or twisted pair cable) or fibre optic cable. The software which makes up the *network operating system* (see below), has to be bought separately. Ethernet networks are frequently used in offices and schools. The transmission rate is 10 Mbits/sec and it uses the principles of *carrier sense multiple access/collision detection* (see page 318).

Peer-to-peer network

including: client station

is a description of a very simple network which provides shared resources, such as printers and storage, but may offer little in the way of additional facilities, such as file security. The name comes from the fact that all the computers on these networks have similar specifications and that all stations on the network have equal status. For example one station may act as a file server, another as the printer server, but both of them are also network stations capable of being used as client stations. A computer on the network, which is available for use by users of the network, is called a *client station*. See also *terminal* and *server*, below.

Client-server relationship

is a method of network organisation in which stations make use of resources available at one or more *servers* (see below). This is the kind of organisation seen in a *star network* (see above), in which one computer has the role of central resource manager for the network. But other forms of network can also operate with a client-server relationship.

Distributed processing

is the sharing of data processing tasks between physically separated processors on a network.

Terminal

also called: network terminal, network station, station
including: point-of-sale (POS) terminal

is a computer or computer controlled device operating on a network. A stand-alone computer used to provide resources for the whole network is a form of terminal which is often called a *(network) station*. See also *server*, below.

A network may have a variety of different kinds of equipment connected to it. For example, a supermarket network will probably have standard computers for its offices as well as the *point-of-sale (POS) terminals* (the checkouts) all connected on the same network. This may be linked to a wider network for the whole supermarket chain. A point-of-sale terminal will have a variety of functions, which may include *electronic funds transfer* (see page 20), as well as *bar code scanning* (see page 106) combined with getting the costs from a database on the network to produce the customer's bill.

Server

including: file server, printer server, CD-ROM server, database server
is a station on a *peer-to-peer network* (see above) which provides a resource
that can be used by any authorised *client station* (see above). There are a
number of types of server.

A *file server* provides central disk storage for any users of the network. The
file server software identifies each user's files separately so that other
users cannot use them. Users can access their own files from any client
station on the network.

A *printer server* allows all the client stations to use a printer controlled by it
and usually provides the facilities of a *print spooler* (see page 286).

A *CD-ROM server* allows all the client stations to obtain data from a
CD-ROM disk currently being used by the CD-ROM server computer.
Often a CD-ROM server will have access to many CD-ROM disks, either
from a collection of several CD-ROM players, or from a *CD-ROM
jukebox* (see page 113).

A *database server* manages a large database. Client stations can access data
in the database and, if authorised, can maintain the database. The
database processing is usually carried out by the server, with the query
being sent by a client station to the server and the results assembled by
the server and returned to the client station. This form of *client-server
relationship* (see above) can ensure the consistency of the database, even
in the distributed environment of a *peer-to-peer network* (see above).

Any expensive resource can be made available to a large number of users by
a server computer. Other examples are a teletext server, which makes
available the current data being broadcast by teletext services; a viewdata
server, which provides and manages a local viewdata service for the network;
a mail server to manage the electronic mail for the network; or even a
weather station server obtaining and distributing current local instrument
readings or satellite weather data.

Work station

is **either** a *station* on a network (see *terminal*, above), **or** a location where a
computer, with its associated equipment, is used, such as a designer's work
area; this kind of work station may be on a network or not.

Network operating system

including: Appletalk, NFS, Novell Netware, Windows for Workgroups, Unix
is the software needed to enable a computer to communicate with other
computers (stations) using a network. All computers on a network must have
the same network operating system software to be able to communicate
through the network. Additional software is required for any servers. In
particular, a file server needs additional software to enable it to provide
secure data storage for users. Widely used network operating systems include
Appletalk, NFS (Acorn computers), *Novell Netware, Windows for
Workgroups* and *Unix*.

Network accounting software

provides statistics about the use of a network by its users. This may be about
the use made of terminals on a multi-user computer system or about the use
of facilities on a *peer-to-peer network* (see above). The information can be
used to charge users for their use of resources or to monitor improper use of
the network.

The information recorded can include such things as the connection time
and the processor time used, a list of times and dates when the computer has
been used on a multi-user system, disk storage space used, printer use, and E-
mail use on a peer-to-peer network.

The accounting software can present the overall activity on the network in
a variety of ways (tables, graphs or a log) and thus assist the network
manager to optimise the system and, possibly, devise charging structures.

Value Added Network Service (VANS)

is a wide area network with additional facilities such as a centrally provided
database or information system for which users pay charges, which are
usually based on their use of the facilities. An example is the charged pages
of the Prestel service.

Gateway

is a link between two dissimilar computer systems, which may be local area
networks. The communications between the systems are usually sent via
public telecommunications links. The gateway converts the data passing
through it into the formats required for each system; in addition, it can
monitor usage and limit access between the systems to authorised users. See
also *bridge*, page 158.

B7   Communications Devices and Control Devices

*This section is concerned with terms used in describing the
transmission of data between computers within networks and
terms found in the study of control systems. Other related
terms may be found in A4 Communications, A9 Control,
B2 Peripherals, B6 Networks or C17 Communications
Technology.*

Communications and control require that information is passed rapidly and
accurately between parts of a system. The origins of present-day
communication systems are the electric telegraph which sent signals as
electric pulses, the telephone by which sound is passed as a varying electric
current, and radio by which the signals are sent as electromagnetic radiation.
   Modern communications systems are highly reliable, accurate and
affordable. From the earliest days of computers until the late 1980s it was
necessary to install special quality telephone lines between linked computers.
Now it is possible to use standard voice quality lines for connecting
computers and remote devices. This is partly due to the use of digital signal
systems and partly due to the use of more reliable materials and devices for
the transmission of signals in the public communications systems. The
installation of digital telephone exchanges in many parts of the world, and
the use of radio links where cables are not available, mean that it is
impossible for a user to know whether a link between two telephones or two
computers is by cables or via some terrestrial or satellite radio link. Where
public communication links are not available, private links are installed.
   The materials for connecting computers are wires of some form, fibre
optic cables, radio links or infra-red radiation. Each has its advantages and
its disadvantages. If wires or optic cables are used, then the individual
locations of equipment may be restricted to sites served by the cables; if
infra-red links are used then receivers and transmitters have to be in sight of
each other; if radio is used then privacy may not be easily achieved. At
present, nearly all local area networks are linked by some form of wire cable.
Where these connect into the wider world, they require some device to make
the connections to the outside world. These connecting devices arrange for
the signals to be sent in an appropriate form, at the correct speed and with the
necessary destination information attached. The computer user determines
the content and destination of the messages but the linking devices determine
the way in which the messages are sent and often the route.

Communications channel

also known as: data channel, data carrier, data link
including: data transmission
is a communication circuit along which data, in coded form, may be
transmitted between two points; it may consist of more than one line. *Data
transmission* is the process of using a data link. See also *facsimile
transmission,* page 22 and *bus,* page 298.

Modem (MOdulator-DEModulator)

is a data communications device for sending and receiving data between
computers over telephone circuits. It converts the digital signals from the
computer into audio tones for transmission over ordinary voice quality
telephone lines and converts incoming audio signals into digital signals for
the computer. It is normally plugged directly into a standard telephone
socket.

Fax modem

is a modem with the ability to send documents as if it were a fax machine.

Fax (facsimile) machine

is a machine for transmitting and receiving copies of paper document pages
over telephone circuits. The process involves scanning a document and
transmitting the resulting data to another fax machine which prints the copy.

Terminal adapter

sometimes called: adapter
is an interface which is plugged into a microcomputer serial port to link into
the *ISDN (integrated services digital network)* (see page 326).

Private Branch Exchange (PBX)

including: Private Automatic Branch Exchange (PABX)
is a private telephone exchange. It provides the interface between a group of
telephone extensions and the public network lines. There is usually a facility
which allows any extension to dial any other extension directly and to dial
into the public network using only a simple connect code and the outside
number. Normally, external callers only get the operator unless they know
the direct dial number for an individual extension.

Digital PABXs can control and interconnect a mix of telephones, fax
machines, teletext devices and computers all operating at different bit rates.

Multiplexor

sometimes spelt: multiplexer

including: frequency division multiplexor (FDM), time division multiplexor (TDM), time slice, statistical multiplexor, intelligent time division multiplexor

is a device that receives data from several independent sources for transmission along a single route to a single destination. A two-way communication multiplexor must be able to separate signals for each of the destinations. The multiplexor for the host computer in Figure B7.1 could be a *front-end processor* (see page 103).

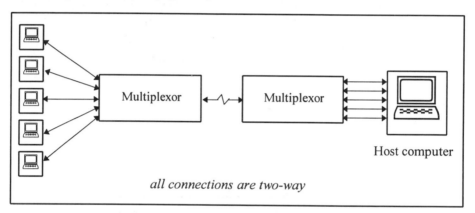

all connections are two-way

Figure B7.1: *Multiplexors connecting remote workstations to a computer.*

A *time division multiplexor (TDM)* transmits the signals from two or more sources in successive short time intervals, called *time slices*. Each source gets the same duration of time interval. Where the multiplexor time allocation is proportional to the activity of each source, it is called a *statistical multiplexor,* or an *intelligent time division multiplexor.*

A *frequency division multiplexor (FDM)* uses the available route link to transmit the data from the different sources at the same time. This is achieved by dividing the available channel *bandwidth* (see page 322) into a number of narrow bands, each of which is used for a separate transmission but at a slower speed.

Signal concentrator

also known as: message concentrator, concentrator

is any device, such as a multiplexor, which is used to enable a single channel to be used for carrying multiple communications.

Wire connector

including: copper cable, coaxial cable, twisted pair (TP), unshielded twisted pair (UTP)

is a standard form of wire cable used to provide the connections in a network. *Copper cables* are commonly used as connectors for local area networks, since they are readily available and have suitable electrical characteristics. Various types of copper cable are used, including:

Coaxial cable, which is made to a variety of specifications, is the same kind of cable that is used for connecting a television aerial to a television set. It has two conductors. One is a wire down the centre of the cable, which may be a single strand, insulated from the second, which is made up of many strands braided around the insulation for the inner wire.

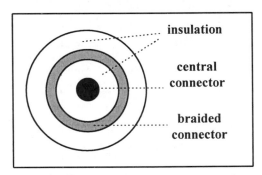

Figure B7.2: *Section of coaxial cable*

Twisted pair (*TP*) cable is commonly used for data transmission. In its simplest form it is a pair of insulated copper wires twisted together surrounded by a copper braid and external insulation. Some cables are made up of a number of twisted pairs surrounded by an overall (earthed) braid screen. In another form, stranded copper wires are twisted together in pairs with an earth wire. These pairs may be grouped to form a single multi-connector cable. These cables all have different specifications and, used in the correct situation, provide minimum interference data transmission.

Unshielded twisted pair (*UTP*) is similar to the twisted pair cables described above, but have no earthed shield. In suitable circumstances they can be used for data transmission.

Fibre optic cable

also known as: optical fibre

is a very fine glass strand that allows rapid transmission of data, using modulated light beams. It is usual to put many strands together in a single cable, each one capable of carrying one or more data signals. Fibre optic cable provides interference-free, secure data transmission and, unlike metal wires, is not subject to corrosion.

Wireless communication
including: infra-red, microwave transmission, satellite
covers a whole range of possible methods of data transmission, which can be used for linking computers within networks or for links within computer systems.

Infra-red communication uses the same systems as domestic remote control of televisions. Examples of its use include the control of robotic devices and remote keyboards. It is necessary for there to be direct unobstructed line of sight between the transmitter and the receiver. Strong sunlight will interfere with infra-red signals.

Microwave transmission is used as a method of communication within public telephone services. Many organisations use private installations to transmit data between key sites. Unlike the cellular phone systems which are broadcast systems, microwave transmissions use highly directional transmitters and receivers with dish aerials.

Satellite links are used for international communications by many providers of public telephone services. Unlike satellite broadcast systems, these links use highly directional, narrow beam, two-way transmissions. A single channel is capable of simultaneously carrying a very large number of separate transmissions.

Cable TV
sometimes: cable
is a form of communications network that provides television programmmes into consumer's homes through underground cables. The cables are usually coaxial cable, but some installations use fibre optic cable. The cables installed for cable TV could easily be used for a variety of other communications purposes and could become part of an *ISDN (integrated services digital network)* system (see page 326).

Terminator
is a device fitted to the end of a network cable which is not plugged into a network terminal. In some network systems, any cable end not terminated can cause the network communications to fail. Similarly *SCSI (Small Computer Systems Interface)* cables (see page 309) need to be properly terminated. A terminator may look like a cable connector with only one socket, its purpose being to prevent signal reflections in the, otherwise unterminated, cable.

Repeater

including: multi-part repeater, router, bridge, brouter
is a device to link two cable segments. Because of the loss of signal strength in network cables, a repeater amplifies the signals it receives before passing them on.

A *multi-part repeater* can be used to create a spur off the network.

A *router* is a form of repeater. In some systems it is merely used as another
    name for a repeater; in others, it is a device that identifies the
    destinations of messages and sends them on via an appropriate route.

A *bridge* is a connection between two local area networks. The use of a
    bridge produces a logical network, which appears to all users as a single
    network although it may be made up of several physically distinct
    networks. All users have access to all the resources on the resulting
    enlarged network, in particular the various *servers* (see page 151). See
    also *gateway*, page 152.

A *brouter* is a device which combines the functions and properties of a
    bridge and a repeater on a local area network.

Signal level

including: signal amplifier, signal booster
is the measure of the strength of a communications signal. In the same way that sound and light become weaker with distance, electrical signals passing down a wire become weaker as they travel along the wire. For this reason *signal amplifiers* or *boosters* are built into communications networks at appropriate intervals. These increase the signal level before passing the signal on to the next part of the network.

Handshake

is the exchange of signals between devices to establish their readiness to send or receive data, for example the transmission of data from a computer to a printer. Handshaking is one of a number of methods of ensuring that both the sender and receiver are ready before transmission begins.

Signal converter

*including: analog signal, digital signal, Analog to Digital (A to D or A/D)
converter, digitising, Digital to Analog (D to A or D/A) converter*
is a device which converts serial signals from one form to another. Signals may be *digital*, consisting of discrete bit patterns, or *analog*, consisting of a continuously varying voltage. Both kinds of signals are used to represent data. Some devices generate analog signals or need to be supplied with data

in analog form, while others generate or have to be supplied with data in digital form.

An ***Analog-to-Digital*** (***A-to-D***) ***converter*** converts analog signals into digital signals for subsequent processing. This conversion is sometimes called ***digitising***. For example, the analog output from a microphone has to be digitised before it can be stored or processed by a computer.

A ***Digital-to-Analog*** (***D-to-A***) ***converter*** converts serial digital signals into analog signals. For example, the digital data for a computer display has to be converted into analog signals if it is to be used as input to a television.

Baud

including: baud rate, bits per second (bps), bytes per second (bps), bit rate, characters per second (cps)

is the unit used to measure the speed (the ***baud rate***) of serial data transmission, for example the transmission of data along a telephone line or the speed of serial transmission to a printer. Generally, one baud is one bit per second, but it is important to note that there is no simple relationship between baud rate and the rate of data transfer between devices. Under any communications protocol additional bits have to be transmitted to provide start and stop bits, error detection and other communications controls. In addition, methods of communication, such as multiphase signalling, and data compression can both increase the amount of data that is transmitted in a given time.

Other measures of speed of data transfer are:

Bits per second (***bps***), sometimes called the ***bit rate,*** is a measure of the speed with which data moves between various parts of a computer. High bit rates are given in Kbit/s ($2^{10} = 1024$ bps) or Mbits/s ($2^{20} = 1048576$ bps). [Note: ***bps*** is sometimes used to mean ***bytes per second***, in which case it is generally taken to be the same as characters per second.]

Characters per second (***cps***) is a measure of the speed of character data transfer between devices. It is frequently also given as a measure of the speed of printers.

Transducer

is an electronic component which converts one form of energy to another. For example, a thermistor converts a temperature into electrical energy with a varying voltage, a photo cell converts brightness of illumination into a voltage. The term is generally applied to devices which produce electricity rather than those which convert electricity into another form of energy.

Sampler

also known as: digital sampler

is an elctronic circuit which takes samples of an electronic signal at intervals and stores them for future processing. In particular, they are used to take frequent measurements of analog signals for converting an analog signal into a digital signal, when it is known as a digital sampler.

Sensor

including: analog sensor, digital sensor, active device, passive device

is a *transducer* (see above) which responds to some physical property such as pressure, rate of flow, humidity, the proximity of ferrous metal. The sensor produces an electrical output which is either *analog* or *digital*. Some sensors, called **passive devices**, require no external electrical source. Those which require an external voltage are called **active devices**.

Servo mechanism

also known as: servo

is a mechanical mechanism for remote control of machines. A simple form is the motors which operate the control surfaces of a radio-controlled model aircraft, where the person flying the model plays an active part continuously adjusting the position of the control levers. Servos can be controlled electronically through computer circuits which may incorporate feedback to achieve automatic control; in these situations human participation may be very limited.

Actuator

is any device which can be operated by signals from a computer or control system causing physical movement. For example, devices for opening windows in a compute-controlled ventilation system.

Stepper motor

sometimes : stepping motor

is an electric motor which moves in small rotational steps. Suitably controlled and geared, a stepper motor can provide very small discrete movements, for example, the movement of the paper rollers and the print head in a printer. The control circuits may well involve the use of *feedback* (see page 39).

Part C:
How Computer Systems Work

C1	Systems Design and Life Cycle	162
C2	Systems Documentation	171
C3	Management and Manipulation Of Data	182
C4	Programming Concepts	190
C5	Programming (Flow of Execution)	204
C6	Programming (Subprograms)	211
C7	Program Syntax	219
C8	Program Documentation	226
C9	Developing, Testing and Running Programs	238
C10	Programming Languages	248
C11	Data Representation	257
C12	Numeric Data Representation	270
C13	Systems Software	279
C14	Machine Architecture	291
C15	Buses and Interfaces	306
C16	Physical Components	311
C17	Communications Technology	315
C18	Truth Tables and Logic Gates	328

This part is concerned with those terms which are frequently considered to be associated with Computer Science as opposed to the terms in Part A, which are concerned with the needs of computer system users, and Part B, which provides some technical information which may be helpful to both computer users and to students following courses requiring some knowledge of computer systems and peripherals.

The range of terms covered and the depth of treatment of individual terms has been influenced by knowledge of the difficulties encountered by students, who are studying courses which involve some Computer Science, whatever the name of the course.

C1   *Systems Design and Life Cycle*

Related topics can be found in A16 User Documentation,
C2 Systems Documentation, C8 Program Documentation
and C9 Developing, Testing and Running Programs.

There is an enormous difference between an individual writing a computer program for their own use and the large-scale commercial production of software. Many stages that can be ignored by an individual become crucially important. There is the need to establish precisely what the customer requires; to organise the design and coding so that teams of people can work together; to keep track of the many changes that will inevitably be necessary; to provide suitable documentation for the future maintenance of the software, and suitable documentation for the user.

For a purpose-built computer system, designed for a single user (a large company, perhaps), the problems will centre around establishing exactly what it is that the customer requires, avoiding the traditional complaints *"Yes – but what I really meant was ..."* and *"Yes – and while you're about it, can you just ..."*. For software that will be marketed in volume, such as word-processors, spreadsheets and so forth, there will be the commercial pressure to ensure that features absent from competing software are on offer, at the same time as ensuring that the software will run with the minimum amount of extra memory or peripherals. It will usually be necessary to ensure that existing users of earlier versions of the software can easily and cheaply upgrade to the new version (rather than being tempted to a competitor's product). At the same time, it will be commercially advantageous to make it easy for users of a competing product to transfer – by offering the ability to read files prepared in other software packages, or by designing the command structure so that it has similarities with competing products.

When commercial software packages are designed to be run under the control of a particular operating system (such as Windows, or UNIX), the designer of the operating system may have defined 'rules' for applications software that ensure that future upgrades to the operating system can be achieved in a way that does not result in existing software ceasing to operate.

It should be clear that the design of computer systems (which may include hardware as well as software) is a task that requires considerable management and discipline. This has been reflected in the relatively recent change of title from simply 'programming' to 'software engineering'. The construction of large, complex systems (on which safety as well as profits

may depend) is very similar to the construction of civil engineering projects
such as bridges or buildings.

Applications program

including: applications package, generic software, productivity tool
also known as: applications software
is an information system designed to carry out some task (such as keeping
accounts, editing text, maintaining a mailing list) which is primarily
independent of computers, and would need to be carried out even if
computers did not exist – this is in contrast to *systems programs* (see page
280) which are concerned with the operation of the computer. An
applications package is a complete set of applications programs together
with the associated documentation. Where the application is appropriate to
many areas (word processing can be used for example in personal
correspondence, the production of business 'form letters', academic research,
compilation of glossaries, writing books etc.) it is usual to describe the
program as ***generic software*** or as a ***productivity tool***.

Applications system design

*including: systems analysis, systems design, feasibility study, system
specification, functional specification*
is the process involved in the design of applications software packages.
Typically this begins with an analysis of any existing system and of the
requirements of the new system (***systems analysis***). A ***feasibility study*** of
potential computer involvement may be made, estimating costs, effort,
effectiveness, reliability and the benefits to be expected from a new system.
The desired system will be specified in a ***systems specification*** that sets out
the hardware and software requirements, and the organisational and human
implications. This may include a separate ***functional specification*** that
describes exactly how the system will behave. Only when all these stages
have been completed will work begin on the production of the software.

Audit trail

including: journal file
is an automatic record made (in a ***journal file***) of any transactions carried out
by a computer system, such as updates to files. This may be required for
legal reasons (so that the auditors can confirm the accuracy of the company
accounts); for security reasons (so that data maliciously or accidentally
deleted can be recovered); or simply to monitor the performance of the
system.

Benchmark

is a standard set of computer tasks, designed to allow measurements to be made of computer performance. These tasks can be used to compare the performance of different software or hardware. Examples of tasks are, how long it takes to re-format a 40-page word processed document, how many pages can be printed in one minute, how long it takes to save 1000 database records to disk. Users seeking to buy software or hardware may be able to obtain some information about the performance of possible purchases.

Benchmarks may also figure in *acceptance testing* (see below) of a computer system, by specifying performance that must be achieved before the system is considered finished. See also s*oftware metric*, below, for a description of the theoretical equivalent of the more practical benchmark.

Configuration management

is the automatic tracking and monitoring of changes to software during development, so that everyone involved is aware of the features of the latest version.

Default

including: default option, default value
is an assumption made by computer software in the absence of explicit instructions to the contrary. This may be a ***default option*** – your files are listed in alphabetical order, unless you request date or size order – or a ***default value*** – the computer prints one copy of a document, unless you request multiple copies. The best software is designed so that the most frequently-used options are all available as defaults, so that users are not troubled by the need to continually specify such values. It is often possible for users to customise software, by selecting their own choice of defaults.

Developmental testing

including: alpha test, beta test
Commercial software is traditionally developed to an incomplete state, with some questions of design, command sequences, defaults, etc. left unresolved. It is then issued in an ***alpha test*** version to a restricted audience of testers within the developer's own company. When the results of this in-house testing have been studied and appropriate changes made, a ***beta test*** version is released to a number of privileged customers in exchange for their constructive comments. Beta test versions are usually close to the finally released product. They are made available to computer magazine reviewers, authors of independent 'how to' instructional manuals and developers of associated software or hardware products, who can work over a period of

time with a near-complete package, so that the final launch can be accompanied by valuable and informed publicity.

Formal methods
including: formal specification
is the name given to the mathematical techniques used to prove that software works, without the necessity of testing every possible route through the programs. With large complex computer systems, it is uneconomic and virtually impossible to test that the system behaves properly under every possible combination of circumstances. Individual parts of the system will have a precise *formal specification* including inputs that they will recognise and outputs that they will produce.

Integrated package
is one that combines a number of distinct applications, such as a word processor, a spreadsheet and a database, in a single package. This allows easy exchange of data between individual components, for example incorporating a spreadsheet of sales figures into a word processed report. It is usually necessary for users to learn only one form of commands for common tasks, such as those for loading and saving files.

Jackson Structured Development (JSD)
including: Jackson Structured Programming (JSP)
is a method invented by Michael Jackson in 1983 for the analysis and design of data processing and real-time systems. It emphasises the need for orderly structure in the development and design of systems.
Jackson Structured Programming (JSP) is a structured programming technique that uses diagrams as a step to developing programs. *Structured programming* (see below) emphasises an orderly approach to program development, breaking down large tasks into smaller sub-tasks. Jackson structured programming is a particular form of this diagrammatic method which enables the design process to be efficiently managed.

Modular design
including: module
is a method of organising a large computer program into self-contained parts, *modules*, which can be developed simultaneously by different programmers or teams of programmers. Modules have clearly defined relationships with the other parts of the system, which enables them to be independently designed, programmed and maintained. Some modules may be independently executable programs, while others may be designed to provide facilities for the suite of programs to which they belong.

Object oriented programming (OOP)

including: object, message, object oriented design (OOD), object oriented language (OOL)

is a type of programming where the programmer defines not only the type of data, but also the allowable operations that can be carried out on that data. Such a definition, of data and permitted operations, is known as an *object*. Objects pass *messages* between each other, with one object making a request of another. This generally results in more reliable software, because each object is 'responsible' for checking that the message it receives is 'sensible'. Developing programs using *object oriented design* allows a team of programmers to work simultaneously, and also allows further development of existing programs without jeopardising existing parts of the program. Obviously, object oriented programming requires an *object oriented language* such as *Smalltalk* (see page 254) or C++.

Operational mode

including: batch processing, transaction processing, multi-access, time-sharing, real-time system, interactive processing, remote access, tele-processing, off-line processing, on-line processing, time-sharing

is the way a computer system is used and operated. Decisions about operational modes are made during system design. Often the *operating system* (see page 284) manages the functioning of the operational modes in use.

The terms in this section are not necessarily exclusive, and more than one might be applicable to any particular computer system.

In *batch processing* all the data to be input is collected together before being processed as a single efficient operation. This method is also used when computer users submit individual *jobs* (see page 287) which are processed together as a batch.

Transaction processing deals with each set of data from a user as it is submitted. This is normally used in commercial systems where a transaction may be a booking, an order or an invoice. Each transaction is completed before the next is begun.

Multi-access systems allow several users apparently to have individual control of the computer at the same time. One method of implementing a multi-access system is by allocating a period of time to each user, this is called *time-sharing*. See also *time slice*, page 288.

Real-time system is one which can react fast enough to influence behaviour in the outside world; for example, this is necessary in air-traffic control systems and desirable in on-line reservation systems.

Interactive processing provides the user with direct, immediate responses from the system. There is often some kind of dialogue with the system. Examples include the booking of airline tickets, requesting information about a bank account through a cash dispensing machine.

Remote access or *tele-processing* is the use of a geographically remote computer system via communications links. See also *remote job entry*, page 287.

Off-line computer processing occurs when devices are not under the immediate control of the main computer, for example data entry to disk or tape storage.

On-line processing allows the user to interact directly with the main computer.

Implementation
including: parallel running, pilot running, direct changeover, big-bang, phased implementation

is the process of starting to use an information system in a real situation after having designed and developed it. It may enable final testing in a real situation. Four different approaches are used depending on the size of the system and the properties of the data being processed.

Parallel running requires the new system to operate for a short period of time alongside the older system. The results can be compared to ensure that the new system is working correctly.

Pilot running requires the new system to operate alongside the old system but only processing part of the data. The results can be compared to check that the system works correctly but pilot running cannot test how the system will operate with the larger quantities of data of the real situation.

Direct changeover or *big-bang* requires that the new system replaces the old system without any overlap. In some cases the nature of the system prevents parallel or pilot running and a direct changeover is the only option, for example is an emergency control system.

Phased implementation involves replacing part of the old system while other parts continue to use the old system. This enables training and installation to be spread over a longer period of time. An example is a supermarket chain, which would not install a new system in all its branches at the same time, but phase it in as the branches are refurbished. The first phase of the implementation could also be used as parallel running.

Software

consists of programs, routines and procedures (together with their associsted documentation) which can be run on a computer system. See also, *applications program*, page 163 and *systems software*, page 279.

Software life cycle

is the stages in the life history of a large-scale piece of software, produced in a disciplined way. There is disagreement over the precise number and description of the stages, but a fairly typical list is shown in Figure C1.1. Many people add the extra stage *obsolescence* to this list

SOFTWARE LIFE CYCLE	
Stage	*Description*
System requirements	identifying what the customer wants ...
Software requirements	... and turning this into a software specification
Overall design	specifying the whole system
Detailed design	splitting it into containable modules
Module design	deciding what each part will do ...
Module production	.. and turning this into a computer program
Module testing	making sure each module works alone ...
Integration and system testing	... and together with all the other modules
Acceptance testing	getting the customer to agree that it works
Release	the software is sold, or delivered to the customer
Implementation and operation	it works ... ... or some parts do not and have to be corrected
Maintenance	maintenance usually includes upgrading the software to meet new requirements

Figure C1.1: *Software life cycle*

Software metric

is a number or other measure that can be associated with a piece of software to describe its efficiency, performance, ease of development, and other properties. *Benchmarks* (see above) measure how software actually behaves, while software metrics attempt to describe performance from a study of the code alone. Simple and sometimes not very helpful metrics include the number of lines of code and the space occupied in memory.

SSADM

abbreviation for: Structured Systems Analysis and Design Method
is the standard method of analysis and design of large-scale software packages used within government departments in the UK.

System development cycle

including: system cycle, system life cycle
is the complete cycle of activities involved in the creation of a new or modified computer system, including several activities described elsewhere in this section. There are differences of opinion about the precise number and description of stages, but a typical set is shown in Figure C1.2. Compare this with Figure C1.1: *Software life cycle* which is very similar, but describes only the software components of a computer system.

SYSTEM DEVELOPMENT CYCLE

Stage	*Description*	*see also*
Specification	of the user's requirements	*system specification*, above *functional specification*, above.
Analysis and design	of the system	*systems analysis and systems design*, above *Jackson structured development*, above *object oriented programming*, above *structured systems analysis and design method*, above.
Implementation (of the design)	using the design from the previous stage	*modular design*, above.
Testing	of the implemented design	*developmental testing*, above.
Implementation (of the system)	with the existing system	*implementation*, above.
Documentation	of the whole system	*user documentation*, page 88 *systems documentation*, page 171.

Each stage involves iterative review until the result is acceptable.

Figure C1.2: *System development cycle*

Structured programming

including: structured planning technique, top-down programming, stepwise refinement, bottom-up programming

is a methodical approach to the design of a program which emphasises breaking large and complex tasks into smaller sections. This is also referred to as ***structured planning technique***.

Top-down programming or ***stepwise refinement*** is a particular type of structured programming, where the problem is defined very simply and then split into a number of smaller sections. Each of these sections is successively split and refined until they are small enough to be programmed. It is an axiom of this approach that new ideas which were not in the original global design should not be added.

Bottom-up programming involves programming a number of small modules and building them into a larger structure. In practice it is often difficult to ensure that an efficient system is developed by this method. See also *modular design*, above.

C2   *Systems Documentation*

This section is concerned with the written comments and graphical illustrations which form the description of a system. The symbols and layout conventions referred to are those given in British Standards BS4058:1973 and BS6224:1982.

Related topics can be found in A16 User Documentation, C1 Systems Design and Life Cycle, C8 Program Documentation, C9 Developing, Testing and Running Programs.

Software systems will require some modification during their lifetime. If this is to be done satisfactorily, it is vital that good, complete and understandable documentation is available. Requests to modify software may arise for a number of reasons, which could include changes in company procedures, requests for improvements, errors in the software which were not found at the testing stage and changes in government regulations (for example, new taxation law). The resources required at the maintenance stage of the **Systems Life Cycle**, which is covered in C1 Systems Design and Life Cycle, frequently equal and indeed sometimes exceed the initial resources required to deliver the software in the first instance.

The original team that did the analysis and design, and the implementation, of the software may well not be available to carry out the maintenance stage. This makes it all the more important that good, up-to-date documentation is available throughout the life of the software.

A standard form of documentation may be followed, which may be specified by the company involved. There are a number of recognised system development methodologies, for example **SSADM (Structured Systems Analysis and Design Method)**. These specify, at various levels of detail, what documentation should be produced and in what form. Software tools also exist, such as CASE (Computer Aided Software Engineering) tools, which can help to produce consistent documentation of changes.

Documentation produced at the design and analysis stage will include the **requirements specification**, which is sometimes 'signed off' as a formal agreement between the customer and the software group. As the design develops, a range of diagrams will be produced; these will include:

- diagrams showing the relationships between the data (**entity-relationships** or **entity-relation diagrams**)

- diagrams showing the relationships between the data and the processes or programs that manipulate and transform the data (**data flow diagrams** or **system diagrams**).

The design task will be tackled in a hierarchical way, gradually breaking it down into smaller parts (sub-tasks), using methods such as **JSD (Jackson Structured Development)**. Often diagrams, such as those used by Jackson System Development, use different shapes to indicate the use of a particular device or medium, in the same kind of way that icons are often used in a graphical user interface.

As the programs are designed and developed there will be other documentation for the programs. These have particular forms and are covered in *C8 Program Documentation.*

Maintenance documentation
including: technical documentation
is written for the computer professional rather than the user. It will include both *systems documentation* (see the introduction to this section, above) and *program documentation* (see page 227). Some parts will be highly technical, for example, the specifications of peripherals and their configuration. The reader of this *technical documentation* will need to have expert knowledge.

Requirements specification
is that part of the system documentation which sets out the customer's requirements for the system. It may be drafted as a formal, contractual agreement between the customer and the software system developers. In some respects, it will provide measures against which the performance of the implemented system will be assessed.

Entity-relationship diagram
including: entity-relationship
is a diagram used to show how data (entities) are related to each other. For example, how the different layers of data in a database are related and how access to one layer of data will automatically achieve access to related data items and related layers. An *entity-relationship* is a formal statement of the way in which one data item is related to another, or of the way in which a class of data items is related to items in another class.

Figure C2.1 gives an example of an entity-relationship diagram in which the relationship between student and course is many:many, because each student may attend many courses and each course will have many students. And the relationship between tutor and course is 1:many, because each tutor will teach many courses but each course will only have one (main) tutor.

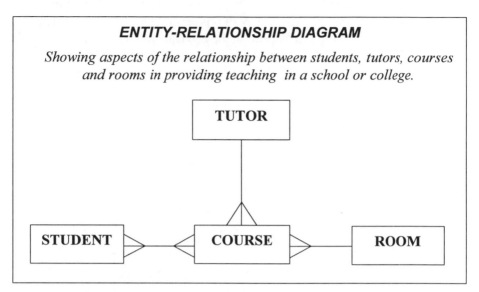

Figure C2.1: Entity-relationship diagram

Flowchart

including: flow line

is a graphical representation of the operations involved in a process or system. *System flowchart symbols* (see below) are used to represent particular operations or data, and *flow lines*, which connect the flowchart symbols, indicate the sequence of operations or the flow of data. Flow lines may use arrows to indicate sequence, or a top-down, left-right convention may apply if there are no arrows.

System flowchart

also called: data flow diagram (DFD), data flowchart, system flowchart diagram, system diagram

is a diagram used to describe a complete data processing system. The flow of data through the operations is diagrammatically described, down to the level of the individual programs needed to achieve the system requirements. The details of programs are not included, since these are covered in the *program documentation* (see page 227).

System flowchart symbol

is a symbol used in a system flowchart diagram. Different shapes indicate the various kinds of activity described by the diagram. Sometimes highly formalised shapes are used, each having a specific meaning; in other situations very simple boxes with words are used. Provided the meaning is clear, either method is an equally acceptable way of representing a process or system. Examples of how these symbols might be used are given in Figure C2.9, where rectangles are used for all processes, and Figures C2.10 and C2.11 which use more formal shapes.

Input/output symbol

also known as: data input/output symbol
also used as: output symbol, input symbol
is used for any input or output of data however achieved.

Figure C2.2: *Input/output symbol*

Interactive input symbol

is used to indicate data input by keyboard or other operator-controlled input system such as a bar-code reader. It may also be used for on-line interrogation.

Figure C2.3: *Interactive input symbol*

Document output symbol

also known as: output document symbol
is used to indicate that data is to be printed.

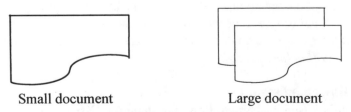

Small document   Large document

Figure C2.4: *Document output symbol*

Process symbol

also known as: data processing symbol
is used for the processing of data, for example, by a computer program.

Figure C2.5: *Process symbol*

File symbol

sometimes called: data symbol
including: on-line data file symbol, (magnetic) disk file symbol,
(magnetic) tape file symbol
A number of different symbols are used when processing data files. In most instances the symbol shapes make it easier to recognise the process defined within the symbol.
On-line data file symbol is used for data held on any on-line file, whatever the purpose.

Figure C2.6: *On-line data file symbol*

The ***(magnetic) disk file symbol*** is used whenever the data is held on a disk .

Figure C2.7: *(magnetic) Disk file symbol*

The ***(magnetic) tape file symbol*** is used whenever the data is held on a tape.

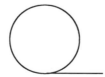

Figure C2.8: *(magnetic) Tape file symbol*

Flowcharts of a payroll system.

The flowcharts in Figures C2.9, C2.10 and C2.11 describe the part of a payroll process where the wages information for each employee is processed. The transactions are validated, sorted and then used to update the wages master file.

The descriptions (printer, disk, etc.) may be altered, according to the particular medium being used; alternatively, the descriptions may be omitted completely, if a less specific flowchart is required.

System flowchart (using simplified symbols)

Figure C2.9: Flowchart of payroll process, using simple symbols

System flowchart (using British Standard symbols)

This flowchart (Figure C2.10) uses British Standard symbols to show the process described above. The annotation on the right of the flowcharts in Figures C2.10 and C2.11 have been used to describe the function of the symbols. A similar annotation method can be used to provide an explanatory commentary on the algorithm or process represented by the flowchart diagram. An alternative set of symbols is used in Figure C2.11.

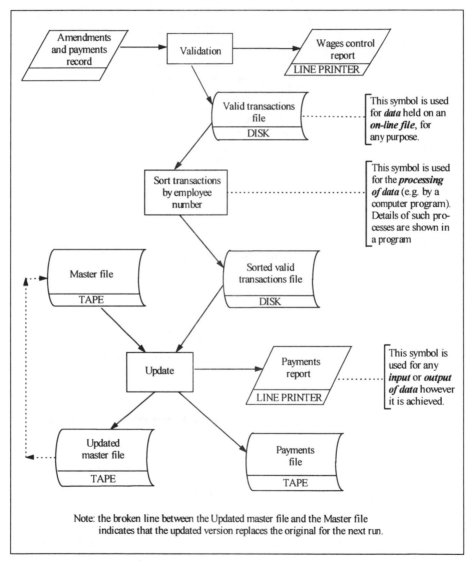

Figure C2.10: Flowchart of payroll process, using British Standard symbols

System flowchart (using British Standard alternative symbols)

This flowchart (Figure C2.11) uses alternative symbols to describe the process shown in Figure C2.10. There are also other, less commonly used, symbols. The document symbols can also be used for the input of data to a system by means of documents (e.g. written orders).

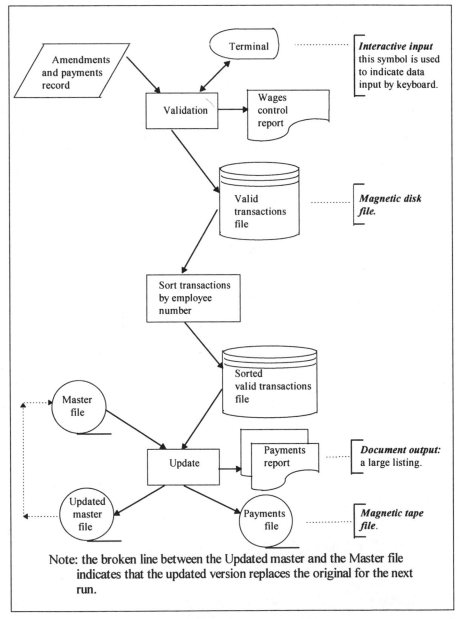

Figure C2.11: Flowchart of payroll process, using alternative symbols

Structure diagram

is a means of representing the design of a program or system. It consists of a number of levels, each of which describes the whole design, but at increasing levels of detail.

The structure diagram, Figure C2.12 (below), shows another way of representing the payroll process shown in Figures C2.9, C2.10 and C2.11. This is based on the *JSD (Jackson structured development) notation* (see page 165). The hierarchical structure diagram is displayed in a top-down, left-to-right manner. At each successive level (labelled 1,2,3,...) the tasks are described in greater detail. The lower boxes expand the description of the task defined in the box in the level above to which they are connected. This process of expansion is continued to varying depths in different parts of the diagram until it is judged that sufficient detail is given.

The numbers are used to identify the boxes uniquely. The actual numbers are not significant although they can be used to indicate levels; in this case the first digit indicates the level, for example 3.59 would indicate a box at level 3.

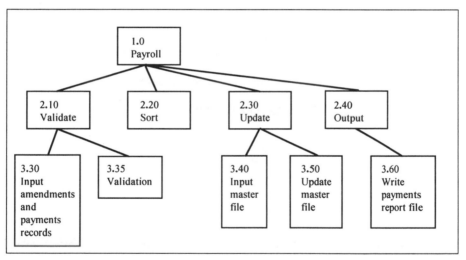

Figure C2.12: *A structure diagram for the payroll process*

At greater levels of detail it can be helpful to draw the expanded version of a section in the structure diagram, in this case the validation section, as a separate diagram, Figure C2.13.

In this example horizontal and vertical connecting lines are used. It is of no importance which type of connecting line is drawn although it is normal to be consistent.

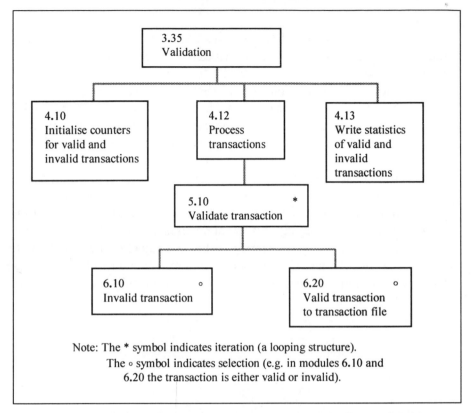

Figure C2.13: *Expansion of process 3.35 in figure C2.12*

Block diagram

is a diagram made up of boxes labelled to represent different hardware or software components and lines showing their interconnections.

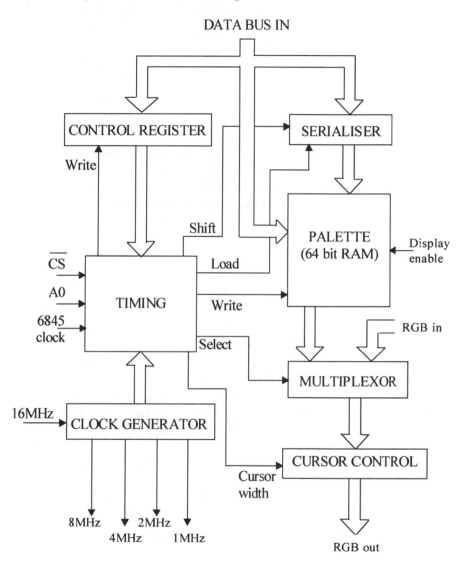

Figure C2.14: *An example of a block diagram (courtesy Acorn Computers)*

C3   *Management and Manipulation of Data*

*Related topics can be found in A1 Data Processing, A2 Word
Processing, A3 Spreadsheets, A5 Databases and Information
Retrieval, B3 Memory, C11 Data Representation and
C12 Numeric Data Representation*

Computer users tend to keep their programs separate from the data they
operate on. The data is usually held as one or more *files* on backing storage,
and the systems software encourages the user to believe that the file is held
here (for example, on a disk) all the time. In fact, when a program wishes to
use the data in a file, it is necessary for the portion of the file being worked
on to be copied into primary storage in order to work on individual items of
data. The systems software is responsible for copying between backing and
primary storage, ensuring that the correct portion is readily available, without
explicit action by the user. Because of this automatic management, it is
necessary for users to access files in a formal way.

If the file is a new one, it must first be *created*, and this might include
specifying how large the file will become, and how it will be organised.
Before any use of an existing file, it is necessary to *open* the file, when a
section will be copied to primary storage, and other programs will be notified
that the file is in use. Any changes will be made to the copy, and when access
is requested to a part of the file not currently in primary storage, the systems
software is responsible for making the changes to the permanent version, and
loading a fresh copy of the required portion.

When access to the file is no longer needed, it must be *closed* so that any
remaining changes are written back to the permanent version, and other
programs can be notified that the file is no longer in use.

A file may be *deleted* from backing store, but it is usual for the systems
software simply to mark the file in some way, so that the space it occupies
may be used for other files, rather than physically erase the contents.

File Allocation Table (FAT)
is a table held on a disk which records how the space on the disk is used.

File operations
including: read, write, update, insert, append, read-only
are those activities that can be performed on an existing data file.

Reading is the operation of taking a copy of a data item from a file.

Writing is the operation of saving any changes to a file.

Updating is altering an existing data item already written in the file.

Inserting is adding a new data item to an existing file. This implies moving all later items to make space.

Appending is adding a new item at the end of an existing file.

In multi-user systems problems can arise if more than one user is allowed to access a file at any one time. Only the first user who requests access to a file will be allowed to update it or append to it. Until the first user has released the file, subsequent requests for access may be denied or allowed *read-only access* to the file or indivdual records.

File access

including: serial access, sequential access, direct access, random access, index-sequential access

The way in which a file is to be accessed by users influences how it is stored, and the information the systems software needs to hold in order to allow for efficient reading and writing.

Serial access is where the items are read, one at a time, from the physical start of the file, in the order in which they are stored. Items may vary in length, provided there is some marker to signal the end of one item and the start of the next

Sequential access is where the items are read, one at a time, from the logical start of the file, in key value order. Because the records in a file held on a *serial access device* (see *magnetic tape*, page 117) need to be sorted into the order in which they are to be processed, serial access is sometimes referred to as sequential access.

Direct access is where any item can be retrieved immediately, provided its position in the file is known. This often means that items must have a known length, so that software can calculate where in the file the required item is located. Direct access files are commonly called *random access* files because they are usually held in storage that has random access. See also *magnetic disk*, page 113, and *random access memory*, page 120.

Index Sequential Access Methods (ISAM) index the records of a sequential file to allow both approaches: as an example, consider searching an index-sequential file of surnames. To locate 'Smith' an index is first consulted to discover the first item beginning with 'S', after which the file is searched sequentially. For this to work both the file and the index must be in alphabetic order.

Search

including: hit, hit rate, serial (or linear) search, binary search,
is the process of examining a file to see if a given data item occurs in it. A
successful location of an item is called a **hit**, and the success rate the **hit rate**.
Unless the file is in some useful order, searching may involve examining every
entry in the file until the item is found or the end of the file is reached, a **serial**
or **linear search.** Efficient *sorting* methods (see below) are important in
searching. If the file is in alphabetic order, a particularly efficient search
method is the **binary search** (Figure C3.1).

Archimedes
Aristotle
Armstrong
Arnold
Asquith
Aubrey
Auden
Austen
Austin   ≤········ *first comparison – goal is later*
Aytoun
Bacon   ≤·················· *third comparison – later*
Bagehot   ≤······················· *successful fourth comparison*
Balfour   ≤··············· *second comparison – earlier*
Ball
Barbour
Barker

In searching for the entry associated with 'Bagehot' in this alphabetically-
ordered table, a first comparison is made half-way down the list: this
indicates that the 'goal' is later in the list. Halving again and again, as many
times as necessary, locates 'Bagehot' after 4 comparisons (this number
would find any item on a list this length). A serial search would take 12
comparisons.

Figure C3.1: *An example of a binary search*

Sorting

is the process of arranging data items in a pre-determined order (such as alphabetical or numerical). When the data items are themselves structured – a record in a file, for example – one particular part of the structure must be specified as the item to be used in determining the ordering: this item is known as the *key* (see page 264). In a file of names and addresses, for example, the 'surname' might be used as the key.

File

including: file name extension
is a collection of related data. It is traditional to think of files as being structured as a collection of identically structured *records* (see page 262) made up of *fields* (see page 263).

To be accessed, a file has to have a name which is recognised by the system. Disk operating systems determine the conventions for file names. All file names carry some kind of extension, ***file name extension***, which may or may not be user controlled. The file name extension identifies the kind of data in the file. for example graphic data, wordprocessed document. See also *file type*, page 266.

Archive file

is one containing data no longer in use, but held for historical purposes, perhaps for auditors. It is often stored away from the computer system, in a secure location.

Backup file

is a copy of a current file kept as a security measure in case the original is corrupted in any way. As with an *archive file* (see above), it is often kept in a secure location away from the computer system.

Master file

including: transaction file
is the principal source of data for an application. It holds data which is mostly static or but which can be added to or amended by updating as necessary during processing. In a traditional commercial batch-processing application, such as a payroll, the master file (of all employees) is updated by reference to a ***transaction file*** of hours worked in the current month, leave, sickness, promotions, etc.

Reference file

is a special type of *master file* (see above) which is not updated during the job being processed. It contains fixed data that does not change. When changes are necessary, this will be achieved by a separate program.

Grandfather, father, son files

are the three most recent versions of a file that is periodically updated, for example the *master file* (see above) in a batch-processing application such as a payroll. The most recent, the '*son*' file, is used for the next run of the program; if an error occurs that corrupts this copy of the master file, the '*father*' version is still available, and can be used with an archive copy of the *transaction file* (see above) from the previous run, to re-create the damaged 'son' version. The '*grandfather*' version provides an additional level of security.

Index file

is a file used to access a large datafile quickly. It contains key field data from the file that the index is for. The key data is in a format which can be searched quickly and the attached addresses are used to access the data.

Data compression

is the technique of reducing the space occupied by a large file. There are many different methods, suited to different types of data.

The first paragraph of the introduction to this section (C3 Management and Manipulation of Data), contains 717 characters, including spaces; it can be reduced in size, without losing any of the information it contains, by replacing certain common pairs of letters by a single character (we have illustrated this by using numbers). For example, there are 18 occurrences of the pair 'th'. If these are replaced by '0', 18 characters have been saved. Making the changes listed in Figure C3.2, the introduction is reduced to 606 characters, a saving of 111 characters or about 15%. The file must be re-expanded before it can be used, of course, but space has been saved in storage.

DATA COMPRESSION

Comput9 us92te6 to keep 0eir program2separ73from 03d7a 0ey op973on. 03d7a i2usually held82on3or mo1 *file2*o4backi5 storage,86 03system2softwa1 encourage203us9 to believ307 03fil3i2held he1 (for example, o4a disk)8ll 03time. I4fact, whe4a program wishe2to us303d7a i4a file, it i2commo4for 03portio4of 03fil3bei5 worked o4to b3copied into primary storag3for mo1 rapid8ccess. 03system2softwa1 i21sponsibl3for copyi5 betwee4backi586 primary storage, ensuri5 07 03cor1ct portio4i21adily8vailable, wi0out explicit8ctio4by 03us9. Becaus3of 0i2autom7ic management, it i2necessary for us92to8cces2file2i4a formal way.

Replacements:

0 = th	1 = re	2 = s'N'	3 = e'N'	4 = n'N'
5 = ng	6 = nd	7 = at	8 = 'N'a	9 = er

(a space is represented by 'N')

Figure C3.2: *A simple example of data compression*

Validation

including: data vetting, range check, check digit, batch total, control total, check sum

is computerised checking to detect any data that is unreasonable or incomplete. It is also known as *data vetting*. There are many methods, chosen to suit the data being processed. Some operate on single data items: a *range check* would signal any data items outside a plausible range (a worker's age that was less than 15, or over 75, perhaps); *check digit* is an extra digit added as part of a numeric data item (like a part number): it is derived from the other digits in a way that can be repeated.

Other methods operate on batches of data: a *batch total* of the number of separate records in a batch might be manually calculated and added to the data, as a check that none had been missed; a *control total* formed by adding up some field from each record could accompany the batch as a double-check. Where the data is computer software, a *check sum* formed by simply adding up all the instructions, treated as numbers, is often added to a file to make sure that it has been copied without error. See also *hashing,* below.

Hashing

including: hash total, hash table, collision

is the process of calculating a numeric value from one or more data items. While this value obviously depends on the value of the data item(s), it does not depend on the meaning attached to them. It can be used as a *control total* (see *validation*, above) to check for errors in copying the data, when it is known as a *hash total*.

It is also an important technique in storing values in a data structure known as a *hash table*. The calculated value can be used to mark the position in the table where the data item should be found, enabling it to be accessed directly, rather than forcing a sequential search.

A *collision* occurs when two data items give the same value under hashing, and should therefore be stored in the same place in a hash table.

Corruption

is the introduction of errors into data or programs during storage or copying. It is usually due to physical causes, such as electrical *interference* (see page 325) or faulty equipment.

Download

including: upload

is to transfer data or programs from a larger computer (such as a mainframe) to a smaller (such as a personal computer). The reverse process is called *uploading.*

Export

including: import

is to create a data file using one piece of software, so that it can be read by another piece – the software that reads the 'exported' file is said to be *importing* it.

Merge

is to combine two or more ordered data structures, such as files, into a single ordered one.

Overflow

including: underflow, stack overflow

is a general term describing what happens when something becomes too large to be processed satisfactorily. For example, the result of a numeric calculation may become too large to be stored in the space reserved for numbers (*numeric overflow*); or a data structure, such as a stack, may have space reserved for just 100 entries, so that attempting to add a 101st would cause **stack overflow**. **Underflow** is also possible, a number too small to be represented in the computer, or an attempt to remove an item from an empty stack.

Overwriting

is the erasing of a data item by writing another in its place.

Raw data

is data as input to a computer, before any *validation* (see above) or processing.

Rounding

including: rounding error

is the approximation of a numeric data item by its nearest equivalent, to a given number of significant figures or decimal places. For example, 1.36 rounded to one decimal place is 1.4. **Rounding error** is the error introduced by rounding (+0.04 in the example).

Truncation

including: truncation error

is the approximation of a numeric data item by ignoring all information beyond a given number of significant figures or decimal places: for example, 1.36 truncated to one decimal place is 1.3. **Truncation error** is the error introduced by truncation (-0.06 in the example). This use of the term 'error' comes from mathematics and is important in situations where numbers are represented in a fixed-length format but should not be confused with other uses of the term. See also *error*, page 240 and *floating-point notation*, page 275.

C4 Programming Concepts

The terms defined in this section cover a variety of techniques and concepts used to communicate ideas and algorithms. These terms are used both to communicate ideas before a program is written and to describe the program design so that other programmers can maintain the program at a later date. Related terms can be found in sections C5 Programming (Flow of Execution), C6 Programming (Subprograms), C7 Program Syntax and C9 Developing, Testing and Running Programs.

The construction of any effective computer program is time consuming and complex, requiring the application of a wide range of techniques, skills and processes. The programmer has to work at a very detailed level to make the computer do what is wanted, so that the resulting program works reliably and at a reasonable speed.

The actual computer program run on the computer has to be in the machine-code used by the computer. There are ways of speeding up and simplifying the production of this program, such as using higher-level computer languages, program generators and specialised computer languages designed to produce particular types of programs, for example database managers. Many of the principles used by these various methods involve the same standard techniques that are used in traditional programming and much of the technical language used is of value to anybody involved in developing computer software.

Regardless of the method used to develop computer software, the designer has to balance the properties of cost, speed, ease of use and reliability of the final product. A slow program can be used with a larger computer, but at a greater cost in computer time. Similarly a complicated program will be more expensive to test. But if software is well designed, using a professional approach, then more efficient software can be developed at lower cost.

A computer programmer has to be prepared to choose between alternative programming strategies in order to get a usable program. The obvious method of solving a problem may be inefficient, as the user will not be prepared to wait while the computer carries out some apparently simple task. To avoid this, the programmer may use a variety of strategies (expressed as algorithms), some of which may be complex, but without which it may not be possible to produce a usable program. One skill a programmer must have is the ability to understand and adapt a wide range of existing algorithms to new situations.

The user will expect a program to work reliably and produce no errors. The programmer may use standard algorithms developed and tested by other people as one way of reducing possible errors in a program. The program must be able to deal with any mistakes the user makes without introducing any errors, for example in the input data.

Address

including: memory location, absolute address, offset, relative address, base address

Each piece of data or program instruction is stored separately in the computer's memory and it is located by its address. The address is the number for the position of a word of storage in the main memory. This number is used by a program as the identification of a particular *memory location*, which may contain a data item or the next instruction, when a machine-code program is branching.

If the address is the real address used by the internal electronics of the computer, it is known as the *absolute address*. Many machine-code programs and operating systems use a method of addressing, which allows a program to have its own (imaginary) addresses and convert these to the real addresses as the program is executed. The real addresses are worked out from a starting address number, called the *base address*, by adding another number, called the *offset* or *relative address*, to it.

One use of relative addressing is storing arrays. The location of any particular element of the array can be calculated from the element number and the base address of the (array) variable.

Array (machine-code programming)

The use of arrays is a fundamental technique in machine-code and low-level programming, since they make it possible to handle large amounts of related data efficiently. Each element in an array will be held sequentially in memory and so an index register or relative addressing can be used to access each element in turn. Since the array is stored as a single block of computer memory the programmer has a variety of methods which can be used to manipulate the data easily, for example copying the entire block as one operation. See also *array,* page 258.

Algebraic notation

including: infix, prefix and postfix notation, reverse polish notation
is the way mathematical and logical processes are described when writing a
computer program. Infix, prefix and postfix notations are different ways of
writing the algebraic (and logical) expressions used by a program.

Mathematicians normally use *infix* notation (where the operators are
placed between the operands, such as **A+B**). *Prefix* notation places the
operator first (such as **+AB**) while *postfix* notation places the operator last
(such as **AB+**). See Figure C4.1.

EXAMPLES OF DIFFERENT ALGEBRAIC NOTATIONS

What has to be worked out: Work out the perimeter of a rectangle
                                      which is: twice (**Length** plus **Breadth**)

*The formula in **Infix** notation:*   2*(**L+B**)

*The formula in **Prefix** notation:*   *2+**LB**

*The formula in **Postfix** notation:*   2**LB**+*
*(also called **Reverse Polish** notation)*

Figure C4.1: *Examples of algebraic notation*

Prefix and postfix notations are easier for a computer to execute. Modern
computers are sufficiently powerful that most users do not need to use either
prefix or postfix notation.

Reverse polish notation is a form of postfix notation where brackets are
not permitted (and not needed). No rules about precedence are needed for
different operations, which are carried out in the order met in the expression.

Reverse polish notation has the advantage that any algebraic expression can
be processed strictly from left to right. It is widely used by compilers which
convert the infix notation that a programmer has used into reverse polish
notation. This reverse polish notation is then easily converted into a machine-
code program. It was devised by the Polish mathematician Jan Lukasiewicz.

Program algorithm

is a sequence of steps designed to perform a particular task. An algorithm
may be constructed to describe the operation of a complete system or to
describe a particular part of it. Standard algorithms have been developed to
do specific common tasks, such as a particular method of sorting a set of
data. Many have been published and are available for general use.

Algorithms include precise details about the operations to be performed and in what order. An algorithm is a sequence of instructions including information such as when sections are repeated or choices made. See also *algorithm*, page 42.

Algorithms can be written in any suitable form, such as a programming language, *pseudo-code* (see page 227) or as diagrams. Often they are written in pseudo-code, which is easily communicated and easily translated into any suitable programming language, see Figure C4.2.

AN ALGORITHM IN PSEUDO-CODE

To count the number of words in a line of text:

```
begin  count words
    set  words = 1
    set  character = space                              for a space at the start
    while  not end of line
    begin
        make  previous character = character            for unnecessary spaces
        get next character from line
        if  character = space
            and  previous character not space           two spaces together
        then  add 1 to words
    end
    if  character = space  then  subtract 1 from words   space at end of line
end  count words
```

Algorithms become complicated when covering all possibilities.

Figure C4.2: An example of an algorithm in pseudo-code

Code

including: program code

refers to the actual set of instructions which form a program. This is either the source text of a program, which is later compiled, or the actual instruction codes of a machine-code program.

The term *program* (see page 219) is often applied to a complete software system (including items such as spellchecker dictionaries) but **program code** applies specifically to the instructions which make up a particular part of the overall system. See also *relocatable code*, page 199, and *absolute code*, page 199.

Coding sheet

is a special form on which program instructions may be written. It has columns to ensure that instructions are presented in the correct format. These are now very rarely used since most programmers now type their programs directly into the computer using a *text editor* (see page 280).

Assignment

is an instruction that gives (assigns) a value, which could be the result of a calculation, to a specified variable. The value is placed in the memory location corresponding to the given variable.

AN ASSIGNMENT STATEMENT

Working out an area in a program:

area:=height*width;

assigns the answer of 'height' times 'width' *to the variable* 'area'

Figure C4.3: *Example of an assignment statement*

Event

is an external change which is notified to the program by the operating system. This may be a key being pressed or a mouse button being clicked.

The term event has a specific connotation related to multi-tasking operating systems used by microcomputers. Events are occurrences which may apply to any of the programs running and are put into context by the operating system communicating with the programs. Events should not be confused with normal input which is directed to a particular program nor with *interrupts* (see page 300) which are usually dealt with by the operating system. One effect of an interrupt may however be to generate an event.

Events are an important element in the design of multi-tasking programs where the operating system handles the input (from the keyboard) and output (to the screen). When a new input is received, a message is sent to the program informing it of the event and allowing it to take appropriate action.

Flag

including: set, unset, status word, status byte

is an indicator that has two states, often called **set** or **unset**. It enables the program to record whether a particular event has occurred, for example whether (or not) a list of numbers has been sorted, whether an interrupt has been sensed (or not sensed).

In a high-level language a variable may be used as a flag. If a *Boolean* or *logical data type* (see *data type*, page 265) is used, the two states, true and false, are equivalent to the flag states set and unset. To begin with the flag may be unset (false) and when a particular case is detected it is set (true); when the action has been completed it is unset again (back to false).

Only one bit is needed to store a flag, so a machine code programmer may use the bits in a single word to store several flags, which can be easily manipulated in machine code using a *mask* (see page 196 and *masking*, page 304). Most central processors have a **status word** or **status byte** which is the group of flags used in the control of the arithmetic/logic unit. When individual bits are used as flags, the two states are referred to as 0 or 1.

Carry flag

including: overflow flag

is a flag within the *status word* (see *flag*, above) of the central processor that is set to 1 (or true) when a carry condition occurs, otherwise it is set to 0 (or false). These may be tested by the programmer if some special action may be appropriate, such as producing an error at that point.

Similarly the **overflow flag** is set to 1 (or true) when overflow occurs during an arithmetic operation, because the result of a calculation is too big for the computer to store.

Initialise

including: initial value

is to set counters or variables to zero, or some other starting value, usually at the beginning of a program or subprogram. These values are known as **initial values**. A common programming error is to fail to initialise a variable. In this case the program will execute correctly but will produce wrong results.

Default option

is the action to be taken automatically by the computer if no specific instruction is given. For example, in some versions of BASIC arrays do not need to be declared, in which case they are given bounds 1 to 10. This is the default option.

Logical operation

including: AND, OR, NOT, XOR, mask, shift

is the use of *logic* (see *logical operator*, page 224) within a program.
Logical operations are frequently used to determine the future progress of a
program within selection statements, such as IF statements, REPEAT and
WHILE loops.

Logical operations include *AND*, *OR*, *XOR* and *NOT* which, when used
with Boolean values, produce the results described in *logic gates* (see page
331). For example when using a simple database of information about birds,
a search might be written:

> IF "webbed feet" AND "white feathers" THEN show picture ELSE next
> item

> Both the expressions "webbed feet" and "white feathers" can be
> either true or false; what happens next depends on the truth value
> derived from 'ANDing' them.

Logical operations can also be performed on *bytes* or *words* (see page 269)
when a group of *bits* (see page 272) is processed together. Logical
operations simply compare each bit and the result is assigned to the
equivalent bit of the result. An example of their use is the manipulation of a
status word (see *flag*, above) by the operating system.

THE MANIPULATION OF A BIT PATTERN

The byte holds colour information:

> *The intensity of red is held in the colour byte below in the third and
> fourth bits from the right:*

0 0 0 1 **1 0** 1 1	*The bold digits **1 0** are the red intensity*
0 0 0 0 1 1 0 0	*A **mask** to select the bits we require*
0 0 0 0 1 0 0 0	*The result of an **AND** operation on the mask and the colour byte: unwanted bits are set to 0*
0 0 0 0 0 0 1 0	*The result of a **right shift** of two places*
equals 2 (denary)	*The intensity of the colour red is 2.*

Figure C4.4: *A logical operation on a bit pattern*

These operations can be performed using a *mask*, which is a user defined binary pattern, to select which bits are to be changed while the other bits remain unchanged. See Figure C4.4.

The bits in a byte, word or register can also be shifted. A *shift* moves the whole bit pattern one or more places to the left or right. Bits that move out are lost and empty spaces are filled with a '0'. See also *shift*, page 302.

Heuristic program

is one that attempts to improve its own performance as a result of learning from previous actions within the program. See also *heuristics*, page 68.

Machine-code instruction

including: instruction set, operation code, address field, operand (field).
is a binary code which can be directly executed by the computer. Each type of computer has a set of binary codes which are recognised by its processor as instructions, the *instruction set*.

Each type of processor has a different instruction set. These are the only instructions that can be used to control the computer. Other instructions (such as those written in BASIC or Pascal) must be converted into appropriate machine-code instructions before they can be executed by the computer.

Each instruction is a binary pattern which can be decoded by the control unit. It consists of several fields, including the *operation code* field and usually an *address field* (see *single address instruction*, below).

The operation code field is the part of the binary code for the instruction to be carried out (for example 'add' or 'jump').

An address field gives the *address* (see above) where the data to be used in the operation can be found. It is sometimes called the *operand field*, or simply the *operand*. See also *address calculation*, page 294.

Look-up table

is a table used to convert one set of values to another set.

The table normally has two columns. The first column holds a list of data items and the second column holds a list of related values. For example, the first column might hold product codes and the second column their prices.

An example is a tax table (for VAT). Each product has a tax code, which is looked up in a look-up table to find the tax rate to be used. Look-up tables are particularly useful for non-linear values and tax rates are often non-linear.

Another example is a SINE table. Values of sine are calculated for a range of values and stored in the memory. Each time a sine is required it is found in the look-up table rather than being worked out again. This speeds up the program because calculating sines is very slow.

Single-address instruction

also known as: one-address instruction
including: two-address instruction, multiple-address instruction
is the most common format of a *machine-code instruction* (see above). It consists of two fields, the operation code field and the address field.

A ***multiple-address instruction*** has more than two fields. There is always an operation code field and at least two address fields (giving several pieces of data which can be used by a single operation). In particular a ***two-address instruction*** has three fields, the operation code field and exactly two address fields.

Other designs of processor may have different structures. For example, stack-based processors do not need address fields at all, just the operation code. Another example is microprocessors, which often use several bytes of storage, instead of one word, for each machine-code instruction. These are loaded separately but then treated as a single-address instruction.

For general-purpose computers, single-address instructions are more economical than other formats.

Mnemonic

including: symbolic addressing
is a code for an operation which is easily remembered. The meaning of the instruction is normally abbreviated into a related alphabetic code.

Mnemonics are particularly used in assembly languages where each binary *operation code* (see *machine code,* above) is replaced with a mnemonic, for example ADC could represent the binary instruction for ADD WITH CARRY. Mnemonics rather than binary numbers make writing programs faster and make errors easier to find. Assemblers are used to convert the instruction mnemonics into the binary machine-code instructions (see *assembler*, page 282).

The use of mnemonics or words to specify the address of a store location is called ***symbolic addressing***. This is used in assembly language programming where the address of a store location is specified by means of an *identifier* (see page 223), normally in the form of a word or mnemonic, rather than the numeric value of the memory address. See also *symbol table*, page 284.

Overlay

including: overlays

is the process by which only parts (the *overlays*) of a large program are brought from backing store for processing, as needed. Only those overlays currently requiring processing are held in main store. The major part of the program (which also manages the overlays) is always held in the main store.

The use of overlays is a technique which enables programmers to reduce the amount of memory needed by a program. Similar techniques are *segmentation* (see page 289) and *paging* (see page 296) which is used by operating systems to make efficient use of available memory.

Relocation

including: relocatable code, absolute code, position independent code

is the moving of a program from one area of memory to another by the operating system. This allows the operating system to make best use of memory, for example during compilation. Code which can be moved in this way is known as **relocatable code**, whereas **absolute code** must reside in a particular area of memory.

When a program is relocated, any memory addresses must be suitably altered, in particular any addresses in *jump* instructions (see page 210). This means that programs may need to be written in a special way to be relocatable. See also *relative address* in *address* page 191.

Ideally, when we relocate a program we would not want to alter it, which will take time. It is possible, using special techniques, to write a program that will operate correctly wherever it is loaded into memory. Such a program has **position independent code**.

Self-documented program

is where the program code describes the operations being carried out. This can be done by the use of comments, statements with meaningful variable names, formatting and clearly visible structures.

These features are in addition to the normal program documentation but are valuable because they help to avoid mistakes being made when a programmer modifies the program. Modifications should always be based on the full program design documentation, otherwise the other effects of introducing changes cannot be predicted.

The use of a fourth generation language helps this process, because these languages describe the underlying design of a system rather than the detail of its implementation. They rely on powerful compilers to convert the design into an executable system. See also *fourth generation language*, page 250.

Packing

is the compression of data in order to make the best use of storage space. If a computer has a large word length, much space can be wasted when occupied by small pieces of data. For example a character may only need 6 bits to store it, so a computer with a word length of 24 bits could pack 4 such characters into one word of storage which would otherwise only store 1 character. Packing is sometimes done automatically by the operating system.

Program characteristics

including: ease of use, robustness, flexibility, reliability, portability, port, ease of maintenance, (hardware) platform
are the general properties (which may be good or bad) of programs or systems, which determine how successful the program may be in general use. The good properties that programmers will attempt to produce are:

Ease of use means that users will be able to operate the program with limited training and support.

Robustness is the ability of a program or system to cope with errors and mishaps during program execution without producing wrong results or stopping. Events (such as a jammed printer) should not make the computer system fail. If failures do occur, errors can be introduced and customer dissatisfaction will be caused.

Flexibility is the ability of a program or system to be easily reconfigured by the user or adapted for use in a different situation. This may enable a program or system to be sold more widely or to be adapted to changing circumstances.

Reliability is how well a program or system operates without stopping due to design faults.

Portability is the ability of a program or system to be used on different computer hardware. Many large commercial systems remain in use for much longer than the original hardware and will be adapted or ***ported*** to new types of computer hardware, thus saving the expense of rewriting the system. Most software packages will only work on particular combinations of hardware and operating system, which are sometimes referred to as (***hardware***) ***platforms***.

Ease of maintenance allows modifications that have to be made during the life of a system to be carried out easily and cheaply. *Program maintenance* (see below) is a major expense in the use of a computer system. *Structured programming* (see page 170) enables software to be designed in a way that enables ease of maintenance.

Program maintenance

including: corrective, adaptive, perfective maintenance
is the modification of a program or system after its implementation has been completed. This may be needed to correct errors found in the system, *corrective maintenance*. Maintenance may be necessary to adapt the system to changes within the organisation using it, to external changes such as new legislation or to allow the system to operate with new hardware, *adaptive maintenance*. Additionally, it may be advantageous to make changes which will enhance the performance of the system, *perfective maintenance*.

Maintenance cannot normally be carried out by the user and specialist staff are employed, often the team that designed and wrote the original system.

Maintenance is much easier if the program is well designed, well structured and well documented (see *structured programming*, page 170). *Ease of maintenance* (see above) is a desirable characteristic of a computer system.

Terminator

also known as: rogue terminator, data terminator
including: rogue value
is a specified value, not normally expected in the data, that is used to mark the end of a list of data items. The program can process the data in order until it reaches the terminator. The number of data items can vary and the number of data items does not have to be known in advance.

The term *rogue value* often implies a *numeric value* (see *numeric data type,* page 273). It may also describe a special value, at some point in the data, used to indicate a particular situation, for example a deleted record.

Common values used as rogue terminators are 0, -1 and 9999. If the data is being entered from a keyboard then simply pressing the enter key can be the terminator (a blank input). When data is stored as a datafile a special terminator, called the *end of file marker* (see page 265), is used to show where the data finishes.

Pretty printer

including: printf, PRINT USING, format

is a subroutine which displays a line of text (on the screen or on paper) in a neat way. This may mean splitting the line between words, justifying it and displaying numeric variables to a defined number of decimal places.

Many operating systems provide pretty printers as machine-code subroutines for use by programmers and some programming languages have predefined functions or procedures (such as the function ***printf*** in C and ***PRINT USING*** in some versions of BASIC). See Figure C4.5.

DISPLAY AND PRINT FORMATTING

*Using the **writeln**, **PRINT USING** and **printf** functions*

If the variables a, b and c have the following values: a:=3.14159
                                                            b:=1.5
                                                            c:=1.5

*In **Pascal**:*

writeln('Answers   ',a:4:2,b:4:2,c:4:2);

will display: Answers   3.14   1.50   1.50

*In **BASIC**:*

PRINT USING "Answers   #.##   #.##   #.00",a,b,c

will display: Answers   3.14   1.5   1.50

*In **C**:*

printf("Answers   %0.2f   %0.2f   %0.2f",a,b,c)

will display: Answers   3.14   1.50   1.50

The examples display variables   **a** rounded to 2 decimal places, as   3.14
                          and   **c** padded to 2 decimal places, as 1.50
                          but   **b** has the trailing 0 discarded by the PRINT USING statement, a facility not available as standard in the equivalent C and Pascal statements.

Figure C4.5: *Examples of display and print format statements*

A pattern, known as a *format,* is used to determine features such as total width and the number of decimal places (Figure C4.6).

DISPLAY FORMATS

#.##	Numbers will be displayed rounded to 2 decimal places.	2.52
#.00	Numbers will be displayed to 2 decimal places with trailing zeros if needed.	2.50
00000	Numbers will be displayed as a 5 digit integer with leading zeros if needed.	00123
#.##e+00	Numbers will be displayed to 3 significant figures using scientific format.	2.56e+02
(£#,##0)	Numbers will be displayed as a currency with brackets for negatives.	(£3,250)
dd/mm/yy	Date in European form with obliques:	02/05/95
mm.dd.yy	Date in American form:	05.02.95
Mmmm d, yyyy	Date in American form with month in words:	May 2, 1995

(the formats used vary between software - these are from a typical spreadsheet)

Figure C4.6: *Examples of formatting numeric and date data*

C5 Programming (Flow of Execution)

Concepts and terms to do with programs in general are in C4 Programming Concepts, other related terms can be found in C6 Programming (Subprograms) , C7 Program Syntax and C8 Program documentation.

Computers derive much of their power from their ability to repeat groups of instructions within a computer program and to choose which instructions to execute. The effect is that the programmer can control the flow (or order) of execution depending on the data being processed.

The instructions which enable a programmer to do this are known as **control structures**. When using a high-level language, specific instructions are provided for control structures. However when using assembly languages the control structures have to be constructed from combinations of simpler instructions and in particular, jump instructions.

The main control structures are **loops** and **conditional statements**. However they are often referred to by the statements commonly used in programming languages such as **if..then, for loop, repeat..until loop, while loop** and **case statement**.

Control structure

is the general term for the different ways in which a group of instructions can be executed.

Control structures allow the group of instructions to be repeated a variable or fixed number of times, or to be selectively executed depending on the data currently being processed.

Loop

including: nested loop, iteration

is a group of instructions which is repeatedly executed. For example, to produce payslips for several workers, the instructions for one payslip are repeated many times with different data.

The instructions may be repeated a fixed number of times (as in a *for loop*, see below) or a variable number of times, with the instructions being repeated until some specified condition is satisfied (as in a *while..do* or *repeat..until loop*, see below).

A *nested loop* is a loop contained within another loop. The inside loop will be executed a number of times for each single execution of the outer loop.

Iteration is the process of repeating a sequence of steps. Iteration will involve a loop which is repeated (iterated) until the required answer is achieved. The first time the instructions in the loop are executed is the first iteration. For an example of how iteration is used in numerical processing, see *iteration (mathematical)*, page 44.

Count-controlled loop

including: for loop, do loop

is a type of *loop* (see above) which is executed a fixed number of times. This may be a constant (if the number of repetitions is known when the program is written) or may depend on the data being processed (but the number of repetitions is still fixed at the start of the loop).

With a high-level language this is often called a *for loop* (*for....next loop*) or *do loop*; names derived from the program statements used to implement it. Traditionally the variables i, j and k are used as the control variables which record the number of repetitions executed. See Figure C5.1.

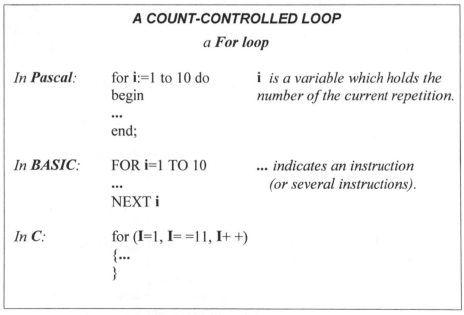

Figure C5.1: Syntax examples: for loop

Infinite loop
including: breaking, escaping
An infinite loop is a *loop* (see above) from which there is no exit and the instructions in the loop will continue to be repeated for ever. This may sometimes be useful, for example in a program controlling a set of traffic lights, which does continuously repeat the same instructions.

In most cases an infinite loop prevents any other use of the computer. Interrupting an infinite loop may mean having to switch the computer off to reset it, but in a multi-user computer system, the operator should be able to terminate the program without affecting other users. This is called **breaking** out of the program or **escaping** from the program. Control will return to the operating system and the user can issue further commands.

An infinite loop which cannot be interrupted results in a *hung* computer (see page 246).

Condition-controlled loop
including: repeat..until loop, while loop
is a type of *loop* (see above) which is executed continuously and only finishes when particular conditions are met. This enables loops to be written where the number of repetitions is unknown. The advantages of this approach include:

- the amount of data being processed need not be known in advance;
- mathematical algorithms can continue until an answer is found;
- more than one exit condition can be used, for example the loop could continue until the result is obtained or an error is found.

Two forms of condition-controlled loops are usually provided by high-level languages. These are often called **repeat..until loops** and **while loops**, names derived from the program statements used to implement them.

Both repeat..until loops and while loops act in a similar way. The repeat..until loop tests for its exit after executing the instructions; while loops test for exiting before any instructions are executed, thus allowing for situations where no action needs to be taken. See Figure C5.2.

CONDITION-CONTROLLED LOOP

*as a **Repeat loop***   *as a **While loop***

*In **Pascal**:*

```
i:=1;                              i:=1;
repeat                             while (i<10) and (flag=false) do
   ...                             begin
  i:=i+1;                             ...
 until (i=10) or (flag=true);        i:=i+1;
end;
```

*In **BASIC**:*

```
i=1                                i=1
REPEAT                             WHILE i<10 AND flag=FALSE
   ...                                ...
  i=i+1                             i=i+1
UNTIL i=10 OR flag=TRUE            ENDWHILE
```

*In **C**:*

```
i=1                                i=1
do                                 while i<10 && flag==0
{                                  {
...                                ...
i++                                i++
}                                  }
while i==10 || flag==1
```

... indicates an instruction (or several instructions).

Figure C5.2: *Syntax examples: repeat and while loops*

If statement

including: else

is the name for a statement allowing selection within a program. A group of statements may be executed or ignored, depending on the data being processed at the time. The name is derived from the program statement used to implement this control structure. See Figure C5.3.

It is possible for the program to choose between two alternative groups of statements by using an additional keyword *else*.

SELECTION

if..then..else statement

In Pascal:
```
if k=1 then
begin
   ...
end
else
begin
   ...
end;
```
k *is a variable that holds the data on which the current selection depends.*

In BASIC:
```
IF k=1 THEN
   ...
ELSE
   ...
ENDIF
```
... indicates an instruction (or several instructions).

In C:
```
if (k==1)
{...}
else
{...}
```

Figure C5.3: *Syntax examples: if statement*

Case statement

is the name for a statement allowing multiple selection within a program. One of several groups of statements may be executed depending on the data being processed at the time. The other groups of statements are not executed. This enables complex selections to be programmed easily and more reliably than using combinations of *if statements* (see above). The name is derived from the program statement used to implement this control structure. See Figure C5.4.

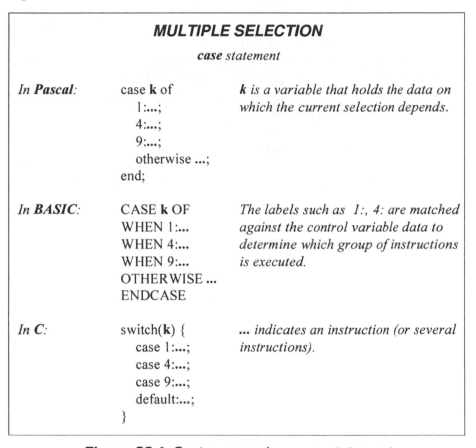

Figure C5.4: Syntax examples: case statement

Jump

also known as: branch

including: conditional jump, unconditional jump

allows the order of execution of the statements in a computer program to be changed. Normally instructions are executed in the sequence they are stored but this can be changed by a jump instruction which enables a program to choose which instruction to execute next.

Machine code program instructions are stored consecutively in memory and the control unit works through them sequentially using the *program counter* (see page 295). A jump alters the program counter and thus changes the next instruction to be executed.

Jumps are not normally used with high-level programming languages because they make the program harder to write without causing *logical errors* (see page 240). However, compilers change instructions such as for loops, while.., and repeat..until into suitable combinations of jump instructions.

A jump may be either *conditional* or *unconditional*. An unconditional jump is always executed. A conditional jump is only executed if required by the result of a test, for example 'is a certain variable zero?' or 'has the loop been executed ten times?'.

C6   Programming (Subprograms)

Concepts and terms to do with programs in general are in C4 Programming Concepts, other related terms can be found in C5 Programming (Flow of Execution), C7 Program Syntax, C8 Program Documentation, and C9 Developing, Testing and Running Programs.

One of the most powerful techniques available to a programmer is the use of subprograms. Subprograms enable a program to be split into a number of smaller and more manageable sections. Because they can be called in any order, any number of times, the use of subprograms is very flexible.

The design technique of splitting a program into subprograms, each designed and programmed separately, has certain advantages:

- Each subprogram is more easily understood, so reducing errors;
- Each subprogram may be small enough to be assigned to one programmer, rather than a programming team;
- The subprograms can be tested separately and more thoroughly than a single large program;
- The subprogram can (and should) be written so that it cannot cause errors in other parts of the system.

Another benefit of subprograms is to avoid having to write the same routines many times. The same piece of program code can be used by different parts of the program, which means it only has to be written and tested once. Routines that perform general tasks, such as controlling the screen display, can be re-used in different programs thus saving programming time, testing effort and expense.

When using high-level languages, subprograms are usually implemented by defining **functions** and **procedures**. In machine-code or assembly language programming, subprograms are often called **subroutines**.

The supplier of the operating system will provide subroutines which allow access to the basic operation of the computer - such as displaying a character on the screen or reading data from a file. Operating systems often provide more sophisticated facilities, such as complex screen drawing routines, loading and saving complete files to backing store and spooling printout. These are all accessed as machine-code subroutines, which enables them to be shared between programs. They are effectively a library of subroutines always available to the user through the operating system.

Subprograms generally require data. With functions and procedures, the data is normally passed using **parameters**. Ideally these parameters and any other variables will be **local** to the subprogram, so that the operation of the subprogram cannot affect variables in any other part of the program. If the results from a subprogram are required by the program, then the variables will be passed **by reference**. It is possible for a subprogram to act on **global variables** but this is generally an unwise process, since it could produce adverse effects in other parts of a large program.

Function

is similar to a *procedure* (see below) but returns a single value. The name of the function is used as a variable having that value. Every time the name is used in the program, the function will be executed and the result will appear like any other variable.

A FUNCTION

In Pascal:

The function **square** *is defined like this*:

```
function square(number:integer):integer;
begin                                  number is the parameter
    square:=number*number;
end;
```

then it could be used as follows:

```
answer:=square(5);
```

or   if **square**(x)=25 then ...

Figure C6.1: Example of a function

Procedure

is a *subprogram* (see below) which is generally written using a precise formal definition. The procedure is defined and given an identifier (or name). This identifier can be used subsequently just like any other program instruction.

A procedure receives data from the program, manipulates it in some way and makes the results available to the program.

Such procedures are usually associated with high-level languages, although sophisticated assembly languages also allow procedure definitions.

Machine-code subroutine

is a subprogram stored in machine code. It may be called from another machine-code program, from an assembly language program or from a high-level language program. The operating system often provides machine-code subroutines for common tasks, such as screen updating and printing, which can be called from any user program in any language.

Usually, when a subroutine is called, the current machine status is stored on the system *stack* (see page 262) and when the subroutine is finished, the previous machine status is restored and the computer can continue running the program from where it left off.

When writing a machine-code subroutine, the programmer is directly manipulating the memory and there is no concept of local variables. If appropriate, the programmer could reserve a section of memory for use by the subroutine.

Common machine-code subroutines are often stored as a *subroutine library* (see below). These machine-code subroutines are often designed as *modules* (see page 165) and are frequently described as machine-code modules.

Macro

including: macro instruction, programmed by example
is a sequence of instructions which are defined as a single element. When a macro is *called* (see *call*, below) the sequence of instructions is used. A commonly used routine can be defined as a macro with an identifier and the user can then simply call the macro, using the identifier, to save time and reduce errors.

Macros are used to provide a limited degree of programmability to applications software. They allow the user to customise the application and make it more efficient for their environment (see *human computer interface*, page 71). For example, when using a word processor, a macro could be used to format and print a document quickly in house style. A macro will usually consist of a sequence of commands used by the software, although some software may provide additional commands to make the macros more useful. Sometimes a macro will be *programmed by example*, storing the user's operations as they occur. See also *macro recording*, page 79.

In a low-level language a macro is also known as a *macro instruction.* Calling a macro (instruction) would insert the set of instructions into the program at that point, so that the program may include the same set of instructions several times. This is different from a subroutine, where the program jumps to the code to be used, although a macro is sometimes incorrectly called an *open subroutine* (see below).

Routine

is a part of a program to do a specific task. It may simply be a section of the main program or might be formalised as a procedure, function or subroutine.

Subprogram

including: subroutine, call, exit, return, subroutine library, open subroutine, closed subroutine

is a set of program instructions performing a specific task, but which is not a complete program. It must be incorporated into a program in order to be used. Different types of subprogram are known as *procedure, function, machine-code subroutine* and *routine* (see above).

The terms *subprogram* and *subroutine* are generally interchangeable, but sometimes each of these terms could mean something more precise, such as implying a machine-code routine.

A program that uses a subprogram must have an instruction to transfer control to the subprogram. This instruction is known as a ***call*** to a subprogram. When a subroutine, procedure or function is called the computer will start executing it.

When the subprogram has completed its task it must transfer control back to the calling program, which can only continue from its calling position. This is generally done by a ***return*** (or ***exit***) statement in the subprogram. A subprogram may have more than one return instruction.

Commonly used subprograms are stored in a ***subroutine library***. This contains a number of prewritten and pretested subprograms, available to a programmer, which perform common tasks such as display a window, sort a set of numbers or save a file.

Subprograms can be used as either *open subroutines* or *closed subroutines* depending on which is more efficient.

In a ***closed subroutine***, separate calls to the subroutine use the same piece of program code. A closed subroutine should make the program shorter, although the program could be slower because of the extra instructions required to call the subprogram and return from it.

In an ***open subroutine***, the instructions become part of the main program. The skeleton code of the subroutine is modified by the parameters passed to it and the resulting code is copied into the program where required. In some situations open subroutines may have advantages, for example avoiding the extra time taken to call closed subprograms.

Recursive subprogram

including: stopping condition

is one that includes, among the statements making up the subprogram, a call to the same subprogram. The subprogram will continue calling itself recursively, so it must have a means of finishing and continuing the calling program. This is done by a ***stopping condition*** which causes the subprogram to exit rather than call itself again.

Some mathematical techniques involve repeating a process an indefinite number of times using the results of the previous calculations. See *iteration (mathematical)*, page 44. One method of managing this is the use of recursion where the same subprogram is called repeatedly (with the revised data). When the result is found, the automatic way in which the computer handles the return from the subprogram ensures that execution will continue from the calling point. See Figure C6.2.

A RECURSIVE SUBPROGRAM

The factorial of N is calculated as:

$$1x2x3x4x....N \quad (up\ to\ the\ number\ N).$$

So	*factorial*(5) is	5x4x3x2x1
which is also		5x*factorial*(4)
and	*factorial*(4) is	4x*factorial*(3) and so on.

*In **pseudo-code** the function **factorial** can be defined:*

```
function factorial(N)
    if N<=1 then factorial:=1 ; return   we stop and go back when we get to 1
    factorial:=N*factorial(N-1)          recursive call
    return                               return to previous call of function
```

Figure C6.2: *A recursive subprogram*

Parameter

including argument, by reference, by value, parameter passing, formal parameter, actual parameter, parameter block
is information about a data item being supplied to a function or procedure when it is called.

With a high-level language the parameters are generally enclosed in brackets after the procedure or function name. The data can be a constant or the contents of a variable. See Figure C6.3.

When a function or procedure is defined, a formal parameter, which is a *local variable* (see page 221), is declared and this can be used in the program code for the function or procedure.

When the function or procedure is used, the calling program must pass parameters to it (***parameter passing***). The ***formal parameter*** links the data in the calling program (which will change) to its use in the function or procedure. The data item supplied, known as an ***actual parameter*** or ***argument***, is passed to the local variable. See Figure C6.4.

Actual parameters can be passed to functions and procedures either ***by value*** or ***by reference***. If a data item is passed by value, a (local) copy of the data is used, which is discarded when the subprogram exits. If the data is passed by reference, the location (in memory) of the data is used. This means that any changes are retained after the procedure or function has been completed. Effectively, a single variable has two identifiers, with the subprogram using a pseudonym for the data item involved.

PARAMETERS

In Pascal:

when the function **length(side)** is called,

the **parameter** is the variable **side**.

when the function **length('Fred')** is called,

the **parameter** has the value **'Fred'**

when the function **SIN(60)** is called,

the **parameter** has the value **60**

Figure C6.3: *Examples of parameters*

PARAMETER PASSING TO A FUNCTION

function definition:

function increment(number);	*local variable is* **number**
begin	
number:=number+1;	*adds 1 to* **number**
increment:=number;	*function returns the value assigned*
end;	*to* **increment**

main program:

begin	
fred:=2;	*variable* **fred** *starts at 2*
bill:=increment(fred);	**fred** *is the* **parameter** *- its* **argument** *is 2*
write(bill);	*variable* **bill** *is now 3*
end;	

Note that the value of **fred** *after execution of the function will be different depending on whether the* **parameter** **fred** *is passed* **by value** *or* **by reference**. *The variable* **fred** *will still be 2 if passed* **by value**, *but will be 3 if passed* **by reference** *(an example of the unplanned effects of using global variables).*

Figure C6.4: An example of parameter passing

Standard function

is a function provided by a compiler or an interpreter which is so common that it is worth providing as part of the language. For example, almost all languages provide standard functions to work out mathematical results such as log, sine and square root.

Re-entrant program

or: re-entrant subroutine, re-entrant subprogram
is one where the same physical copy of the program code can be used by several different tasks. The program must be written so that data about different tasks does not get mixed up. This is particularly important with systems software, where the computer can be executing the subroutine and an interrupt transfers control to a different program which may then use the same

subroutine. If this subroutine is not re-entrant then data may be corrupted and errors may occur.

One example is an interrupt handling routine, which may still be handling one type of interrupt when a different type of interrupt is received.

Another example is the use of a high-level language interpreter on a time-shared system, where a single copy of the interpreter is used by the different users with different data depending on whose time slot is currently being executed .

C7 Program Syntax

This section considers the various elements which make up a computer program rather than how they are used. Related material can be found in C4 Programming Concepts, C5 Programming (Flow of Execution), C6 Programming (Subprograms) and C10 Programming Languages.

A computer program, which must be written in a very precise way, is written in a programming language. Programming languages have a vocabulary of only a limited number of words with precise rules describing how they may be combined.

Unless a program is written in machine code (which is very rare) it needs to be translated into some form of machine code before it can be executed. A program can be **assembled**, **interpreted** or **compiled**, which are all forms of **translation**.

Program
including: program suite
is a complete set of program statements that can be executed by the computer to perform some task. The program statements may be written in assembly language or in a high-level language. In order to be executed, the program will need to be translated by a translator program into machine code.

If a program is not complete, it will not work successfully. A correctly written program can be thought of as a specification of the algorithm that the design process has produced. Large software systems are normally *suites* of several programs to do all the tasks required.

Syntax
is the precise way program statements must be written to be understood by the computer. It is the set of rules for combining the elements of a programming language (such as characters and reserved words) into forms that the compiler, interpreter or assembler can understand. The set of rules does not define meaning, nor the use of the final construction. But it does allow programmers to know if a statement they are making is a correctly structured statement.

Semantics

is the meaning of the individual elements which make up a computer language statement, such as the words, symbols and punctuation. The overall meaning of any statement, which is made by combining these individual elements, is uniquely determined by the semantics of the programming language.

Program statement

is any one of the instructions within a program. Program statement is usually taken to mean a statement in a source language instruction, which is human readable, rather than a binary code instruction. When a program statement is translated it often generates several machine-code instructions.

Block

including: block structured language

is a group of program statements which are treated as a single unit. Special *reserved words* (see below) or symbols are used to show which statements form a block. Blocks enable complex programs to be constructed from simple elements without any confusion about how statements will be executed. See Figure C7.1.

Programming languages which encourage the use of blocks are called **block structured languages**.

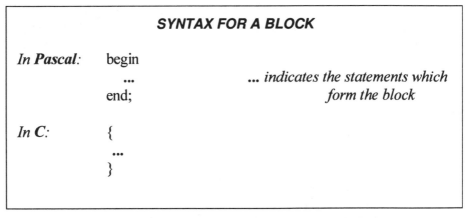

Figure C7.1: Examples of block structure

Declaration

is a statement in a program which gives the translator information it needs. It is not an operation carried out as the program is executed but is needed for the correct translation of the program. For example, in Pascal the declaration:

var area : integer;

informs the translator that whenever the program uses the variable 'area' it must be treated as an integer (a whole number) rather than as a real number, a string or other data type. Declarations provide information about such things as array sizes, variable types, constants, functions, procedures, library routines and memory allocations. See also *directive*, below, and Figure C11.3, page 260.

Variable

including: global variable, local variable, strongly typed languages, dynamic variables, static variables

is the identifier (or name) associated with a particular memory location used to store data. By using a name the programmer can store, retrieve and manipulate data without knowing what the data will be.

Global variables can be used anywhere in the program but local variables are defined only for use in one part of the program (normally a function or procedure). They come into existence when that part of the program is entered and the data they contain is lost when execution of that part of the program is completed. Using local variables reduces the unplanned effects of a variable being used in another part of the program and accidentally being changed. In a large system, global variables should only be used for data that needs to be shared between sections and should be clearly documented at the design stage.

The data that is identified by a variable can be a number (such as integer or real), a character, a string, a date, a set, a file, an array, a sound sample or any other kind of data. This is called the variable type or data type (see page 265). In a high-level language, the type may need to be declared when the variable is first used, so that adequate storage space is provided. In a machine-code program, the programmer has to manage the different types of data although they still need to be identified and defined in the design process.

The special features of the data types provided in many high-level languages enable a programmer to write better programs (see *program characteristics*, page 200). These features include:

Strongly typed languages which *validate* (see *validation*, page 187) the data and prevent the wrong kind of data being assigned to a variable,

Dynamic variables which store the data in the most efficient way, often by using a pointer to locate the data which is held in a different location. The programmer has limited control over how or where the data is stored.

Static variables are stored in a known format in a known location allowing the programmer to use unorthodox methods to manipulate the data. Static variables can also be used to preserve local data between the calls to a subprogram.

Scope

is the range of statements for which a *variable* (see above) is valid. This will normally be the subprogram in which it is declared and any other subprograms embedded within that subprogram. A variable cannot be used outside its scope as it appears not to exist.

This concept enables the same identifier to be used in different parts of the program for different purposes without conflict. This concept defines which variable will apply in any given situation during compilation. In a large software project several programmers may be used but this characteristic of variables means they will not have to co-ordinate their use of identifiers.

Dummy variable

is a variable (or identifier) that appears within a program but which is not actually used. This may be because the syntax of the programming language requires a variable but the data contained is not needed.

One use of a dummy variable, illustrated in Figure C7.2, is the use of an assignment statement to produce an outcome which is desirable and a dummy variable has to be present to accept the (unwanted) result of the assignment.

A DUMMY VARIABLE

*In **BBC BASIC**:*

```
110  PRINT "Press any key to continue"
120  dum = GET
130  CLS
```

*In line **120** the statement **GET** provides the code of the key being pressed and this is stored in the variable **dum**. This value is not needed and is ignored.*

Figure C7.2: *Example of the use of a dummy variable*

The identifiers used in the definition of a *procedure* or a *function* (see page 212) have sometimes been called dummy variables because they will be replaced by other identifiers when the program is executed. Better descriptions for these would be *parameters* (see page 216) or *local variables* (see above).

Identifier

is a name or label chosen by the programmer to represent an object within a program. The object could be a variable, a function, a procedure, a data type or any other element defined within a program. It is wise to make identifiers as meaningful as possible by using longer, more descriptive words (such as 'sales' rather than 'S'). See also *variable*, above.

Constant

is a data item with a fixed value. In a high-level language it is assigned to a variable which cannot be changed when the program is executed. For example if the following declaration is used:

const pi = 3.14159265;

then the programmer can use the variable name **pi** which will make writing the program easier.

Similarly the declaration:

const tax_rate = 17.5;

allows the programmer to use the variable name **tax_rate** which is also easy to change the value of at a later date if circumstances change. However the program would need recompiling. Only one *declaration* (see above) would need altering and not the many occurrences throughout the program.

Machine-code programs also use constants in the form either of a directive assigning a value to a particular mnemonic, or of a data item stored when the program is assembled, which makes it part of the program rather than its data.

It is generally more efficient to use constants, because the data is inserted directly into the program code, rather than variables, which the computer will have to retrieve from memory every time they are required.

Label

is an identifier (normally a name) which identifies a particular statement in a program. Labels are normally only needed to indicate the destination of a *jump* (see 210), which is the next instruction to be used after the jump instruction.

Reserved word

also known as: keyword

is any word in the vocabulary of a programming language which can only have the meaning which is defined in the language.

For example, many programming languages have an instruction FOR which is a reserved word and a variable or other identifier cannot be named FOR.

Directive

is a statement in a program that influences the translation process; examples include, controlling the use of memory, production of a program dump, producing debugging information or the use of declarations. While a declaration provides information for the program, a directive affects the environment of the translation process. See also *declaration*, above.

Operator

including: arithmetic operator, logical operator, relational operator, string operator, binary operator, unary operator, Boolean operator
is a symbol used to indicate that a particular operation is to be performed and provides a shorthand method of indicating in a computer program how data is to be manipulated. An obvious example is the '+' sign to mean 'add', but most programming languages now provide a wide variety of operators for different contexts.

OPERATORS

Two different uses of the '+' operator:

5 **+** 7 means 12

         in the context of the addition of numbers.

But   'Fred' **+** 'Smith' means 'FredSmith'

         in the context of the concatenation of strings.

Figure C7.3: Example of '+' operator

The important distinction between an operator and a program instruction is that an operator manipulates one or more pieces of data. Most operators are *binary operators*, which combine two pieces of data, although *unary operators*, which act on a single piece of data, are commonly used.
Arithmetic operators manipulate numbers by carrying out normal arithmetic tasks such as addition or subtraction.
String operators combine or manipulate strings by performing such tasks as concatenation (joining strings) or replication (replacing part or all a of string).
Relational operators compare data and produce an answer of *true* or *false* (see page 328). This answer can control the flow of a program using IF, WHILE or REPEAT UNTIL statements. Examples of relational operators include equals '=' and less than '<'.

UNARY AND BINARY OPERATORS

*In **Pascal***: *operators are in **bold***

unary operators: **not** end_of_file

— 5

binary operators: result **and** end_of_file

length **+** width

Figure C7.4: *Examples of unary and binary operators*

Boolean operators combine Boolean values using operators such as AND, OR, NOT to produce a Boolean result, *true* or *false*. This result can control the flow of a program using IF, WHILE or REPEAT UNTIL statements. See *logical operation*, page 196.

RELATIONAL OPERATORS

in these examples, the operators **=** *and* **>** *are shown:*

are two numbers equal ?

may be if number **=** 5 then ...

is a string alphabetically after another string?

may be repeat ...

until word **>** 'FRED'

Figure C7.5: *Examples of relational operators*

C8 Program Documentation

This section is concerned with the written comments and graphical illustrations accompanying a program. The symbols and layout conventions referred to are those given in British Standards BS4058:1973 and BS6224:1982. Related topics can be found in A16 User Documentation, C1 Systems Design and Life Cycle, C2 Systems Documentation and C9 Developing, Testing and Running Programs.

Program documentation is the documentation that is produced for those stages of the **software life cycle** which are concerned with module development and integration. Program documentation is particularly important at the maintenance stage of the system life cycle.

Software will need to be modified during its lifetime and the original programming team is unlikely to be fully available to assist with modifications, hence the team making the modifications will need to rely heavily on the original program and system documentation.

Each module will need to be documented individually at various levels of detail, depending upon its size and complexity. Some of this will be within the programs, using comment facilities to describe, for example, the data used and the processes carried out. This notion of a **self-documenting program** is an important element in program documentation. As well as the use of comment facilities, there are other functions, which can improve the readability of code; these include the use of indentation (for example, for the body of a loop) and the choice of meaningful names for identifiers.

The history of a module is important, for example, who wrote it, where and when it was written, when it was modified and by whom, details of modifications made, testing history including some test data and the results obtained. As with other information about a module, some of this can be included in the module listing, often as a standard header of comments.

Diagrams, such as a set of **program flowcharts** or **JSP (Jackson structured programming)** structure diagrams, help to show the flow of a module and can be particularly valuable for showing how modules are integrated into sub-systems and then into the fully integrated software as it is to be delivered.

Another tool which is also helpful at the module design stage is **pseudo-code**, which is a formalised English-like way of describing the steps involved in a program routine.

Program documentation

is the complete description of a program, intended for use in program maintenance. It should include a statement of the purpose of the program, any restrictions on the use of the program, the format for input data, flowcharts, program listing(s), *test data* (see page 244) with expected results, and any generally helpful notes to assist in future modifications. Some parts of program documentation may also be included in *user documentation* (see page 88).

Program flowchart diagram

also known as: program flowchart
including: flow line
is a graphical representation of the operations involved in a computer program. Symbols are used to represent particular operations and *flow lines* indicate the sequence of operations. Arrows on flow lines may be omitted if the flow is from top to bottom or from left to right.

A program flowchart forms part of the permanent record of a finished program; it is needed for maintenance purposes. Examples of *program flowcharts* are given in Figures C8.9, C8.10, C8.12 and C8.13, below. See also *design structure diagram*, below.

ECMA (European Computer Manufacturers Association) symbols

are standard symbols used in system and program flowcharts. Examples of the use of some ECMA symbols in *system flowcharts* are shown in Figures C2.9 and C2.10 (see pages 176 and 177). Their use in *program flowcharts* is shown in Figures C8.9 and C8.10, below. In addition there are British Standards for flowcharts.

Pseudo-code

is a method of describing a program or system design. It uses control structures and keywords similar to those found in programming languages, but without the strict rules of programming languages. It may be presented in a form which looks like a combination of English and a programming language. (See the example of pseudo-code, Figure C8.11, below.)

Decision table

is a table which specifies the actions to be taken when certain conditions arise.

The example, in Figure C8.1, illustrates possible decisions in the problem of how to go to work. N and Y indicate the values of the condition (Yes and No). X indicates that the action is possible. Blank entries indicate that the action is not possible or that no action decision is needed. For example, column three indicates that on a weekday, after 8.00am (which is also after 7.00am) the decision has to be to go by bus without having breakfast.

Condition	Value of condition		
Action	Value of action		

Weekday	N	Y	Y	Y
Before 7.00am		Y	N	N
After 7.00am		N	Y	Y
After 8.00am		N	N	Y
Breakfast		X	X	
Walk		X		
Go by bus			X	X

Figure C8.1: *A decision table*

Listing

also known as: program listing
is the printed sequence of program statements. This may also include lists of the data required for the program.

Design structure diagram

also known as: structure diagram
is a means of representing the design of a program or system. The British Standards Institution, in its document BS 6224, uses the term to refer to any flowchart and defines standards for drawing them. Examples of the use of BS6224 symbols are given in Figure C8.12, below.

Usually, a structure diagram consists of a number of levels, each of which describes the whole design, but at increasing levels of detail. Examples of Jackson Structure Programming (JSP) notation are given in Figures C2.12 and C2.13 (see pages 179 and 180).

Program flowchart symbol

is a formalised symbol used in a program flowchart diagram. Different shapes indicate the various kinds of activity described by the flowchart. Sometimes highly formalised shapes are used, each having a specific meaning; in other situations very simple boxes with words are used. Provided the meaning is clear, either method is an equally acceptable way of representing a process or system. Examples of program flowcharts showing how these symbols might be used are given below. See Figure C8.13, (where rectangles are used for all processes), and Figures C8.9, C8.10 and C8.12, (which use more formal shapes).

Connector symbol

also known as: continuation symbol
is used to indicate that the flowchart is continued elsewhere at an identically labelled connector point. To simplify layouts, connector symbols may be used to replace lengthy flow lines, or to indicate that the flowchart continues on another page.

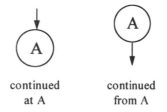

Figure C8.2: Connector or continuation symbol

Input/output symbol

also known as: input symbol, output symbol
is the program flowchart symbol used for any input or output operation. The description in the box may include the device or medium for the process.

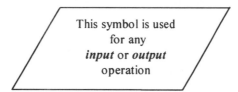

Figure C8.3: Input/output symbol

Decision box

also known as: decision symbol

is the flowchart symbol used to indicate points in a program where decisions are made. There are a number of different ways of representing decisions diagramatically. One set uses the diamond shape in a variety of ways. A decision box may have more than two exits. Four forms are shown in Figure C8.4. Other versions of decisions are shown in Figure C8.5

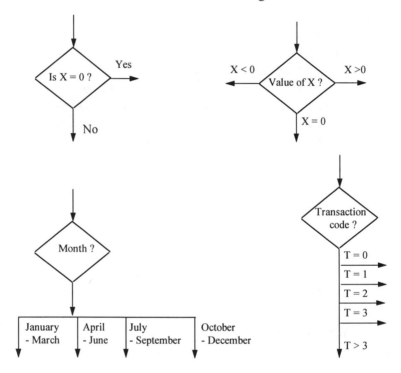

Figure C8.4: *Alternative forms of decision box*

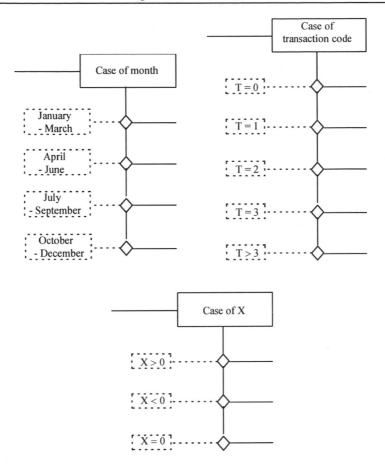

Figure C8.5: *Alternative forms of decision defined in BS6224*

Process box

also called: operation box, process symbol, operation symbol
is a box used as a flowchart symbol for any operation or sequence of
instructions that does not involve a decision. The box can be any suitable size

> This box can be used for
> any ***operation***
> or ***sequence of instructions***
> not involving a decision

Figure C8.6: *Process box or symbol*

Start/stop symbol

is the flowchart symbol used for both starting and stopping points in a flowchart. A flowchart will have only one start point but there may be more than one stop in a flowchart.

This symbol is used for
both *start* and *stop*

Figure C8.7: Start/stop box or symbol

Subroutine symbol

is the symbol used to indicate a call to a subroutine. The flowcharts for the subroutine will be elsewhere.

This is the symbol for

a **subroutine** call

Figure C8.8: Subroutine box or symbol

An example of a program module

This program module reads a series of records from a transaction file and uses the valid transactions to update a master file. Details of invalid transactions are output on a line printer, together with a summary of the numbers of valid and invalid transactions processed. Figures C8.9, C8.10, C8.12 and C8.13 give flowcharts for this module.

1) Program module flowchart (in traditional notation)

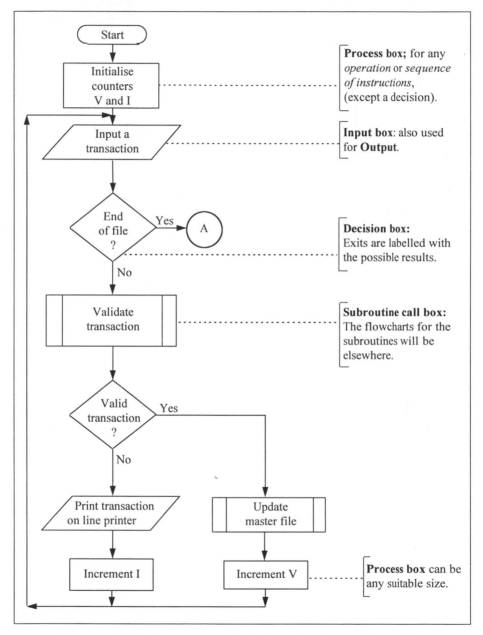

Figure C8.9: Program module flowchart in traditional form

The flowchart continues on the next page.

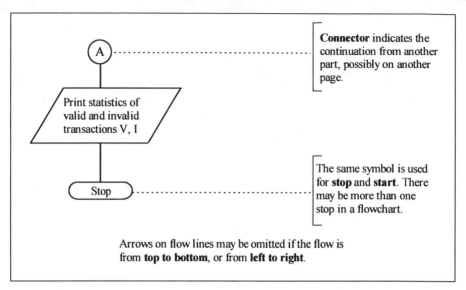

Figure C8.10: Program module flowchart (continuation)

2) Pseudo-code version of program module

In this method of presenting the program module, an English-like approach is combined with the use of a structured layout, which is closely akin to some computer languages.

```
BEGIN
Initialise counters
WHILE more transactions
      BEGIN
      Input transaction
      Validate transaction
      IF valid transaction
            THEN BEGIN
                  Update master file
                  Increment V
                  END
            ELSE BEGIN
                  Print transactions
                  Increment I
                  END
      END
Print statistics of valid and invalid transactions
END
```

Figure C8.11: *Program module in pseudo-code*

3) Program module flowchart (in BS 6224 notation)

The British Standard for flowcharts, or *design structure diagrams* as they are called in the British Standards Institution document BS6224, does not generally use arrows.

Since the flow is from *top to bottom*, and from *left to right* at each junction, when the end of an intermediate structure is reached, a 'fall back' to the original junction takes place.

At a decision junction a small diamond shape is drawn.

If the condition is **true**, flow is from **left to right**.

If the condition is **false**, flow is from **top to bottom**.

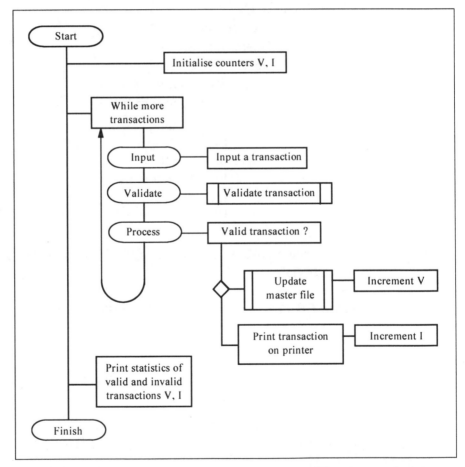

Figure C8.12: *Program flowchart (using BS6224 symbols)*

4) Program module flowchart (simplified notation)

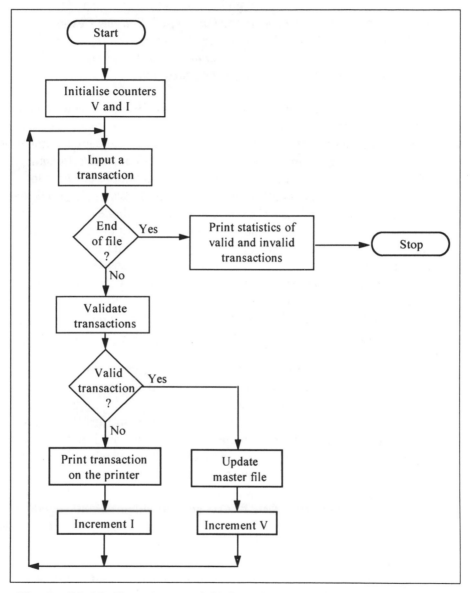

Figure C8.13: *Program module flowchart (using very simple boxes)*

C9 Developing, Testing and Running Programs

*Other related material can be found in C1 Systems Design
and Life Cycle, C4 Programming Concepts,
C5 Programming (Flow of Execution), C6 Programming
(Subprograms) and C7 Program Syntax*

With so many microcomputers in use in everyday life it is easy to think of computers only being used interactively, in which the computer is given an instruction and there is an immediate effect or result. There are a number of other ways of using a computer system which are often more efficient.

With larger computerised systems it may be much more efficient to collect the data and process it later as a batch (**batch processing**). The data required is collected and passed to the computer in a single collection (a batch) that the computer works through from beginning to end. For example, a payroll system often uses batch processing because salaries and wages are paid on a regular basis and involve large amounts of data. Batch processing avoids wasting computer time on manual data input during processing.

Some situations require an almost immediate response (**interactive processing**). For example, booking an airline ticket from one travel agent would need a fast response to ensure that other customers were not unduly delayed looking for the same flight at another agent.

Other situations may require the computer to respond without any effective delay (called **real-time processing**) such as controlling a chemical plant or an air traffic control system.

Since data is valuable, it is unwise to allow users unrestricted access either to the computer system or to the data on the system. If a user modifies an information system, then other users will be hindered when they try to use it and the modification may also introduce faults into the system. Unrestricted access to data gives opportunities for mistakes, conflict between users, fraud and the infringement of data protection legislation. A good reason for tight management control over a large project is to ensure that the work of various individuals does not conflict, which could possibly result in the introduction of errors.

Even with microcomputer based systems, such as a word processing package, a long process of development and testing is undertaken to ensure that the system works well for the customer.

These issues mainly affect the design of a complete computerised system. But of course much of the effort is directed at the program or programs which produce the results. In many cases the development of an information system is, in fact, the development of the computer programs, which make up the system.

The development process for a program involves a cycle of compiling and executing the program to test for errors, investigation of these errors (**debugging**), modification of the program, and repeating the testing cycle. The resulting system is then supplied in a way that should be easy to install and run.

The testing process is carried out with a **test plan**, designed to test the widest range of possible situations, which can be used repeatedly until no faults are found. The program will normally have to be **compiled** to produce an **object program** which can be **executed**.

A range of errors will be detected. Some, such as **syntax errors**, can be easily identified and corrected. Others, such as **logical errors**, will require much more investigation. These can be investigated using **debugging tools** such as **dry runs**, program **traces**, **breakpoints**, **dumps** and **variable checks**.

When the system has passed these tests it can be made available to customers who will run it on their computer system. The user has to be aware that problems may still occur in the **operation** of a computerised system, due to the specific hardware configuration or the interaction between several systems in use at the time.

Source program

including: object program, source language
is the program as written by the programmer using a programming language. It is normally written using a *text editor* (see page 280) and is an understandable document rather than consisting of binary codes. It must be assembled, compiled or interpreted before it can be executed.

When a source program is compiled or assembled a new program is generated called the *object program*. This is the program that is executed. The source program is kept in case any changes have to be made, in which case the modified source program would be recompiled. It is not generally possible to modify the object program if the source program is lost. It is the object code which is sold and this cannot be modified by the user.

The object program is normally in the machine code of the computer being used. There are some exceptions to this, where *intermediate code* (see page 252) is produced. When the program is executed, the intermediate code is easily translated into machine code.

The programming language in which the source program is written is known as the *source language.*

Execution

including : program execution

is the operation of a computer program. Unless the program is being interpreted (see *interpreter*, page 283), it must be in machine-code. If the machine-code is produced by compiling a high-level language program, it is the *object program* (see above) that is executed. If the machine-code is produced from an assembly language program it is the assembled program (see *assembler*, page 282) that is executed.

Error

including: bug, error message, listing file

is a fault or mistake in a program or information system causing it to produce wrong results or not to work. A *bug* is a fault in a program which causes errors. Most computers attempt to indicate the likely source of an error by producing *error messages*. Usually these messages are produced either on the user's screen if the error is attributed to the user, or on the operator's console for more serious errors.

When a program is being developed, many simple errors will be detected during the compilation process. A *listing file* can be generated during compilation; this will contain the source program with error messages and other diagnostic information.

The many types of error can be classified as follows:

Execution errors or *run-time errors* are detected during program execution. These errors, such as overflow and division by zero, can occur if a mistake is made in the processing algorithm or as a result of external effects not catered for by the program, such as lack of memory or unusual data.

Compilation errors are detected during compilation and are usually *syntax errors* (see below).

Linking errors occur when a compiled program is linked to library routines. For example, if a particular subroutine is not present in the library or the wrong number of parameters are provided.

Syntax errors occur either when program statements cannot be understood because they do not follow the rules laid down by the programming language, *statement syntax errors*, or when program structures are incorrectly nested, *program syntax errors* or *structure errors*. Examples of statement syntax errors include wrong punctuation and misspelling of reserved words and variables. Examples of program syntax errors include control structures incorrectly nested or incorrectly terminated.

Logical errors are mistakes in the design of a program, such as a branch to a wrong statement, or the use of a wrong mathematical formula. A logical error will be recognised because the program produces wrong results or an incorrect display. It is unlikely to generate an error message because the error is in the program design.

Debugging

including: diagnostic aid, debugging tool

is the detection, location and correction of faults (or bugs) causing errors in a program. The errors are detected by observing *error messages* (see above) or by finding unexpected results in the test output. The location of the faults may be obvious (identified by the error message) or may require extensive investigation. Tools are available to help in this process, particularly with assembly language programs, where comprehensive error reporting may not exist. These *diagnostic aids* and *debugging tools* include:

Diagnostic programs attempt to detect and locate faults in another program or a system by supervising its operation and providing additional information about possible errors.

Debuggers are programs which provide a range of facilities enabling the programmer to investigate the conditions when errors occur.

Cross-referencers are programs which identify where variables are used in a program. This allows errors such as unplanned use of duplicate names to be identified.

Traces are printouts which show the statements executed as the program is being run and may include the values of variables. The program flow can be compared with the *trace table* (see below) to identify where an error has occurred.

Variable checks list the contents of variables at specific points in the program. This allows their contents to be compared with the expected values, perhaps from a *dry run* (see below). *Breakpoints* (see below) provide a way of stopping the program to look at the contents of variables.

Step mode or (*single stepping*) is the execution of a program one statement at a time under user control. It allows the user to observe the effects of each statement after it has been executed.

Post mortem routines display or print out the values of variables at the point when a program failed. In some systems it is a list which indicates where the program failure occurred and gives the latest values of registers, stacks and other variables.

Breakpoint

is a position within the program where the program is halted as an aid to debugging. Whilst the program is halted, the programmer can investigate the values of variables, memory locations and registers. This provides additional information to help locate errors, particularly run-time errors.

This facility is often used with assembly language programs and may be incorporated into the operating system or provided by a *debugger* (see above). The machine-code addresses of breakpoints can be set, the progress of the program can be monitored and the program will halt when a breakpoint address is about to be executed. A debugger allows the contents of computer memory to be displayed. It may be possible to resume execution after stopping the program at a breakpoint.

A programmer may insert breakpoints in a program as part of a testing strategy. These will be deleted when the tests are successful.

Similar facilities have been developed for use with high-level languages, in particular interpreted languages, but these are less commonly available.

Dump
including: screen dump

is to copy the contents of a file, or the contents of part of immediate access store, to backing store or to an output device. The output is known as the dump, and may be used to test the integrity of a data file, or to assist in program error detection. A dump may also be made as part of a backup process.

A *screen dump* is a representation of the screen stored as a data file or produced as a print-out. A screen dump is an easy way of printing data collected together on the screen and produces a copy of the current screen display.

Patch

is a small fragment of code provided by a software supplier, to enable a user to modify or correct their copy of software without requiring a complete replacement.

Dry run

including: trace table

is working through a section of a program manually. This is useful for locating errors, particularly run-time errors. A dry run can be performed on a section of an assembler program or on a high-level language program. A dry run would usually be carried out on parts of a program rather than on a whole program.

Working from the listing of a section of a program, a ***trace table*** is constructed with a column to identify the instruction executed and columns for the contents of each variable.

TRACE TABLES

*Example of a **trace table** for a very simple program in an assembler language:*

Current Address	Instruction	Accumulator	&98FF	&9800	&9801	Display
&8001	INP &98FF		5			
&8002	INP &9800			15		
&8003	LDA &9800	15				
&8004						

*Example of a **trace table** for a very simple program in a high-level language:*

Line number	Height	Width	Area	Display	
1	5				
2		15			
3			75		
4				75	

*An alternative form of **trace table** for the simple program in a high-level language:*

(Showing the position after line 3 of the program)

Line 1,2,3	Height 5	Width 15	Area 75	Display

Many programmers simply use a box for each variable, making changes to the boxes as instructed by the program but without constructing a formal trace table.

Figure C9.1: *Examples of trace tables*

The programmer follows the instructions from the listing, adding a new line to the trace table each time an instruction is executed. The new line of the trace table should indicate the instruction, by either its machine address or line number, and show any changes to the variables. See Figure C9.1.

Test plan

including: test data

is the schedule for testing a program or a system. It is usually a table showing each item which needs to be tested. The test plan should cover every possible type of input including those which may be made by mistake, such as values that are too large, too small or just silly. The data used, when following a test plan, is called *test data.* Both the test plan and the test data need to be available as part of the documentation of the program or system. For a program the test data will show the inputs to the program and specify what the results should be, if the program works correctly.

Run

including: run-time

is putting a program or information system into action so that it can perform the data processing is was designed to do.

    Run-time is the time during which a program or information system is in operation. Often data has to be provided during run-time and some effects, such as *run-time errors* (see above), can only be detected when the system is operating.

Run-time system

is the complete set of software, including any *library programs* or *routines* (see page 280), that must be present in a computer before a particular program can be executed.

Process state

including: ready, running, blocked, suspended, stopped, completed, deadly embrace

is the status of a program submitted to a computer system for *running* (see *run,* above).

    The concept is particularly useful with multi-programming systems where several programs may be being processed at the same time. This includes multi-user computer systems which will be operating using some form of multi-programming.

    Programs submitted to a computer, either for batch or interactive processing, are added to a job queue and are then in one of a number of process states:

Ready: a program waiting to continue execution by the central processor. Several programs may be ready at any one time, waiting for execution.

Running: a program being executed by the central processor. A central processor can only execute one program at a time, so only one program will be running (except in a computer with several processors). Execution may be interrupted, in which case the program will be either suspended or blocked.

Blocked: a program waiting for a peripheral. The peripheral may be in use by another program or already committed to a task for this program. When the peripheral becomes available, the status returns to *Ready*, allowing the central processor to continue executing the program when it can.

Suspended: the operating system decides that a program has to be interrupted, perhaps because it is taking up too much time. The program status will be returned to *Ready* to await a further time allocation.

Stopped: a program has been *aborted* (see below).

Completed: a program has run to a proper conclusion. It will then be deleted from the job queue.

Deadly embrace is a condition in which no processing takes place at all and the system appears to be *hung* (see below); this could be the result of a number of situations, for example, process A is waiting for process B to complete, which it cannot do until process C is complete, which it cannot do until process A is complete..., the chain could, of course, be even longer.

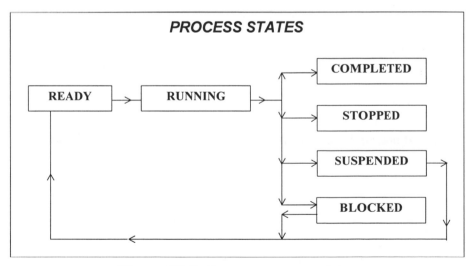

Figure C9.2: *Program process states*

Abort

is stopping the execution of a program or system before it has reached its normal conclusion. The run may be aborted by the program itself, the operating system or an operator.

A program may be aborted if an error is detected or if the operator requests it. An error such as a missing file will cause a program to be aborted. If the program appears to be working incorrectly, the operator may request that it is aborted. Sometimes the operating system may not be able to abort a run; in this case the computer will not respond and will have to be reset. (see also, *hung*, below).

Crash

including: hung, system crash

is when a computer unexpectedly stops working correctly. This could be caused by a hardware failure, an error causing the program to *abort* (see above) or an error causing the computer to be hung.

A *system crash* is a major failure of the computer leaving the computer inoperable and all users unable to continue.

A computer is *hung* if it does not produce any output, and appears to have ceased to operate. This is often caused by an *infinite loop* (see page 206). The operator will then attempt *recovery* (see below) and if that is not possible, the computer will need to be *reset* (see below).

If a crash occurs on a microcomputer, it is possible that any recent unsaved alterations to work or data will be lost.

Recovery

including: warm start, cold start, reset

is the process of returning the system to normal operation after an error. The procedures may differ, depending on the type of program in use and the type of error (whether due to hardware, software or data). Recovery will include identifying any data that has been corrupted and deciding on the restart process:

Warm start where execution is continued from the point at which the error occurred, using data that may already have been processed and stored in memory. Because the computer's memory is not initialised, there is a risk that corrupted data may cause further errors. A warm start enables a fast recovery of the system, if it is possible.

Cold start where the system is started again from the beginning. The computer's memory is initialised and the system should now work as expected. This can be a slow recovery, since the system may have to repeat processing already performed. See also *crash*, above.

Reset where a computerised system is returned to its initial state, as if it had just been switched on or started. This is often used after a program has caused a computer to crash or behave erratically, when the computer may continue to work, but corruption of the contents of critical areas of memory may lead to erratic behaviour and loss of data.

Down time

is the time when a computer system is not available (*down*) to the user. This may be because the computer is being maintained, it has broken down, there is a failure in the operating system or there is a communications failure.

Immediate mode

is the use of a command or program language statement outside a program. The instruction is executed and the results are produced before the next instruction can be entered.

Usually, immediate mode is only available with interpreted systems. Examples include, using a command line interpreter, DOS commands and checking the values of variables when using a language such as BASIC or LOGO.

C10   Programming Languages

Other related material can be found in C13 Systems Software.

A program within the computer is a sequence of instructions, held as electronic patterns in memory, consisting of **machine code**. The programmer starts with a design, or algorithm, of what the program is intended to do, but needs a means of expressing this idea in terms that can be understood by the computer. This expression is usually called the **program**, but needs to be translated into the electronic patterns. The written program is known as the **source code** and is translated (by a **translator** program) into the machine code (or **object code**).

Programming languages are obviously not the same as human languages - most obviously because (at present) they are only written and never spoken. But the term 'language' is a very appropriate one. Languages have a **grammar** (or **syntax**) which states the rules of the language. This makes it possible to recognise 'wrong', ungrammatical uses of language, and avoid spending time and effort trying to understand something which has no meaning. The syntax of a language is not simply a collection of 'correct' uses - it is a set of rules that allow programmers to know if a statement they are making is a correct statement, *even if the statement has never been used before*. Languages also have meanings (or **semantics**). One important difference between human and computer languages is that computer languages are never ambiguous - a statement always has just one meaning (even if it isn't the meaning that was intended).

Historically, the first languages were attempts to simplify the process of programming the electronic patterns directly, which was accomplished by entering these patterns as 1s and 0s - binary digits, or bits. If the pattern 101010 was the code for 'ADD', it was easier to allow the programmer to write ADD and let the computer substitute the appropriate code. Because they 'assembled' instructions that could have been coded directly as bits, these languages are known as **assembly languages** and were translated into instructions by **assembler** programs.

Assembly languages are very close to the actual machine code of a computer. A different assembly language is needed for each type of computer. Because of this close link, such languages are known as **machine-oriented** or **low-level**.

As programming became more sophisticated, **translators** were written which allowed programmers to write instructions that were closer to the way they thought about the problem. A mathematical computation could be expressed in mathematical symbols, and the translator would turn this into the (often quite lengthy) sequence of machine-code instructions to perform that computation. This also allowed the programmer to use a single language for different computers, provided that the language was translated by a translator appropriate for the computer in use.

Because such languages were at a different level from the details of how the machine worked, and because they expressed programming steps in a way more suited to the problem than the computer, such languages are known as **problem-oriented** or **high-level** languages.

Writing a program takes a long time, compared to carrying out the instructions in the program. This means that the translation process need not be very fast, provided that the machine code that is produced is efficient. There are several ways of organising the translation. Some translators take in a written program and produce working machine code; others translate into assembly language, and use an existing assembler for the last stage of translation. A third way is to produce an **intermediate code** which is a sort of language (written by the computer) that is easier to translate into machine code, because it is at a lower level.

Translators which produce another program at a lower level (machine-code, assembly language, intermediate code) which could, with more difficulty, have been written by a programmer, are called **compilers**. Compiled programs can be executed without needing the original translator any more. So, after compilation, a user's program need consist of no more than the translated version.

There is also another way of organising the translation. Some translators are designed to recognise that there are many tasks that will be repeated often in a single program (such as printing to the screen): such translators, called **interpreters**, keep a very efficient version of this frequently-used code ready in the translator, and arrange that it is **this** that is used whenever the task is needed. Interpreters have a speed advantage (the code for common tasks does not need to be generated, as it is already there), but a corresponding disadvantage is that all of the translator program needs to be present when the program is executed. So even a quite small program will need a lot of space in the computer when it is running.

Interpreters often translate and execute the program line-by-line, converting a program statement into a sequence of instructions branching to the appropriate routines in the translator software, and execute these routines without retaining the translated version. In a program with a loop, this means that the same statement will be translated each time it is encountered. For this and similar reasons, interpreted programs are usually slower in execution than compiled ones. Because they need the interpreter always present, they are also usually larger. Both disadvantages are outweighed by their ease of use.

Interpreters begin execution of a program immediately and they can work on an incomplete program, hence they are commonly used for interactive languages, like BASIC, where it is important for beginners to see their results as soon as possible after completing their program. Compilers are best used for languages designed for writing software that will be used many times without change - such as systems software and applications packages.

A translator is just a program itself. For efficiency, the version in use is usually a machine-code version, but it was originally written in a higher-level language, and was itself translated.

New languages are designed when existing ones no longer provide adequate facilities - specialist graphics and statistics languages have emerged, for instance. At present, their translators are often written in a particular high-level language called **C** which has its own specialised features to allow the easy design of such systems software.

A table giving comparative information about some significant computer languages appears as Table C10.2 (see pages 254 and 255).

Assembly language

is one very close to the computer's own machine code. Instead of writing actual machine-code instructions (which would typically need to be entered in binary or hexadecimal), the assembly language programmer is able to make use of symbolic variable names and labels. These are then assembled (by software known as an assembler) into the appropriate machine-code instructions. See also *machine code*, page 253 and *assembler*, page 282.

Authoring language

is one used in the preparation of teaching materials that are to be presented on a computer. The language allows the author to specify what material will be displayed (this might include the use of sound or video) and what questions are to be asked of the student. Answers to these questions will be listed, together with the action to be taken in response to each one, and the section of the teaching that follows; in this way, remedial lessons can be offered to students who score badly, while students giving correct answers can be directed along a faster route through the material. See also *computer aided learning*, page 64.

Backus-Naur form (BNF)
including: replacement rules

is a way of describing the syntax of a computer language. The name comes from its two inventors, although it is sometimes held to be 'Backus *normal form*'. A BNF description is expressed as a series of ***replacement rules*** that describe how some element of the language is built up from choices of simpler elements. See Figure C10.1 for an example.

BACKUS-NAUR FORM

Part of a possible definition of the LET assignment statement in the BASIC language:

<LET-statement> := [LET] <numeric-variable> = <numeric-expression>|
                    [LET] <string-variable> = <string-expression>

This says that the 'LET statement' *can take either of two forms, shown by the vertical bar, which represents alternatives.*

The first form is
> *the word LET (which is optional, because it is shown in square brackets), followed by a numeric variable, followed by the equals sign '=', followed by a numeric expression.*

Items shown in angle brackets '<' and '>' have definitions elsewhere in the full language specification.

For example, it is likely that elsewhere you would find the line:

<string-variable> := <numeric-variable>$

showing that a string variable obeys the same rules as a numeric variable, but is followed by a dollar sign '$'

Items shown in curly brackets '{' and '}' may occur any number of times, including none.

For example the definition of a numeric variable may be:

<numeric-variable> := <letter>{alphanumeric}

showing that the variable name must start with a letter, but that following characters, if any, may be either letters or numbers.

Figure C10.1: *Example of Backus-Naur form*

Fourth Generation Language (4GL)

Although the 'generations' of computers are not precisely defined, it was inevitable that software designers would advertise their software by attaching an appropriate up-to-date descriptive label. Fourth generation languages are thus those that were being invented around the time of fourth generation computers. This is slightly more than an advertising label, however: a characteristic of these languages was the recognition that computing power was becoming more freely and more cheaply available, and that popular software would be that which could reduce the time taken to *develop* users' programs. Thus RPG, the Report Program Generator, was a fourth generation language that attempted to make the production of printed reports easier -- not necessarily making it quicker to print out the report, but making it much faster to specify the format for the report.

High-level language

including: problem-oriented language

is one designed to help a programmer express a computer program in a way that reflects the problem that is being solved, rather than the precise details of how the computer will produce the solution. These languages are often described as **problem-oriented languages**. The programmer will certainly be allowed to use long descriptive names for the variables, and to structure the program into subroutines or functions to help keep the logic of the solution clearly visible. Mathematical notation will be permitted, allowing calculations to be specified in the same way as in written mathematics. When the language is translated, the *compiler* (see page 282) or *interpreter* (see page 283) will take care of the details of the many machine-code instructions necessary to cause the computer to execute the program. Compare this with the definition of *low-level language*, below.

A table giving some comparative information about some significant high-level languages appears as Table C10.2 (see pages 254 and 255).

Intermediate code

Computer programs are generally translated into instructions for the computer to follow in one of two distinct ways, compilation or interpretation. There is also a possible 'mixed' approach, in which the program is first compiled into an intermediate code made up of simpler instructions, which are then interpreted when the program is executed. One advantage of this approach, which has not been as fully exploited as might be hoped, is to reduce the number of translation programs that are necessary: to fully implement (say) 10 different computer languages on 15 machines would normally require 150 translator programs to be written — 15 for each language. Using an agreed intermediate code, 10 translators would be required to get from a language to the intermediate code, and a further 15 translators to get from the intermediate code to the machine code of the computers — a total of only 25 pieces of software. See also *compiler*, page 282 and *interpreter*, page 283.

Low-level language
including: machine-oriented language
Some programming languages are necessarily close to the design of the machine; the available instructions reflect the way the machine is built. *Assembly language* (see above) and *machine code* (see below) are good examples. Such languages are necessary for programming tasks connected with the running of the computer, such as driving displays and printers, or for writing translator programs. For this reason they are described as ***machine-oriented languages***. They are not generally good for problem-solving, for which *high-level languages* (see above) are necessary.

Machine code
is the set of all possible instructions available from the electronic design of a particular computer. These instructions usually reflect the hardware design of the computer, and operate on very basic items of data, such as bytes or even single bits. These instructions may be given memorable names in the associated documentation, but can only be understood by the computer when expressed in binary notation. Hence machine code is very difficult to write without mistakes. In practice, machine-code programming is achieved by the programmer writing in *assembly language* (see above), which is close to machine code.

Query language
including Structured Query Language (SQL), Query By Example (QBE)
Large databases must allow the user – who may not be a skilled programmer – to ask for information to be extracted: for example, "How many invoices more than 3 months old are recorded in the database that have not yet been paid?" Query languages are simplified programming languages, restricted to querying a database.

A few keywords are used to link the names of fields in the database, and to specify values for comparison:

SELECT invoices WHERE date-sent < 16-11-94 AND total-owing > 0

Popular query languages that you might come across include ***Structured Query Language (SQL)*** or ***Query By Example (QBE)***. See also *database*, page 24.

Language	Date	derivation of name	translated	data
Ada	1975-83	after Countess Lovelace	compiled	numeric
ALGOL	1958-68	*ALGO*rithmic *L*anguage	compiled	numeric
APL	1957-68	*A P*rogramming *L*anguage	interpreted	numeric/ characters
BASIC	1964	*B*eginners *A*ll-purpose *S*ymbolic *I*nstruction *C*ode	interpreted	numeric
C	1972	see notes	compiled	numeric/ text
COBOL	1959-60	*CO*mmon *B*usiness *O*riented *L*anguage	compiled	numeric/ strings
COMAL	1973	*COM*mon *A*lgorithmic *L*anguage	interpreted	numeric
FORTH	late 1960's	pun on 'Fourth'	compiled	graphics
FORTRAN	1954-57	*FOR*mula *TRAN*slation	compiled	numeric
Lisp	1959	*Lis*t *P*rocessing	interpreted	symbols
Logo	1966-68	Greek for 'thought'	interpreted	symbols/ graphics
Pascal	1968-71	after Blaise Pascal	compiled	numeric
PILOT	1968	*P*rogrammed *I*nquiry, *L*earnin *O*r *T*eaching	interpreted	characters/ graphics
PL/1	1963-64	*P*rogramming *L*anguage *1*	compiled	numeric/ strings
POP-2	late 1960's	author: Dr. R. J. Popplestone	interpreted	symbols
PROLOG	1972	*PRO*gramming in *LOG*ic	interpreted	symbols
RPG	1964	*R*eport *P*rogram *G*enerator	compiled	numeric/ strings
Simula	1965	from *simulation*	compiled	numeric/ symbolic
Smalltalk	1972-80	to emphasise nature of language interface	compiled	all types
SNOBOL	1962-68	*S*tri*N*g *O*riented Sym*B*olic *L*anguage	compiled	symbolic

NOTES :

The **date** is that of initial development; most languages have been continuously improved since invention.

translated indicates the most usual method, not necessarily the *only* one.

data is that type that the language was originally intended for – with the advent of the micro-computer, most languages have been enhanced to handle text and graphics.

Table C10.2: *Programming languages*

structure	ext	notes
imperative	no	mainly used for large military systems, sponsored by US Dept of Defense
imperative	no	originally for (paper) description of algorithms – an influential language with several distinct versions (Algol-60, Algol-68)
functional	yes	easier to write than to read; it uses symbols not always found on regular keyboards – requires large memory
imperative	no	easy to learn and (in modernised versions) the world's most frequently encountered programming language, especially on micro-computers
imperative	no	systems programming language, derived from 'B' which derived in turn from BCPL, which derived from CPL
imperative	no	easier to read than to write; large memory requirements, hence a mainframe language; highly structured data suited to business use
imperative	no	a Danish attempt to add structure to BASIC programming, but which ignored *data* structuring
unique	yes	very different from other languages: used in control and graphics applications – see separate description in this section
imperative	no	mainstream scientific programming language; language still reflects punched-card input – too early to be a structured programming language
functional	yes	artificial intelligence uses – an influential language, in that many other languages have been derived from it
functional	yes	based on Lisp, but noted for its 'turtle graphics' subset; popular in education, as it 'teaches' thinking as well as programming
imperative	no	mainstream general-purpose structured language of the 1970s and 1980s
imperative	no	an author language for production of computer-aided instruction materials
imperative	no	introduced new simple concepts but never gained popularity
functional	yes	artificial intelligence uses
logical	yes	artificial intelligence uses – a very different language
imperative	no	almost an applications package for business reports
object-oriented	yes	simulation
object-oriented	yes	forerunner of most graphics interfaces
functional	yes	string manipulation language

structure indicates whether the language is used by giving instructions on how to solve the problem (an algorithm, or conventional program) – *'imperative'*; whether it is based on functions or procedures applied to sets of data – *'functional'*; or whether its basic structure is that of an *object-oriented* programming language . **FORTH** and **PROLOG** are both rather different in this respect and are described in the glossary section.

ext indicates whether or not the language is *extensible* by adding new syntax words of the programmer's choice, that are then processed in the same way as the built-in words.

Data manipulation language (DML)

is a form of high level language, usually part of a *database management system* (see page 26) which is designed to allow the user to access (query), store (insert) and change (update) data in a *database* (see page 24).

Report generator

including: RPG (Report Program Generator)

is a piece of software that allows a business user, who is not necessarily a skilled computer programmer, to specify a printed report that draws on values from a database, or the results of calculations performed by the computer. Such software is closer to an applications package than most items considered 'languages', but is generally included in listings of available computer programming languages. The structure of the software allows the user to design the report using statements that are very similar in appearance to programming language statements. The table of computer languages, Table C10.2, includes *RPG*, the *Report Program Generator*, as the commonest example of such a report generator.

PROLOG

is an unusual high-level programming language. It does not fit traditional classifications, as used in the accompanying table (Table C10.2), because 'programming' involves adding a large number of 'facts' and 'rules' to the system, using mathematical logic notation, and asking the PROLOG system to deduce conclusions from these. The name comes from 'PROgramming with LOGic'.

FORTH

is an unusual low-level programming language, well suited to control applications. The language consists of a number of pre-defined 'words' at a level very close to machine code: the programmer then defines new words, which are added to the language, just as if they were part of the original definition. Because speed of execution is important, the language uses *reverse Polish notation* (see page 192), in which to add 1 to 2 you would write: 1 2 ADD

C11   *Data Representation*

Related material, particularly about numbers and their representation, can be found in C12 Numeric Data Representation.

The essence of any computer is its ability to store and manipulate data. The data is stored electronically and this section looks at the principles used to interpret the stored data as understandable information.

Within the computer all information is represented as some combinations of physical properties. What these properties mean depends on how we interpret them. Indeed a particular set of these properties could represent a number, a letter, a word, an instruction or a variety of other things. What a particular set of properties is taken to mean depends on the context it is in when interpreted by the computer's central processor.

In a digital computer these properties are made up of individual elements which can have one of two values (often voltages). It is convenient for us to think of this element as a binary digit (a **bit**) which can be written as either 0 or 1. Binary digits can then be grouped to form patterns which are used as **codes**. These codes provide a way of thinking about how the computer works internally but the technology actually used can vary from computer to computer.

The codes allow us to describe how data is stored and manipulated in a way which is common between computer systems. We can also consider the codes as binary numbers which allows us to use mathematical theory to manipulate the data.

Data representation is about the way in which binary digits are grouped to provide codes, how these are interpreted and how larger groupings are used for sets of data.

Data

is information coded and structured for subsequent processing, generally by a computer system. The resulting codes are meaningless until they are placed in the correct context. The subtle difference between data and information is that information is in context, data is not.

Data structure

is a group of related data items organised in the computer. A data structure allows a large number of pieces of data to be managed as a single set. Each type of data structure makes it easy for the programmer to find and process the data in particular ways, each type of structure having its own strengths and weaknesses. Examples of data structures are *lists*, *trees*, *tables*, *strings*, *arrays* and *files* (see below).

Array

including: list, table, subscript, subscripted variable, array bound, dimension, one-dimensional array, two-dimensional array
is a set of data items of the same type grouped together using a single identifier. Each of the data items is addressed by the variable name and a *subscript*, for example **NAME(4)** is the fourth element of the array **NAME**.

ONE-DIMENSIONAL ARRAY

A one-dimensional array consisting of people's names.

The array has four elements.

Name (1)
Fred
Name (2)
Ann
Name (3)
Jan
Name (4)
Bill

The **data** contained in each element of the array, such as '**Fred**', is in bold.

The **identifier** 'Name' and the **subscript** '1' etc. are in italic.

Figure C11.1: A one-dimensional array

A column of data like this is called a *list* or a *one-dimensional array*.

Arrays may have many *dimensions*, and have a *subscript* for each dimension. So **STOCK(3,5)** is an element in the *two-dimensional array* called **STOCK**. On paper two-dimensional arrays are the same as tables (with rows and columns) and are sometimes called *tables* in the computing context.

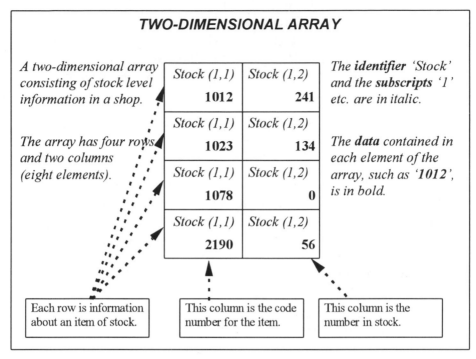

Figure C11.2: A two-dimensional array

Before an array can be used in a program, it must be *declared* (see *declaration,* page 220) and its size defined, so that the computer can allocate a part of memory for the array. xamples of array declarations are given in Figure C11.3. The limits of the array are known as the *array bounds* and it is usual to declare the array by stating its name and giving the maximum values of each dimension.

A *subscripted variable* refers to an individual element of an array, for example **AGE(20)** or **STOCK(3,5)**.

ARRAY DECLARATION

| Two-dimensional array of stock items | One-dimesional array of the results of throwing two dice |

In Pascal:

    var **stock** : array [1..10,1..5] of real;   var **dice_score** : array [2..12] of integer;

In BASIC:

    DIM **STOCK**(10,5)   DIM **DICESCORE**(12)

In C:

    float **stock** [10][5]   int **dice_score** [12]

| This example defines an array (of real numbers) which has two dimensions, with upper bounds of 10 'rows' (the first subscript) and 5 'columns (the second subscript). | This example defines an array (of integers) for a problem using subscripts 2 to 12. Pascal allows the lower bound to be set at 2. |

Figure C11.3: Declaring array dimensions

Tree

including: node, branch, binary tree, leaf node, terminal node, parent node, root node

is a non-linear data structure where the data items can be thought of as occurring at different levels. There are links between items at one level and their descendants at the next. Each data item has data which relates it to its unique parent node.

The data items are usually called *nodes* with the links known as *branches*. A node may have any number of descendants but itself may only be the descendant of one other node. This data structure is often encountered in a directory of files, where directory nodes are linked to sub-directories. It is usual in computing to draw a tree diagram 'upside down' with the root at the top, unlike a natural tree. See Figure C11.4.

Data can be added to the tree (by creating a new node) or removed from a tree (by deleting a node). The tree can be traversed using a variety of algorithms but only by following the links between nodes.

One particular form of tree is the **binary tree** where nodes have at most two branches down the tree. Binary trees are easier to implement on a computer than other forms of tree. Some of the advantages of a binary tree are:

- There is a way of representing all trees as binary trees;
- A fixed amount of space can be reserved for its branches;
- Efficient algorithms exist for adding items to the tree and searching it.

Some nodes in a tree have particular characteristics. Of particular importance are leaf nodes, parent nodes and root nodes.

Leaf nodes or *terminal nodes* are nodes in a tree without any branches further down the tree. In the conventional way of drawing trees (upside-down), the leaves occur at the bottom.

A *parent node* is the node immediately above a given node, at the next level up. There can only be one parent node for each node, but different nodes may share the same parent.

A *root node* is the entry node where we would start before moving around the tree. It is the only node in a tree without a parent node. In the conventional way of drawing trees (upside-down) the root occurs at the top. A tree has exactly one root node. If the data suggests that there should be two or more root nodes, the data structure has to be viewed as several trees.

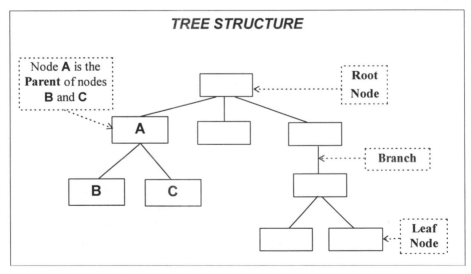

Figure C11.4: A typical tree structure

Stack

including: Last In First Out (LIFO), push, pull, pop
is a list where items are added or deleted from the same end. The operation
of a stack is ***Last In First Out (LIFO)***. The most recent item to arrive is
dealt with first.

Push is the term used for adding an item to the stack. ***Pull*** and *pop* are
terms used for taking an item from the stack. Taking an item from the stack
makes the next item in the stack available. Items in other positions in the
stack cannot be accessed.

Stacks are often represented by an array with a pointer to the top of the
stack where the elements are added and removed.

Linked List

is a list where each item contains the data together with a pointer to the next
item. There may be an additional pointer to the previous item. This means
the items can be accessed in order even if they are not stored in order; they
do not have to be stored in adjacent memory locations.

Queue

including: First In First Out (FIFO), circular queue, circular buffer
is a list where any new item is added to one end, and items are deleted from
the other. The operation of a queue is ***First In First Out (FIFO)***. Items are
dealt with in the order they arrived.

Queues are often represented using an array with pointers to the first and
last elements of the queue.

A *circular queue* is a queue in which the storage area is fixed and the first
item is held in a location which is logically next to the storage location for
the last item of the queue. Data items can be thought of as being arranged in
a circle; for this reason it is sometimes called a *circular buffer*.

Record

including: record format, logical record, physical record, blocking factor
is the basic unit of data stored in a datafile. It is a collection of items, which
may be of different data types, all relating to the individual or object the
record describes and is treated as a unit for processing. Most datafiles contain
records which have the same types of information but about different
individuals or objects.

The contents of a record are described by the *record format* which
specifies the record in terms of its *fields* (see below).

Where it is necessary to distinguish between the content of a record and the computer-stored record, the terms *logical record* and *physical record* are used. Logical record is used to refer to the information held in a record, but a physical record is a *block* (see page 220) of memory in backing store, which can hold one or more logical records.

The number of logical records in each physical record, which will depend on the size of the logical record and the structure of records and blocks on the backing store, is called the *blocking factor*.

Field

including: field name

is part of a *record* (see above) designed to hold a single data item of a specified type. Most datafiles contain records which have the same fields of information but about different individuals or objects. Each field is referred to by a *field name*, which identifies the data in the field and makes it possible to generalise about the data being processed.

FIELDS AND RECORDS

A **datafile** *holding details of club membership.*

Each **record** *would contain* **fields** *for the member's:*

  Name, Initials, Date Of Birth *and* **Telephone Number.**

The **field names:**

  Name, Initials, Date Of Birth *and* **Telephone Number**

  identify the data present, rather than being the actual data, which may be:

  Smith, F, 12/3/78, 458923.

Each **record** *would have the* **Name, Initials, Date Of Birth** *and* **Telephone Number** *of a different member.*

Figure C11.5: *Fields and records in a datafile*

Key

including: key field, primary key, sort key, key field order, composite key

is the field (the ***key field***) within a record used to identify the record, for example a bank account number identifies a customer's account. The key can be used for finding the record within a file or as the sort key for sorting a file into order.

Most datafiles will have a ***primary key***, which is unique and used to locate the *physical record* (see above). If the datafile can be accessed *sequentially* (see *sequential access*, page 183) the records will be accessed in ***key field order***, which is the order they will be in when sorted using the key field.

Datafiles may also have ***secondary keys***, which enable the file to be accessed in a different order, usually using *index files* (see page 186).

A ***composite key*** is made up of several fields and enables a file to be sorted or accessed in a more sophisticated order.

KEY FIELDS

In the example (Figure C11.5) of a datafile holding details of club membership containing **fields** *for:*

Name, Initials, Date Of Birth *and* **Membership Number**

The **Membership Number** *could be the* **primary key** *field because it is unique and identifies who the record is about.*

Name *could be a* **secondary key***.*

Date Of Birth *or* **Initials** *could not be* **key** *fields because without the other fields they are out of context (and the data is unidentifiable and meaningless).*

Date Of Birth *could be a* **sort key** *because the resulting list would be in order of age, which is useful.*

Name *and* **Initials** *(i.e.* **SmithF***) could be a* **composite key.**
If the file is sorted using this as a sort *key, all the* **Smiths** *would be together, in alphabetic order according to* **initial.**

Figure C11.6: *Key fields in a datafile*

EOF marker (End Of File marker)

is a marker written to a file by the operating system immediately after the last record to signal the end of that file to the controlling program. A programmer can use this to process a variable amount of data in a file, processing records until the end of file marker is found. This is similar to using a *rogue terminator* (see page 201).

Variable-length record

is a record where the number of bits (or characters) is not predetermined but is governed by the amount of data to be stored. This is useful where textual data is to be stored, which would leave a lot of wasted space in *fixed-length records* (see below). However fixed-length records are more easily processed.

Fixed-length record

or fixed-format record

is a record where the number of bits in a record is decided in advance at the design stage. This length is constant and cannot be changed later. The length of a fixed-length record is often thought of in terms of bytes or characters.

Data type

including: variable type, field type, alphanumeric data, Boolean (or logical) data, character data, string data, sample data, sound data, video data, video clip, date data, user-defined data type,

is a formal description of the kind of data being stored or manipulated within a program or system, for example, alphabetic data, numeric data or logical data.

Variable type in a high-level language describes the kind of data held by a *variable* (see page 221).

Field type describes the kind of data stored as a *field* (see above) within a datafile.

The specification of data types is important because:

- It provides a limited validation of data;
- Different operations can be performed on different data types;
- Memory can be efficiently allocated to store data.

Different programming languages provide different data, variable and field types. Many allow programmers to specify their own data types; these are called **user-defined data types** and are often combinations of existing data types.

Some systems provide a wide range of data or field types, such as *date*, *sample* (sound recordings) and *video* (moving pictures). These are particularly useful in database systems.

Data, variable and field types can be specified for any data item that has an identifiable structure. Some of the more important ones are detailed below:

Alphanumeric data is a general term used for textual data which may include letters, digits and, sometimes, punctuation. It includes both character data type and string data type.

Character data is a single character represented by the codes from the character set in use on the computer. See also *character*, below.

String data is textual data in the form of a list of characters, for example words and punctuation. String data is made up of character data and will usually vary in length.

Boolean data or **logical data** can only have one of two values, *true* or *false*. This makes it easy to use the values of Boolean variables to control the flow of a program. See also *C18 Truth Tables and Logic Gates*, page 328.

Sample data (digitally recorded **sound data**) and **video data** (a **video clip**) are large complex data structures containing all the information needed to enable a suitable subroutine to play a sound sample or display a video clip.

Date data is in a form recognised as representing a date, for example 1.2.34 or 1st February 1995. Date data must represent a valid date, for example 11/12/84 is allowed, but 31st February 1995 is not.

Numeric data can have a variety of types (see *numeric data type*, page 273).

File type

including: CSV file, TSV file, SID file, RTF file, ASCII file, text file
is the labelling of a file to identify the structure of its contents. This means that the user knows which software can be used with that data and that an applications program knows how to load and interpret the data. In some cases the operating system uses the file type to locate, load and run the application software as well. The file type may be implicit or explicit, where the three characters of the *file name extension* (see page 185) indicate the file type.

Most application programs have their own file types for data stored in their format. Other file types are used to transfer data between applications. Some common file types are detailed below:

CSV files (*Comma Separated Variable files*) are used to transfer tabular data between applications. Each field is separated by a comma and may be enclosed in quotation marks to avoid ambiguity.

TSV files (*Tab Separated Variable files*) are also used to transfer tabular data between applications. Each field is separated by a special character (the tab character) to avoid ambiguity.

SID files (*Standard Interchangeable Data files*) are also used to transfer tabular data between applications. The format also allows other data to be stored. SID files are not common outside the UK education market.

RTF files (*Revisable Text Format files* or *Rich Text Format files*) are a complex format used to store data from a word processor, including information about fonts, sizes, colour and styles. This standard format can be used to transfer data between most word processor packages without losing the formatting information.

ASCII files or *Text files* are used to transfer textual data between programs. The data consists only of individual characters in the standard ASCII code. No formatting information is included and, as a result, ASCII data is a file type acceptable to most programs. This is the most common means of transferring data between application packages. Most packages that allow data to be *imported* (see *import*, page 188) will accept a text file.

Character set

including: character, character code, control character, internal character code

is the set of symbols that may be represented by a computer at a particular time. These symbols are called *characters* and can be letters, digits, spaces, punctuation marks and include non-printing, control characters.

Individual characters are represented by a single code number (the *character code*) stored as a binary integer. Any textual data will be stored as a sequence of these codes. When the data is displayed or printed the code is converted into the appropriate shape.

The shape assigned to a particular code number can be changed and the resulting display will be different. In particular, this occurs when the screen display character set is different from the printer character set, in which case the printout will be different from the screen display.

Many character sets also have codes for *control characters*. These non-printing characters are used for special purposes. Examples of control characters are, end of record and end of file markers in a file, carriage return and line feed for a printer, begin and end transmission with a modem and cursor movement on a screen.

All the symbols available form a character set which could be specific to a particular computer or application. A microcomputer system will usually use *internal character codes*, which are the code numbers produced by pressing the keys on the keyboard. These internal character codes will usually be converted into standard codes for use by applications software.

Many computer systems now have the flexibility to use several character sets as required, for example to provide foreign language characters or for compatibility with earlier systems. In practice most computers use internationally agreed character sets such as:

EBCDIC (*Extended Binary Coded Decimal Interchange Code*) is an older character set used by large computer systems for internal communication and data storage.

ASCII (*American Standard Code for Information Interchange*) was devised for use with early telecommunication systems but proved to be ideal for computer systems and forms the basis for almost all other character sets.

ISO 8859 is the current international standard for computer character sets and has several variations for use in different cultures. The variations are more usually known by their names such as *Latin1 alphabet*, *Latin2 alphabet* and *Greek alphabet*.

Code page 437 and *code page 850* are character sets defined for use with IBM-compatible microcomputers.

ANSI (*American National Standards Institute*) *character set* provides various lines and shapes as additional characters. These simplify the production of screen displays involving lines and shapes.

Teletext character set enables screen displays involving simple graphics to be constructed. These are very compact and can be economically transmitted.

The ASCII code uses 7 bits giving 32 control codes and 96 displayable characters (an eighth bit could be used for error checking). Most modern character sets are extensions of the ASCII code, using 8 bits, which provides the possibility for more characters, but letters, digits and common punctuation characters retain the same code numbers. The most noticeable effect of character set variations is that some characters appear to change, for example a '£' may appear as a '$' or as a '#'.

Collating sequence

is the order in which a computer will sort character data. This could be the order in which a particular application sorts data, but it is often the sequence of characters in the order of their character codes. Obviously letters such as A to Z will be in the usual alphabetic order, but various computer systems may differ in whether 'A' comes before 'a' or whether '1' comes before 'A' depending on the codes used in the system. The use of a standard code such as ASCII avoids such differences between computer systems.

Byte

is a group of bits, typically 8, representing a single character. This is normally the smallest grouping used by a computer. A byte may also be used to represent a small number.

Word

including: word length

is a group of bits which can be addressed, transferred and manipulated as a single unit by the central processor. The size of a word, the *word length*, is determined by the width of the data pathways within the computer and is usually larger than a *byte* (see above) possibly consisting of 16, 24, 36 or even 64 bits. Large word sizes may mean that a computer can work faster than a computer with a smaller word size, but is less efficient when the data does not need to use the full word length.

C12   Numeric Data Representation

*This section defines terms associated with some of the
methods used to store numbers in ways which can be
efficiently processed. Other related material can be found in
C11 Data Representation.*

Much of the data stored in a computer are numbers of some kind. Numbers
create special problems for the computer scientist because they vary in type
and size in an unpredictable way.

A number, such as '123', could be treated as the three separate **characters**
'1' '2' '3', but if it is necessary to store its **value**, 'one hundred and twenty
three', then there are several of ways of doing this. Storing numbers as values
has the advantage that it is easier to perform arithmetic efficiently on numbers
that are stored as values rather than as characters.

A number could be very large or very small, positive or negative, a whole
number or a fraction. Whatever it is, it must be converted to a binary pattern
for storage and manipulation in a computer. For a given number of bits there is
a finite number of patterns available to represent number values and this
places limits on the numbers that can be stored. Figure C12.1 shows the
number of patterns available for different numbers of bits.

**THE NUMBER OF PATTERNS PROVIDED BY DIFFERENT NUMBERS
OF BITS:**

1 bit	example: 1	2 patterns (0 and 1)
2 bits	example: 11	4 patterns (00, 01, 10 and 11)
3 bits	example: 101	8 patterns (000, 001, ... 111)
4 bits	example: 1101	16 patterns (0000, 0001, ... 1111)
7 bits	example: 1101100	128 patterns
8 bits	example: 11011001	256 patterns
....	....	....
16 bits	....	65,536 patterns
....	....	....
32 bits	....	4,294,967,296 patterns
....	....	....

Figure C12.1: Numbers of bit patterns

The way numbers are stored involves a compromise between the **range** of values needed and the **accuracy** with which these values can be represented.

For a limited range of whole numbers each number can be represented exactly using one of the available code combinations. As the required range of numbers increases, eventually there will not be enough codes for each code to represent a single value. A longer word length (more binary digits) could be used to extend the range of values, but there will always be a limit at some value, and using a very long word length all the time would mean that the computer would be slower and could only run smaller programs.

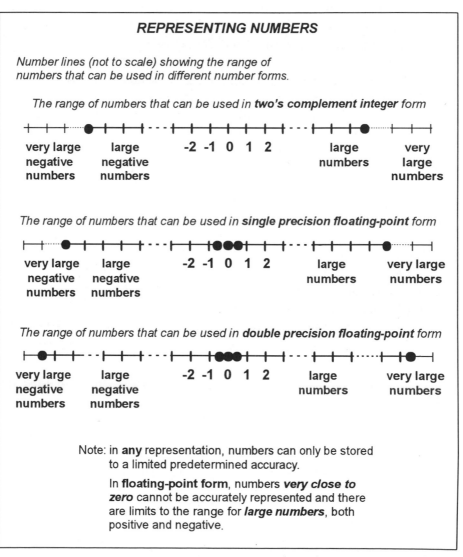

REPRESENTING NUMBERS

Number lines (not to scale) showing the range of numbers that can be used in different number forms.

*The range of numbers that can be used in **two's complement integer** form*

very large negative numbers | large negative numbers | -2 -1 0 1 2 | large numbers | very large numbers

*The range of numbers that can be used in **single precision floating-point** form*

very large negative numbers | large negative numbers | -2 -1 0 1 2 | large numbers | very large numbers

*The range of numbers that can be used in **double precision floating-point** form*

very large negative numbers | large negative numbers | -2 -1 0 1 2 | large numbers | very large numbers

Note: in **any** representation, numbers can only be stored to a limited predetermined accuracy.

In **floating-point form**, numbers **very close to zero** cannot be accurately represented and there are limits to the range for **large numbers**, both positive and negative.

Figure C12.2: Number ranges for different number forms

To store an even larger range of numbers with the same set of codes, two, or more, numbers close to each other will have to use the same code, which could introduce errors into the results of calculations. Similarly, if provision is made for negative numbers, the largest value that can be stored will be halved.

Even larger numbers require different methods of representation which may also introduce errors into the computer results because similar numbers will share the same codes. To represent very large numbers and fractions, **floating-point representation** is used. This enables a wide range of numbers to be represented to a known accuracy. Figure C12.2 illustrates the range of numbers that can be represented in different forms.

An additional constraint is that the computer has to perform arithmetic with the resultant codes; in particular it has to be able to add and subtract them. The methods used to represent values have to be related to the way the computer does arithmetic, in particular the way it deals with negative numbers.

A programmer normally has control of the types of representation used. A program can be optimised to work as fast as possible, to handle numbers with great accuracy or to handle a wide range of numbers. Some compromise is normally essential since these properties are often mutually exclusive.

Bit (BInary digiT)

including: least significant bit (LSB), most significant bit (MSB)
is a single digit from a binary number, it is either a 0 or a 1. It is the smallest unit of storage since all data is stored as binary codes.

The *least significant bit* (*LSB*) is the bit in a binary number with the least place value and the *most significant bit* (*MSB*) is the bit in a binary number with the greatest place value.

Binary notation

is the number system using base two and the digits 0 and 1. It is a convenient way of representing numbers in an electronic computer. Most computers do arithmetic using binary numbers and other representations need converting into binary form before the computer can do anything with them. For example: 123 (denary) is 1111011 (binary). See *denary notation*, below.

Denary notation

is the familiar number system using base ten and the digits 0 to 9. It is often incorrectly referred to as decimal notation.

Integer

is any whole number, whether positive or negative.

Real number

is any number represented with a fractional part. In most high-level languages, real indicates that *floating-point notation* (see below) is to be used when the number is stored or manipulated. This implies that the number may contain a fractional part and that it is processed to a limited number of significant figures.

Numeric data type

including: numeric variable type, numeric field type, integer type, int type, real type, float type, complex type, single precision, double precision
is a formal description of the kind of numeric data being stored or manipulated within a program or system, for example *integers* (see above), *real numbers* (see above), complex numbers.

    Numeric variable type or *numeric field type* specify the kind of numeric data held by a *variable* (see page 221) in a high-level language or as *fields* (see page 263) in a file.

    In many cases the same numerical value can be stored using any of the representations available; the one that is chosen by the programmer will be the most appropriate to the task being programmed. Some of the more important numeric data types are detailed below:

Integer type data are whole numbers, either positive or negative. Internally the computer it will usually store integer type data as binary integers in *two's complement* form (see below). It is sometimes called *int type*.

Real type data are numbers which include a fractional part. Internally the computer will usually store real type data using *floating-point representation* (see below). It is sometimes called *float type*.

Double precision type data provides a more accurate representation than the usual *single precision* type data, by using twice the number of bits to store and manipulate the data. Double precision is usually applied to real type data.

Complex type data are complex numbers. Some programming languages allow complex type data, which provides for the direct manipulation of complex numbers.

Negative numbers

including: sign and magnitude, sign and modulus, sign bit,
complementation, complement, one's complement, two's complement
are represented within the computer by binary patterns which enable the
computer to do arithmetic easily. Generally one bit, called the **sign bit**, is used
to indicate the sign of the number. Common methods of representing negative
numbers are described below:

Sign and magnitude (or **sign and modulus**) is a method of representing
numbers by allocating one bit of a binary word, usually the *most
significant bit* (see above), to represent the sign of a number whose
magnitude is held in the remaining bits of the word.

In the 16 bit number:

1000101010101000

The **1** at the left-hand end is the sign bit,
the remaining 15 bits are the magnitude (or modulus) of the number.
For the sign bit, **0** is usually positive and **1** negative.

Complementation is a method of representing positive and negative numbers.
This system requires numbers to be represented by a fixed number of
bits. There are two forms of complementation, one's complement and
two's complement, which are illustrated below. Two's complement is
preferred because subtraction can be performed by adding the two's
complement of the number to be subtracted.

43 (denary) is represented as an 8-bit binary number by **00101011**

One's complement is formed by changing each 1 bit to a 0 and changing each
0 bit to a 1.

the one's complement of **00101011**   (+ 43) is   **11010100**

and this complement, **11010100** could be used to represent − 43,

but more often the two's complement is used.

Two's complement is one greater than the corresponding one's complement.

the two's complement of **00101011**   (+ 43) is   **11010101**
                                                          (11010100 + 1)

and this complement, **11010101** is normally used to represent − 43.

Fixed-point notation

is the form of notation in which numbers are expressed by a set of digits with the decimal (or binary) point in its correct position. During operations in the computer the position of the decimal (or binary) point is generally maintained by instructions in the program. The size of fixed-point numbers is limited by the construction of the computer, but operations are generally very fast and preferred for most commercial data processing work.

Floating-point notation

including: exponent, mantissa

is a form of notation in which numbers are expressed as a fractional value, the *mantissa*, together with an integer *exponent* of the base. The use of floating-point notation increases the range of numbers which can be represented, although the number of significant figures remains constant for any given system. Generally, the advantage of the extra range available when working in floating-point notation is gained at the expense of processing time and precision. Floating-point numbers are often called real numbers in a computing context, although this meaning is different from the strict mathematical use of the term real number.

FIXED-POINT AND FLOATING-POINT NOTATION				
Fixed point				*Floating point*
	Sign	Mantissa	Exponent	Equivalent to
In Denary: 142.687	+	.142687	+3	0.142687×10^3
−0.0034128	−	.34128	−2	-0.34128×10^{-2}
In Binary: −101.011	−	.101011	+11	$-0.101011_2 \times 2^3$
+0.0010111	+	.10111	−11	$0.10111_2 \times 2^{-2}$

Figure C12.3: Fixed-point and floating-point notation

Normalise

is to change a number in floating-point form into an agreed floating-point notation format. Using a standard format for floating-point notation has some advantages, such as:

- avoiding the problem of having two different binary codes meaning the same thing;
- the form chosen is usually that which provides maximum precision;
- multiplication is performed more accurately.

Binary Coded Decimal (BCD)

is a coding system in which each decimal digit is represented by a group of 4 binary digits. This is sometimes useful because it maintains the relationship between the place values in decimal and the values stored in the computer. It is not efficient for the computer to store and manipulate numbers in this form but may have advantages in some applications.

Figure C12.4: Denary to BCD

Octal notation

is the number system using base 8 and the digits 0-7. It has similar advantages to *hexadecimal* (see below) in that it is related to the binary pattern (each octal digit represents 3 bits). Most people use hexadecimal in preference to octal.

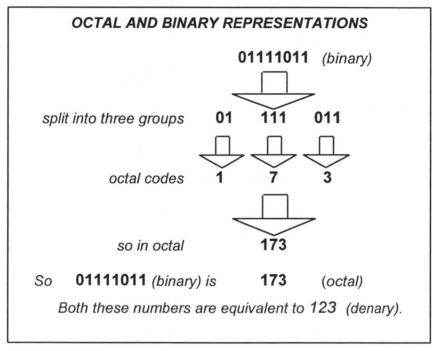

Figure C12.5: Binary to octal

Hexadecimal notation

also known as: HEX

is the number system using base 16 and the digits 0-9 and A B C D E F. It is often used in computing because long binary patterns can be written as short hexadecimal numbers without losing the relationship between the value and the individual bits in the pattern, with each group of 4 bits being represented by one hexadecimal digit.

Figure C12.6: Binary to hexadecimal

C13 Systems Software

Other related material can be found in C10 Programming Languages.

A computer system requires a layer of software which enables users to operate it without having to know about the underlying processes that are going on all the time inside. This includes the **operating system** and other forms of **systems software**.

A computer needs separate instructions for even the most elementary tasks. Computer users are interested in solving their problems without having to program every detail into the computer. The systems software is provided by the manufacturer and enables a user to give a few simple instructions which the systems software translates into the millions of minor operations needed for the computer to function in an easy-to-use way.

Every computer is provided with an operating system which controls the vital parts of the computer's operation - using the keyboard, screen display, loading and saving files and printing are some examples.

Additional programs (such as disk formatters) are provided which are useful in the operation of the computer. They do not enable the user to get answers to problems (**application programs** do that) but they do make using the computer easier, by allowing resources to be organised and controlled better. They improve efficiency by making the computer easier to use.

Systems software can be classified in a variety of ways depending on whether it:

- is necessary to run the computer (**operating system software**);
- provides other useful functions for operating the computer (**utility programs**);
- provides for frequently required tasks (**library programs**);
- enables software to be produced and maintained (**compilers** and **assemblers**).

Software which is essential to the performance of the computer is usually sold with the computer. Other systems software may be purchased separately to enable the computer to be used for particular types of task.

In brief, systems software is the collection of programs available for the total control of the performance of a computer system.

Systems program

is one of the programs that control the operation of a computer system, enabling the computer system to be developed and to be more efficient (examples of systems programs are compilers, monitor programs, disk formatters, network software and print spoolers). Many systems programs are part of the *operating system* (see below).

Systems programs can be contrasted with *applications programs* (see page 163), which perform some task. These tasks, such as producing a letter, are not part of the actual operation of the computer.

Utility program

is a *systems program* (see above) designed to perform a commonplace task, for example the transfer of data from one storage device to another, sorting a set of data, or a disk editor for directly editing the contents of a disk.

Software library

also known as: library, program library
is a collection of software held either permanently accessible on backing store or on removable media such as tape or disk. It will include complete software packages, package modules which will only be required occasionally, and machine-code routines for loading into user programs.

Library program

including: library routine
is one available to all users of a multi-user computer system, typically to carry out common tasks (such as file maintenance) required by everyone. Some tasks may be carried out by *library routines* which users can incorporate into their own programs. See also *software library*, above.

Text editor

also known as: editor
including: screen editor, line editor
is a program that enables the user to input, inspect and alter text files, which may be programs or data. Text editors are particularly used by computer programmers who need to produce text files suitable for compilation or assembly. Most text editors have special features which make the programmer's task easier.

In a *screen editor* the user interacts with a file by moving the cursor to the required position in the file, which is displayed on the screen, as in a word processor. In contrast, a *line editor* requires the user to specify a particular line of the file, for example a line number in a BASIC program.

Bootstrap

including: booting, boot file, CONFIG.SYS, AUTOEXEC.BAT

is a short sequence of machine-code instructions used for loading the program which starts up the computer. It is normally held in read-only memory and activated when the machine is switched on. This process is sometimes referred to as ***booting***. It loads or initialises the operating system ready for use.

The users of a microcomputer are often given the opportunity to start it up automatically as they want it. This is done by placing the required commands in a file (called a ***boot file***). This file can be executed automatically by the computer after it has booted the operating system.

MS-DOS and similar operating systems use two files as part of the start-up sequence. These files must be called ***CONFIG.SYS*** and ***AUTOEXEC.BAT***. These files do not have to be present, but if they are then they are automatically used. The file CONFIG.SYS is a datafile containing values and settings to be used by the operating system; it may include the file names of files to be used by the operating system. The file AUTOEXEC.BAT is a list of commands (see *batch file*, below) which the user wishes to execute when the computer is started up.

Command line interpreter

including: batch file, command file

is the portion of the operating system which analyses a system command typed by the user and performs the appropriate actions. Most operating systems work by asking the user for commands to be typed in, as a line of text after a *prompt* (see page 83), analysing them and taking action. Modern operating systems provide a *graphical user interface* (see page 71), which is often easier to use, but usually the command line interpreter is still available.

Some graphical user interfaces simply convert information from the mouse into an equivalent system command processed by the command line interpreter. Commands may be read from a text file (called a ***batch file*** or ***command file***), provided remotely from a peripheral or another computer through an interface or even provided from within a program. These commands are all automatically processed by the command line interpreter.

Translator

is a computer program used to convert a program from one language to another (for example from a low-level language to machine code). This is a general name for the three types of translation programs, *assemblers*, *compilers* and *interpreters* (see below). See also *C10 Programming languages*, page 248.

Assembler

including: assembly, assembler program, assembly language, macro assembler, cross-assembler

is a program that translates a program written in assembly language into machine code.

An *assembly language* is a special type of programming language where the instructions are closely related to the computer being programmed (rather than a common language which is similar on any type of computer). In general, each assembly language instruction is changed into one machine-code instruction but programming can be simplified by the use of *macro instructions* (see page 213).

The program is written in the assembly language of the computer being used and then translated (*assembly*) into the machine code of that computer by software called an assembler (or *assembler program*).

The assembler program is specific to a type of computer and is often provided as part of the systems software, since the assembly process automates the task of producing machine-code software required to operate the computer.

A *macro assembler* is a more complex type of assembler that offers the facility of expanding *macro instructions* (see page 213).

A *cross-assembler* is an assembler that runs on one computer, but that produces machine code for another. It enables software developers to produce programs for computers that are still being designed or to convert software between different types of computer.

Compiler

including: compilation, lexical analysis, syntax analysis, code generation, cross-compiler

is a program that translates a high-level language program into a computer's machine code or some other low-level language. Generally each high-level language instruction generates several machine-code instructions. It produces an independent program which is capable of being executed by itself. This process is known as *compilation*.

Compilation involves analysing the language structure of the source program, determining if it is valid, and producing suitable machine code. This involves a number of steps including:

Lexical analysis which is the stage in the compilation of a program which puts each statement into the form best suited to the syntax analyser. The standard components of each statement, such as PRINT, IF, etc., are replaced by their tokens (a unique fixed length code) and programmer-defined names are entered into a *symbol table* (see below). The lexical analyser also removes unnecessary characters such as spaces.

Syntax analysis which is the stage in the compilation where language statements are checked against the rules of the language, errors being reported if a statement is not valid.

Code generation produces a machine-code program which is equivalent to the source program.

A *cross-compiler* is a compiler that runs on one computer, but that produces code for another. It enables software producers to develop programs for computers that are still being designed or to convert software between different types of computer.

Interpreter

translates and executes a program one statement at a time. The program may be in a high-level language or an intermediate code.

The interpreter is actually a machine-code program. It is used as an easy, if slightly inefficient, way of executing programs not in the machine code of the computer. For example, when an interpreted program contains a loop, the speed of execution will be slow because the analysis of each statement has to be repeated for each time round the loop, however there are advantages in using interpreted languages. See also *programming languages*, page 248.

Loader

including: linking loader, linking, linker, link editor
is a program that copies an *object program* (see page 239) held on backing store into main store ready for execution.

Often common routines are provided already compiled in a *library* (see above), and when the program is loaded these routines also have to be loaded and links made to these routines. This is performed by a *linking loader*.

Alternatively, the library routines can be added when the program is compiled or as an additional *linking* operation between compilation and loading. A *linker*, or *link editor*, is the software tool which allows already compiled object code files or modules to be combined with the compiled program and then converted directly into an executable file. This also involves completing address links to the program.

Disassembler

is a program that translates from machine code back to an assembly language. They are generally used to decipher existing machine code by generating equivalent symbolic codes. This is useful for programmers maintaining and modifying machine-code programs.

Symbol table

also known as: name table

is the table created and maintained by a compiler or assembler relating programmer-defined names to machine addresses. It may also hold information about properties of data, such as data types.

When translating a program the compiler or assembler works through the program for the first time (the first pass) replacing some parts with tokens and building the symbol table which contains the actual address in memory of each variable, label or subroutine. The program is then processed a second time (the second pass) when each identifier can be replaced with its actual address in memory.

Parsing

is the breaking down of high-level programming language statements into their component parts during the translation process, for example identifying reserved words and variables.

Emulator

is a program that allows a computer to behave as if it were a different type of computer. An emulator enables:

- software to be developed which will run on computers not yet built;
- software to be used on a type of computer other than the type it was designed for;
- software to be tested when it would otherwise use expensive resources;
- a computer to be used as a peripheral, appearing to the host computer to have the characteristics expected. This enables microcomputers to act as terminals to larger computer systems.

Operating system

including: disk operating system, DOS

is a program or suite of programs that controls the entire operation of the computer. It is normally provided by the manufacturer and deals with the basic functions of the computer, such as detecting what has been typed in, displaying data on the screen and loading and saving to backing store. Most modern operating systems include *utility programs* (see above) which make the operation of the computer easier, such as a program to format a disk. At a technical level the operating system handles the basic and central functions such as *input* and *output* operations (see *BIOS*, below) and *interrupts* (see page 300).

The design of the operating system is often modular, allowing new features to be added and new hardware to be accommodated. One part, the portion of the operating system that deals with access to and management of files and programs stored on disk, is often provided separately. This is the ***disk operating system*** (commonly abbreviated to ***DOS***). The *network operating system* (see page 152) provides similar facilities for use with local area networks.

Many modern operating systems also provide a *graphical user interface* (*GUI*) (see page 71), either incorporated into the operating system or provided separately.

These are general terms and most manufacturers have their own proprietary names for either the operating system or the disk operating system. Among these are:

Advanced Disk Filing System (ADFS) is the name specifically given to the disk operating system in BBC Master, Archimedes and Acorn computers. It superseded the ***DFS (Disk Filing System)*** in the older BBC microcomputer.

CP/M is the name given to an important early operating system for microcomputers based on the family of Z80 microprocessor chips. The Z80 processor and CP/M are now obsolete.

MS-DOS is an operating system written by Microsoft originally for the IBM-PC. It is now the most common operating system used with PC-compatible microcomputers. It provides an operating system for the Intel 8086, 186, 286, 386, 486 and Pentium microprocessors. A version called ***PC-DOS*** was supplied as the operating system on the original IBM-manufactured Personal Computers.

OS/2 is a development of the PC-DOS operating system for IBM PCs and compatible microcomputers using more powerful microprocessors than the original Intel 8086. This operating system allows *multi-tasking* (see page 288) which makes it more suitable for use in a complex or network environment.

Presentation Manager is the graphical user interface developed by IBM and Microsoft for use with the OS/2 operating system.

Risc-OS is the operating system and graphical user interface developed by the computer manufacturer Acorn for their computers. The operating system and graphical user interface are integrated making the system easy to use with all operations being performed using the graphical user interface.

UNIX is an operating system originally written for large machines. Versions are now available for a variety of machines ranging from mainframes to microcomputers. It was designed to improve software portability. It has been highly successful as an operating system for minicomputers, because it is particularly suited for running multi-user and networked systems. It is also easily adapted for the specific requirements of each multi-user or networked system.

Windows is the graphical user interface developed by the software producer Microsoft for computers using the MS-DOS and PC-DOS operating systems. It is very successful, with a vast number of Personal Computers using it. Almost all new Personal Computers are now supplied with the Windows software. Many users do not need to be aware of what operating system is used as the Windows interface appears to do most of the required system operations.

BIOS (Basic Input Output System)

is the part of the operating system that handles the input and output of the computer. It enables the operating system to use the particular features of the hardware being used. The name specifically refers to a single part of some operating systems which can be easily altered to allow the same operating system to be used by a variety of hardware designs and manufacturers. If the BIOS is altered, the other parts of these operating systems will not need any alteration.

Spooling

is the temporary storage of input or output data on magnetic disk or tape, as a means of compensating for the slow operating speeds of peripheral devices or when queuing output from different programs to one device, such as a printer (see *printer spooler*, below).

Printer spooler

including: print spooler, print job, print queue

is a program which stores data ready to be printed. Each set of data to be printed is known as a ***print job***. When the print job has been received from a program and is complete, the printer spooler can send this data to the printer. Several programs or terminals can send data at the same time for printing;

because the data is stored in files by the printer spooler and sent to the printer when appropriate. A printer spooler is normally part of the operating system.

If a printer spooler is used, programs do not have to wait whilst printing is being done (printers work more slowly than computers do). This is particularly important with microcomputers and interactive computing, as users do not want to waste time waiting for data to be printed out. See also *printer server*, page 151.

The *print queue* is a list of things waiting to be printed by a printer spooler. Normally it is a list of the files holding data ready for printing. Each file will hold the data from a particular task which will be sent to the printer by the printer spooler when the printer is free. A task could be a single letter or a large batch of commercial documents.

Job

including: job control language (JCL), job queue

is a data processing term for a package of work regarded by the computer as a single unit. Typically, a data processing department will run programs on behalf of its clients. These programs may be small (a single report) or large (a complete payroll). Once started, each program will proceed automatically to completion and from the data processing department's point of view, each is a single task or job to be run.

A specialised language, the *Job Control Language* (*JCL*), is used to control the execution of a job in a computer. It enables the operators to specify the requirements of a job (such as which printer to use) when the job is executed. The programmer does not need to deal with these decisions when writing programs. A job control language also enables a series of small jobs to be linked together and executed in one larger and more efficient operation.

In a *multiprogramming* system (see below) or a *batch processing* system (see page 166) the jobs wait in a *job queue* until the computer system is ready to execute them. This will normally be in the order they are submitted although in some systems priority levels can be assigned to a job to ensure earlier execution than other jobs.

Remote Job Entry (RJE)

is the use of a remote terminal to initiate a *job* (see above) on a computer within the network to which the terminal is attached. One example is the use of a terminal in a supermarket to transmit the record of the day's transactions to the central computer for the chain and initiate the appropriate funds transfer and ordering routines. Another very simple example is a request for a bank statement from a customer using a cash machine.

Multiprogramming

including: time slice

is a method of benefiting from the speed of a central processor compared with slower peripheral devices, allowing two or more programs to be processed apparently simultaneously but actually in bursts, controlled by an operating system. For example, while one program is waiting for an input or output operation to be performed or is using a peripheral, another may have access to the central processor. To control this process, priorities may be assigned to jobs.

A *time slice* is the predetermined maximum length of time during which each program is allowed to run in a multiprogramming system.

Multi-tasking

including: single-tasking

is a method of organising computer use which allows several different tasks or applications to be available at the same time. The users of a *multi-access system* (see page 166) will be working on different tasks apparently at the same time, although only one program is actually being executed at any one time. Similarly a modern microcomputer operating system allows a user to have several tasks apparently running at the same time, with the user switching freely between applications or tasks.

Some operating systems will not support multi-tasking, these are called *single-tasking* systems and only allow one program to be in use at any time.

Scheduling

including: round-robin

is the method by which central processor time is allotted in a multi-access system. The scheduling algorithm may be as simple as the *round-robin* which deals with each user equally in turn, or as complex as a scheme of priorities distinguishing between users and between tasks.

Processing mode

is the way in which the processing tasks carried out by a computer system are organised to make the most of the potential of the system. Sometimes the choice of mode is given to the user. For example, the user may have a choice between single-tasking or *multi-tasking* (see above) when running a program, or a choice between *foreground* or *background processing* (see below).

Different processing modes can also be selected by the central processor for different types of tasks. For example some types of instruction may only be available to the operating system, reducing the possibility of a user program affecting the rest of the computer's operation.

Foreground/background processing

including: foreground job, background job

is a method of organising a computer system so that certain important tasks (*foreground jobs*) may claim the sole use of the computer when required, while other less-pressing tasks (*background jobs*) utilise the remaining time.

For example this enables a user to continue typing at a word processor (the foreground job) whilst the computer sends data to a printer (the background job) using processing time which is idle whilst waiting for user input.

The same concept applies to a *multiprogramming system* (see above), where the foreground job will have priority, but if the processor is idle (for example, waiting for disk access) then a background job will use that time.

Segmentation

including: segment, interleaving

is splitting a large program into a number of smaller programs or *segments*. Each segment is a complete program that is executed separately. The function of the large program is achieved by running segments consecutively. Segmentation allows a large program to be executed on a computer with insufficient memory to store the whole program.

The segments of several programs can be *interleaved*, which allows several large programs to be run concurrently in parts, to make optimum use of resources. These techniques are not widely used now due to the relatively large memory of modern computers. Similar techniques are *overlays* (see page 198) and *paging* (see page 296).

Systems Application Architecture (SAA)

including: Common User Access (CUA), Systems Network Architecture (SNA)

is a set of standards for achieving both consistency and compatibility between software running on various types of IBM computer, including a consistent user interface. A number of standards are defined for the various parts of the Systems Application Architecture including:

Common User Access (*CUA*) which is the set of standards for the screen and keyboard layout, labelling and functions.

Systems Network Architecture (*SNA*) which is the standard for distributed processing, providing for communication between terminals and a host computer.

Executive program

also known as: monitor program, supervisor program

is a control program that schedules the use of the hardware required by the programs being run in a multi-task or multiprogramming situation.

Garbage collection

including: fragmentation, defragmentation

is a 'housekeeping' task carried out by software. Many applications packages and systems software programs do not immediately rearrange their immediate access storage when data is deleted and the 'free space' becomes distributed throughout memory. In order to re-use this efficiently software will need to 'collect the space together' and this tidying up is called garbage collection.

A similar problem occurs with some *disk operating systems* (see above) where files may be split (and stored on different parts of the disk). This *fragmentation* usually happens when a disk is almost full. The access speed of the disk and hence the performance of the system will be improved if the separate elements of these files are collected together, a process known as *defragmentation*.

C14   Machine Architecture

Other related terms can be found in B3 Memory,
C15 Interfaces and Buses and C16 Physical Components

The structure of a computer, or more properly the **Central Processing Unit
(CPU)**, and how the particular components are related to each other is called
Machine Architecture. The working of the computer can still be considered
in terms of binary patterns and codes. The physical characteristics of the
central processor affect the way the computer is used and also determine the
speed, power, cost and suitability of the computer for a particular
application.

The choice of integrated circuits and other components can determine
how fast the computer will operate. This is important when selecting a
computer for a particular application. For example, an important part of the
specification of a personal computer is its **microprocessor** (such as a, '386',
'486', 'Pentium', '68010' or 'ARM600') since this tells the purchaser
something about the complexity of the programs it will run. Other parts of
the central processor can affect a computer's performance for particular jobs,
for example a **floating-point unit** will make a computer much faster at
solving scientific problems, but may be of little value in an office context.

An important factor in the design of the central processor is the selection
of the binary patterns used internally. For example the number of bits used as
an address affects the maximum size of the main memory and the number of
bits used to store a number affects very large and very small numbers.

Ways exist of getting round these problems, but always at the expense of
performance and at a price. Various techniques may be employed within the
hardware of the central processor to enhance performance, but further
development of a type or series of computers will be limited by these
technical factors and the initial design decisions.

Central Processing Unit (CPU)
including: central processor, processor
is the main part of the computer, consisting of the *registers*, *arithmetic logic
unit* and *control unit* (for each of these parts of the central processing unit
see below). Usually the central processing unit includes the main memory
(see *immediate access store*, page 111). It is sometimes called the ***central
processor*** or ***processor***. Many computers have more than one processor.

A special form of central processing unit is the *microprocessor* (see below) which is used in microcomputers and small computerised devices, for example the control circuits of washing machines.

Microprocessor

including: Complex Instruction Set Computer (CISC), Reduced Instruction Set Computer (RISC)

is an integrated circuit where the components of the *central processing unit* (see above), excluding the main memory, are combined as a single unit. Microprocessors are manufactured in large numbers for use in microcomputers and small computerised devices. The general user has to obtain software suitable for that type of processor, since software cannot usually be used on different types of central processor.

Two of the main approaches to the design of microprocessors are the **Complex Instruction Set Computer (CISC)** and the **Reduced Instruction Set Computer (RISC)**. A complex instruction set computer design produces a complicated and expensive integrated circuit capable of performing a large variety of complex operations. A reduced instruction set computer design produces a simple, cheap integrated circuit with a basic range of operations. It is however much faster and relies on its speed to perform complex operations by using several machine instructions.

There are many types of microprocessor available including the:

Z80 microprocessor which was used in many early microcomputers and computerised control systems. It is now obsolete.

6502 microprocessor which was used in some early microcomputers including the BBC microcomputer. It is now obsolete.

8086 microprocessor which was used in the earliest IBM PC and similar computers. It is now obsolete.

186, 286, 386, 486 and **Pentium** microprocessors which are further developments of the original 8086 microprocessor. Each succeeding newer design is much faster than its predecessor but they share a similar instruction set so that most software written for earlier IBM PC compatible computers can still be used without modification. These microprocessors were originally designated 80186, 80286 etc.

ARM2, ARM3, ARM250 and **ARM 600** microprocessors are used in Archimedes and Acorn computers. They are based on RISC (see above) design principles and so are fast operating and inexpensive. Their design is modular and variants are produced to control devices such as laser printers and personal organisers.

68000 microprocessor and its variants are used in the Macintosh series of computers.

Transputer is a microprocessor which includes the *immediate access store* (see page 111), hence its nickname 'computer on a chip'. Combining processor and store in the same chip makes it very easy to build parallel processing arrays containing many processors.

Instruction set

is the complete collection of instructions which are used by a particular type of central processor. These are the instructions available for use in machine-code or assembly language programs for that computer. The instruction set is part of the design of a central processor or microprocessor and so the machine code of different types of computer are rarely compatible.

Arithmetic Logic Unit (ALU)

including: arithmetic unit, arithmetic register, accumulator
is the part of the central processing unit where data is processed and manipulated. It is also called the ***arithmetic unit***. The processing and manipulation of data normally consists of arithmetic operations or logical comparisons allowing a program to take decisions.

Most operations involve the ***accumulator***, a special storage register within the arithmetic logic unit. It is used to hold the data currently being processed by the central processor. Any data to be processed is temporarily stored in the accumulator, the results ending up in the accumulator before being stored in the memory unit.

Most computer calculations are based on addition methods and so the 'accumulator' is where the computer does its 'additions'. A computer performs subtraction by two's complement addition and multiplication by combining addition with shifts for column alignment.

The ALU usually includes ***arithmetic registers*** (see *register,* below) which are special store locations used to hold operands and results temporarily during calculation.

Control unit

including: fetch-execute cycle, instruction cycle, instruction decoder, fetch phase, execute phase
is the part of the central processor which manages the execution of instructions. A characteristic of all computers is the ability to follow a set of instructions automatically. The control unit fetches each instruction in sequence, decodes and synchronises it before executing it by sending control signals to other parts of the computer. This is known as the ***fetch-execute cycle***. See also *program counter,* below.

The fetch-execute cycle is the complete process of retrieving an instruction from store, decoding it and carrying it out. This is also called the *instruction cycle*. Part of the control unit is the *instruction decoder* which decodes the machine-code instructions during the fetch-execute cycle and determines what actions to take next.

The cycle consists of two phases, the *fetch phase* where the instruction is copied into the control unit and decoded, followed by the *execute phase* in which the instruction is obeyed.

Adder

including: full adder, half adder, sum bit, carry bit

is part of the arithmetic logic unit (ALU) which has the specialised job of addition within the central processor. Its proper name is *full adder*, a logic design which takes two binary numbers and adds the equivalent bits, adding in any carrys. Full adders are made from smaller components called *half adders* which simply take two bits and add them together producing the answer (called the *sum bit*) and a *carry bit* if the result is greater than one. See also *standard logic networks*, page 340, for *half adder* and *full adder*.

Only some very specialised computers, such as *super-computers* (see page 100) or computers using *floating-point units* (see page 297), have specific components to do any arithmetic other than addition. The arithmetic unit can do subtraction by adding complements but has to do multiplication and division using a special program (often written in *micro-code*, see page 301) which uses combinations of addition and subtraction.

Address calculation

including: vector, index register

is working out which *memory location* (see *address*, page 191) is to be accessed by a machine-code instruction. Part of a machine-code instruction is called the *address field* (see page 197) which contains data about which memory location the instruction is to use. There are a number of alternative methods for determining the address of the memory location, such as:

Direct addressing uses the data in the address field without alteration. This is the simplest method of addressing and also the most common.

Indirect addressing uses the address field to hold the address of a location which contains the required address. The action of a program can easily be changed by altering the data in the location pointed to by the instruction. The location holding the real address is known as a *vector*.

One use of a vector is to provide access to library routines. Program control is passed to the address in the vector. The locations of the vectors are defined for other programmers to use. Routines can be changed without all the programs using them also being changed. This is because the address of the vector remains the same, but its contents can be altered to point to the new start address for the routine. See also *vectoring*, below.

Immediate addressing uses the data in the address field, not as an address, but as a constant which is needed by the program. An example is a routine counting up to 10, which may have the constant '10' supplied in the address field of an instruction. Although the address field cannot hold numbers as large as those that can be stored as data in a memory location, because space has to be left for the *operation field* (see page 197), this is a particularly convenient method of loading constants into the accumulator.

Indexed addressing modifies the address (either a direct or an indirect address) in the address field by the addition of a number held in a special-purpose register, called an ***index register,*** before the address is used. Index registers are quickly and easily altered providing an efficient way of accessing a range of memory locations, such as in an array.

Address modification is changing the address field of a machine-code instruction as the program is running, so that each time the instruction is executed it can refer to a different memory location.

Register

is a location, normally used for a specific purpose, where data or control information is temporarily stored. Some registers are used in the different parts of the *fetch-execute cycle* (see *control unit,* above) whilst others may be available for use by the program being executed. Registers usually are much faster to access than the immediate access store, since they have to be accessed so often.

The various registers include:

Program counter in the control unit that contains the address of the next machine-code instruction to be executed. ***Instruction Address Register (IAR)***, ***next instruction register*** and ***Sequence Control Register (SCR)*** are alternative names for the program counter.

Address register in the control unit that holds the address part (see *address field*, page 197) of the instruction being executed.

Memory Address Register (*MAR*) in the central processor that stores the address of the memory location currently in use. In the fetch phase this would be the address of the instruction being loaded and in the execute phase the address of the data being used. The memory unit has access to the MAR and switches the address selection circuitry to access the appropriate location.

Memory Buffer Register (*MBR*) in the central processor that stores the data being transferred to and from the immediate access store. It acts as a buffer allowing the central processor and memory unit to act independently without being affected by minor differences in operation. A data item will be copied to the MBR ready for use at the next clock pulse, when it can either be used by the central processor or stored in main memory. *Memory Data Register* (*MDR*) is another name for the memory buffer register.

Memory management

including: Memory Management Unit (MMU)

is organising the flexible use of the computer's main memory, the *immediate access store* (see page 111). This can be done by the *Memory Management Unit* (*MMU*), often a single integrated circuit in a microcomputer, which allows the addresses used by the *central processing unit* (see above) to be stored at a different physical location. The memory management unit automatically converts the logical address provided by the central processor into the physical address in memory.

This allows programs in a multi-user or multi-tasking computer system apparently to use the same memory locations. The memory management unit places them in different physical parts of the immediate access store. Four memory management techniques which can be used are bank switching, virtual memory, paging and direct memory access:

Bank switching is used for overcoming the limitations of computers that can only address a limited amount of immediate access storage. Several 'banks' of storage are provided, each one occupying the same place in the computer's memory map. Only one bank may be active at any one time, and the required one is selected as required by the software.

Virtual memory is used when the required amount of immediate access store is not available. Part of a disk drive is allocated to be used as if it were main memory. When accessing these memory locations the software has to copy the contents of the relevant disk block into a reserved area of main memory, having first copied its existing contents back onto disk. This is very slow and the software will attempt to use the immediate access store if possible.

Paging is the organisation of memory into fixed size units, called ***pages*** (for example a page of 32K bytes). The immediate access store is organised as a number of physical pages. The logical pages used by the central processing unit can be assigned, by the memory management unit, to any page in physical memory. A form of *virtual memory* (see above) can be used with less frequently used pages being stored on disk, but when required they are reloaded into the immediate access store as a complete page.

Page turn is the movement of a page to or from backing store. The movement of pages is counted in page turns, which are sometimes confusingly called ***page faults***. Monitoring the rate of page turns can lead to improved efficiency by indicating where unnecessary movement is taking place. Rapid up-loading and down-loading of pages is known as ***threshing*** and can be recognised by a very high rate of disk access. In extreme cases something close to a *deadly embrace* (see page 244) may occur, because tasks cannot continue for any effective time before being interrupted and while new pages are loaded.

Direct Memory Access (***DMA***) is the use of part of the immediate access store independently from the operating system or the memory management unit. This is usually used in the design of games for use on microcomputers, where the screen display is accessed directly allowing a faster and more complex display.

Floating-point unit

including: maths co-processor, Floating-Point Accelerator (FPA)

is a component that can be added to the central processor to make arithmetical operations faster. It provides registers sufficiently large to handle floating-point representation of numbers as single units. It contains micro-code routines optimised to perform floating-point arithmetic operations very quickly.

Floating-point units are manufactured as a single integrated circuit for use in suitable microcomputers where they are called ***maths co-processors*** or ***Floating-Point Accelerators*** (***FPA***).

Floating-point units increase the performance of a computer when carrying out large numbers of calculations. They do not improve performance of text processing nor of peripheral handling. They are widely used in graphics applications to perform the calculations needed to plot screen images, for example in a computer aided design system.

An alternative approach to complex mathematical problems is the *array processor* (see below).

Array processor

is a central processor designed to allow any machine instruction to operate simultaneously on a number of data locations (data arrays). This design enables problems involving the same calculations on a range of data to be solved very quickly. Examples of suitable problems are weather forecasting and airflow simulation around a new aircraft. See also *floating-point unit*, above.

Parallel processing

is the simultaneous use of several processors to perform a single job. A job may be split into a number of tasks each of which may be processed by any available processor.

Bit map

including: disk map, screen map

is a pattern of bits describing the organisation of data. For example, the arrangement of data on a disk might be represented to the operating system as a bit map in which each bit represents one sector on disk: a '1' for sectors in use, a '0' for unused sectors.

A bit map for a disk is called a **disk map**. A graphic screen prepared in a painting or drawing package may be held as a bit map, often called a **screen map**, each bit relating to the setting of an individual pixel on the screen.

Bus

including: highway, address bus, data bus

is a common pathway shared by signals to and from several components of a computer. For example, all input and output devices would be connected to the I/O (input/output) bus. In practice each bus has two parts, an **address bus** which carries identification about where the data is being sent, and a **data bus** which carries the actual information. The principle of a bus is that the same wires go to each component in turn. The components watch the address bus until an address which they recognise, by using an address *decoder* (see page 342), is present. When this occurs they take action, either retrieving the data from the data bus or placing new data on the bus for the central processor.

Highway is a rarely used alternative name for a bus.

Buffer

including: buffering, single buffering and double buffering

is an area of computer memory allocated to transferring data between the computer and a peripheral. Sometimes a buffer is used between components within the computer, (see *memory buffer register,* above). Using a buffer provides a barrier between devices with different working speeds or data organisation.

It is much more efficient to send or receive data as a *block* (see page 123) of many words or bytes. Magnetic disks and tapes require data to be read or written in such a way that a block of data is moved in a single operation. The computer and the peripheral have to be capable of sending or receiving a whole block of data at high speed when required.

The management of block data transfer is done by *buffering*. An area of memory is allocated as the buffer, and when information is to be transferred, it is stored in the buffer until an entire block is compete. This block is then sent, leaving the area it occupied free for assembling the next block of data. When a block is received into a buffer, the data is processed before the next block is requested and transferred.

With *single buffering*, one device has to wait for the block to be received before using the data (and the other device has to wait whilst it is processed). This is inefficient and slow. An improved method is *double buffering*, where two areas of memory are allocated, and as one buffer is emptied the other can be filled up. This reduces the time a device has to stop while waiting for the data transfer.

Some peripherals may communicate with single bytes of data, for example keyboard input or musical sounds. The buffer for these peripherals may be organised as a *circular queue* (see page 262) enabling data to be added or removed as required.

Channel

including: channel number

is any physical path followed by data, particularly between a central processing unit and a peripheral device or, by extension, between the user's program and a file on backing store.

Although different peripherals work totally differently, the computer is simply sending or receiving data, but along different physical routes. These routes are all called channels and are normally given a number (a *channel number*) by the operating system. A program can alter the peripheral used simply by altering the channel number and allowing the operating system to redirect the data stream, allowing great flexibility in switching between peripherals and adding peripherals to the system.

An example is a music system, where a generated tune could be saved to a suitable disk, or played by a variety of output devices. Each output device can be linked to a separate output channel of a *MIDI interface* (see page 53) which switches the output to one or more devices simply by setting and altering channel numbers.

Cycle

including: cycle time, processor cycle time, machine cycle time, program loop time, millions of instructions per second (MIPS)

is the sequence of actions to perform a particular hardware operation, which is either repeated continuously or performed whenever it is required. In many cases the time taken for an operation is constant and is known as the *cycle time*. It useful when calculating the speed of a particular computer task.

The *processor cycle time* or *machine cycle time* is the cycle time for one *fetch/execute cycle* (see above) and is governed by the speed of access to the immediate access store. Processor cycle time gives a rough guide to the speed of a computer, although other factors, such as word length, are also important. Processing speed is sometimes expressed in *millions of instructions per second* (*MIPS*), which is also only a rough guide, and is normally based on the average number of machine-code instructions executed.

The *program loop time* is the time taken by a single repetition of a *loop* (see page 204) and is useful for calculating the expected speed of a routine.

Interface

is the hardware and associated software needed for communication between processors and peripheral devices, to compensate for the difference in their operating characteristics (e.g. speeds, voltage and power levels, codes, etc.). A number of internationally accepted standard interfaces (and their associated protocols) have been defined, these include: RS232, IEEE 488, SCSI and Centronics (see *C15 Interfaces and Buses*, page 306).

Interrupt

including: timer

is a signal, generated by a source such as an input or output device or a systems software routine, which causes a break in the execution of the current routine. Control passes to another routine in such a way that the original routine can be resumed after the interrupt.

This enables peripherals to operate independently, indicating to the operating system, with an interrupt, when they need to communicate with the central processor. An example is a keyboard, which only sends data to the central processor when a key is pressed. The central processor continues with other tasks until, on receiving an interrupt, it *polls* (see *polling*, below) the various peripherals to establish the reason for the interrupt. If the interrupt is from the keyboard, the central processor collects the data, the code for the key which has been pressed, and stores it in the keyboard *buffer* (see above) before continuing. Timing circuits, called *timers*, are also used to generate interrupts at fixed intervals, for example, to refresh the screen display.

Micro-code

including: micro-program, micro-instruction

is machine-code instructions which are executed by calling small programs held elsewhere in the computer. To the user a micro-code instruction behaves like a machine-code instruction but the control unit implements it by passing control to the micro-code routine. The micro-code is stored within the central processor for speed of access. Micro-code enables the instruction set of a computer to be expanded without the addition of hardware components, but it will be slower than a machine-code instruction.

Each micro-code routine is a ***micro-program*** consisting of a sequence of ***micro-instructions***, typically defining a machine-code instruction.

Parity check

including: parity bit, even parity, odd parity

is a test applied to binary data to ensure that it has been stored or transmitted without error. It is possible for technical failures to corrupt (or alter) the data in a computer system. This may be caused by electrical interference, dust or corrosion. Corrupt data can be detected by a parity check and the user alerted to the problem.

A bit in each word or byte of data is reserved to be a ***parity bit***. This parity bit is altered to make the number of '1's in the data either even (for ***even parity*** systems) or odd (for ***odd parity*** systems). If the data is corrupted, the even (or odd) total is unlikely to apply so that, when the data is checked, the error will be detected.

Parity checking may be used inside the computer (to check the internal workings of the computer), when data is transmitted to a peripheral (such as backing store or a printer) or when data is being transmitted over longer distances using a network or telephone system. Usually when sending data using a serial interface (for example, to a printer or modem) parity checking will be used and the user must ensure that both devices use the same parity check.

Pipelining

is the concurrent decoding of two or more machine instructions. While part of one instruction (for example, an address field) is being decoded, another part of a second instruction (for example, an operation code) may also be decoded, as a means of increasing the speed of execution of a program.

Shift

including: shift register

is an operation that moves the bits held in a register, called the ***shift register***, either to the left or to the right.

There are three different types of shift, arithmetic shift, logical shift and cyclic shift (also called a rotation). They are distinguished by what happens to the bits that are shifted out of the register at one end and what is moved in to fill the vacant space at the other end.

Arithmetic shift to the right causes a bit at the right hand end of the register to be lost at each shift, and a copy of the sign bit is moved in at the left hand end. This operation preserves the sign of a number and has the effect of dividing a binary number by 2 at each shift, regardless of the notation system or whether the number is negative or positive. The division will be inaccurate because of the truncation caused by the loss of a digit at each shift.

Arithmetic shift to the left causes the bit at the left hand end of the register, the sign bit, to be lost at each shift. A zero bit is moved in at the right hand end. If the bit to be moved into the sign bit position is different from the one that was there before the shift, an overflow flag is set.

The use of two's complement notation ensures that shifting right gives correct results for multiplication by 2 until an overflow is flagged, because the number is too large to be represented in this size of register.

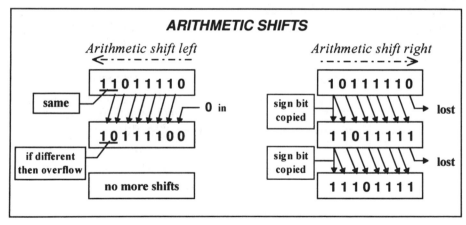

Figure C14.1: *Arithmetic shifts*

Logical shift is where the bits shifted from the end of the register are lost, and zeros are shifted in at the opposite end. It is called a logical shift because it is suitable for *logical operations* (see page 196) rather than for arithmetic.

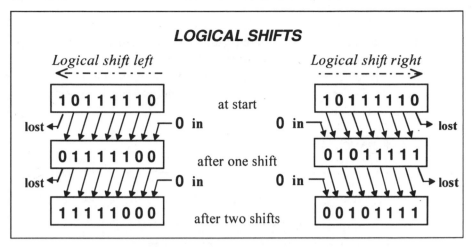

Figure C14.2: Logical shifts

Cyclic shift or **rotation** is where the bits shifted out at one end of the register are re-inserted at the opposite end.

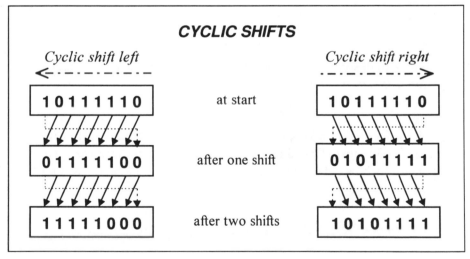

Figure C14.3: Cyclic shifts

Masking

is an operation that selects certain of the bits in a register for subsequent processing. Usually, another register of equal length holds a bit pattern called a mask with each bit set to 1 where a corresponding bit is to be selected and 0 otherwise. For example, if a 16-bit register holds a machine-code instruction divided as follows:

OPERATION CODE							ADDRESS								
1	0	0	0	1	0	1	0	0	1	1	0	1	0	1	1

the operation code can be selected by constructing the following mask:

1	1	1	1	1	1	1	0	0	0	0	0	0	0	0	0

Using the *AND operation* (see page 196) gives a result of:

1	0	0	0	1	0	1	0	0	0	0	0	0	0	0	0

If necessary, the result can then be *shifted* (see *shift* above) to the right by 9 bit places to put the operation code at the right hand end of the register.

The idea of using a mask in this way is so fundamental that the same words are used to describe similar selections at a much higher level, such as in using a *data manipulation language* (see page 256).

Polling

is the sequential checking of a range of possibilities to identify which should be dealt with next. This allows the operating system to manage a range of choices, such as determining what has caused an *interrupt* (see above) or which terminal in a multi-user system is waiting for processing. Usually a message is sent to each routine in turn and the routine has to respond positively to claim the attention of the operating system. The routines are polled in order so that each routine can claim (if required) its full share of the processor.

Vectoring

is the technique for passing control in a computer program through an intermediate address or vector. For example, on detecting an interrupt, instead of the computer passing control directly to a service routine, it may first jump to a location which in turn hands control to the routine. By altering the contents of this intermediate location, alternative service routines may be introduced without affecting programs that have already been written for that system.

Von Neumann architecture

also known as: Von Neumann concept or machine

is the name given to traditional computer architecture which forms the basis of most digital computer systems. A single control unit manages program control following a linear sequence of "fetch-decode-execute-output".

John von Neumann (1903-57), who was a member of a team working on first generation computers, is credited with the idea that programs and data were indistinguishable, and hence could be stored in the same memory unit. In early computers, programs and data were stored in separate memories and the process of entering or altering programs was very tedious. Treating programs as just one form of data made changing programs easier and opened the way for compliers, whose input was text and whose output was a program in binary code.

Von Neumann is also credited with the introduction of the flowchart and with the concept of 'assertion boxes'. These say *what should be true* before or after a step in a program as opposed to *what should be done* at that point in the program.

C15   Interfaces and Buses

Related terms can be found in C14 Machine Architecture,
C16 Physical Components, C17 Communications
Technology

What goes on inside a computer is of little interest to most users. For those who are interested in the basic concepts of the internal workings, machine architecture is covered in the preceding section. It is when they connect peripherals to a microcomputer that most users are affected by the computer's architecture.

All peripherals are connected to a computer through an **interface**, but each type of computer may have to be fitted with slightly different interfaces depending on the computer's internal design. Some peripherals require their own dedicated interface, but in situations where a variety of peripherals may be connected, the interface may provide an **expansion bus**. The expansion bus allows several peripherals (of a suitable type) to be linked in a chain to one computer interface.

Inside a microcomputer all the components are connected together by a bus. Any peripherals have to be connected to this bus. An **interface board** plugs into a special socket connected to the bus. The electronics on this interface board need to be tailored to fit the electrical connections used by that particular computer's bus. So each design of bus requires its own particular interface boards.

Each peripheral is provided with an interface and is connected, generally through a cable, to the equivalent type of interface on the computer. For the computer and the peripheral to communicate with each other, the interface in the peripheral and the interface in the computer need to be of the same type.

Some peripherals use a **bus interface**. Several peripherals attached to the same bus can share one computer interface, making it easy to use many different peripherals and change peripherals as needed. The computer can identify each peripheral by an address which is set when the peripheral is first installed.

Interfaces may be plugged into the main printed circuit board of the computer, called the **motherboard**, or into an extension of the motherboard. The degree to which a microcomputer can be expanded depends on the physical space available in its case, which limits the size of the interface board, and the number of sockets available; these are normally called **slots**.

Bus (microcomputer)

including: S100, ISA, AT, EISA and MCA buses

is the common pathway shared by signals between the internal components of the microcomputer. Each design of microcomputer uses different electrical signals and physical layouts. This is important when new components, such as *interface boards* or *cards* (see below), are being added, since they will have to be manufactured to fit that type of computer.

Typical designs of standard microcomputer buses are the S100, ISA, AT, EISA and MCA buses. Interfaces designed for one type of bus will not fit another type.

S100 bus is now obsolete but was widely used in small personal microcomputers and was so called because it could link a maximum of 100 components.

ISA (***Industry Standard Architecture***) bus, ***EISA*** (***Extended Industry Standard Architecture***) bus, ***AT*** (***Advanced Technology***) bus and ***MCA*** (***Micro Channel Architecture***) bus are all standard designs used by various types of IBM-compatible microcomputers.

Local bus

including: video bus, VESA and PCI buses

is an additional bus in a microcomputer normally with a specific function. Some functions of modern microcomputers (such as maintaining the VDU display and sending data to and from the disk drives) can require the computer to move vast amounts of data. This can use between 10% and 50% of the microcomputer's power. One way of cheaply increasing the power of a microcomputer is to provide a special bus for one or both of these functions, so relieving the load on the main bus. This special bus doing a specific function is known as a local bus. If the local bus is simply maintaining the screen display then it is sometimes called a ***video bus***.

VESA (***Video Electronics Standards Association***) and ***PCI*** (***Peripheral Component Interconnect***) are both standard designs of local buses used by various types of IBM-compatible microcomputers.

Motherboard

including: mainboard, daughterboard, carrier board

is the printed circuit board (PCB) that holds the principal components in a microcomputer system. The motherboard contains at least the main bus. The other components, such as the microprocessor and clock chips, will be either plugged into the motherboard or soldered to it. The motherboard is also known as the ***mainboard***.

Some components may be mounted on their own printed circuit board, called a ***daughterboard*** which will be plugged into the motherboard. Components attached using daughterboards can easily be replaced or upgraded and are not limited by the sockets or circuitry provided by the motherboard. Daughterboards are sometimes called ***carrier boards.***

Expansion slot

including: slot, expansion card, card, memory card, PCMCIA card
is a socket which is provided in a computer to allow additional components, such as additional disk drives and network interfaces, to be added to the computer later. These sockets are also called ***slots***. The more slots that are provided, the greater the number of extra components that can be added.

Expansion slots allow ***expansion cards*** (or ***cards***) to be added. These expansion cards are usually *interface boards* (see below) but can also provide extra facilities such as a small hard disk drive or a co-processor. Similarly many computers can accept ***memory cards*** which allow the computer's main memory to be increased.

In most microcomputers, the expansion slots are connected directly to the main bus. This means that the expansion board must be designed for that particular bus design (or architecture). One important agreed standard is the ***PCMCIA* (Personal Computer Memory Card International Association)** ***card,*** which is the size of a credit card, for fitting into the expansion slots of small portable computers. Although originally intended for memory expansion cards, a variety of peripheral cards, including modems and hard disk drives are now available.

Interface board

also known as: interface card
including: parallel port, serial port
is the necessary hardware (see *interface*, page 300), mounted on a small printed circuit board (PCB), needed for a microcomputer to communicate with a peripheral device (or another computer). Appropriate ***interface cards*** can easily be plugged into the *expansion slots* (see above) of the microcomputer.

Some international standard interfaces are used by microcomputers. These include a ***parallel port*** and a ***serial port***. Although these are general terms, when referring to microcomputers they refer to particular international standards. The parallel port is often a Centronics interface and the serial port frequently uses the RS232 interface. The wide range of interface standards include:

Centronics interface, an interface initially designed for use with printers, is a form of parallel port. The latest versions have been developed to allow the interface to be used for both input and output, enabling it to be used for data transfer between computers or for the easy attachment of a range of peripherals; this is sometimes called 'the PIO' (parallel input/output) interface.

RS232 interface is a widely used international standard serial interface. The serial port is often referred to as 'the RS232 port'.

The *V.24 interface* and the *RS432 interface* are almost identical to the RS232 interface.

IDE interface, another common standard, is used to control the hard disks in a microcomputer. The IDE interface is built into the hard disk it is controlling, which reduces the cost of adding hard disks to microcomputers. In high performance applications, other interfaces such as the *SCSI bus* (see below) are more likely to be used.

One particular type of interface board is the *expansion bus* (see below) and another important standard interface is the *MIDI interface* (see page 53) for sound.

Bus interface

also known as: expansion bus

is an *interface* (see page 300) which provides an additional *bus* (see above) external to the computer to which several peripheral devices can be connected. This makes it easy to use a range of peripherals or to change the peripherals being used. Each device has an address, which is set on installation, so that the microcomputer can distinguish between the various peripherals. The most common bus interfaces are the SCSI (Small Computer Systems Interface) and the IEEE interface, which are internationally defined standards. Peripherals fitted with one of these interfaces can be connected to any microcomputer fitted with the same type of bus interface; this means that peripherals do not have to be designed for one model of microcomputer but can be interfaced with many different types of computer. Many different pieces of equipment can be connected to the computer at the same time via the same bus.

IEEE bus conforms to standards defined by the Institute Electrical of and Electronic Engineers (USA). It is used outside the computer to connect scientific equipment to a computer. The computer will have an IEEE interface to convert signals on the IEEE bus into signals suitable for the main computer bus. As it is a common standard, many types of equipment are manufactured with the logic and connections needed for the IEEE bus. These pieces of equipment can easily be connected to computers with an IEEE bus.

SCSI (Small Computer Systems Interface) bus was designed to connect a wide range of devices to microcomputers at minimum cost, in particular disk drives and scanners which need a high data transfer rate. It is widely used in general microcomputing. Each SCSI interface can connect up to seven peripheral devices.

Docking station

is a device containing a range of peripherals and interfaces for use by a portable computer. For lightness and to reduce power consumption, *portable computers* (see page 102) have few peripherals other than disk drives and use a small LCD screen rather than a large monitor. One solution to this lack of peripherals is a docking station which may be part of a network. When plugged into the docking station, the portable computer has access to a large monitor, printer, extra disk drives and other peripherals, such as modems. The portable computer can be quickly disconnected and used elsewhere.

Print buffer

is an area of computer memory where data to be printed is held until the printer is ready to print it. It enables a program to continue operating without waiting for each character to be printed, as it can send its data to the buffer. The buffer is normally managed by the operating system. When a printer, which works much slower than a computer, is ready to print the next data, it can signal this by means of an *interrupt* (see page 300) to the operating system. The operating system will remove the data from the buffer and send it to the printer. See also *buffer*, page 298.

C16 *Physical Components*

*Related terms can be found in section C14 Machine
Architecture.*

The computer industry has produced a range of electronic components to
perform specific functions within a computer system. Some of these
components, such as the clock, simply provide the controlling electronics
needed by a computer, whilst others allow a particular type of computer to be
designed for a specific role.

Many of these components are integrated circuits and are designed to a
standard size which makes them easy to incorporate into computer designs.

The development of standardised components means that they can be
mass produced rather than being individually constructed. This has the
advantage that components are much cheaper and that it becomes economic
to design a variety of computers with particular characteristics.

Although computer systems are usually viewed conceptually as a 'black
box', it is useful to appreciate the functions of some of the individual
components.

Clock
including: clock rate
is the electronic unit that synchronises related components by generating
pulses at a constant rate. Clock pulses are used to trigger components to take
their next step, so keeping all components in time with each other. The ***clock
rate*** is the frequency at which the clock generates pulses. The higher the
clock rate, the faster the computer may work. One limiting factor for machine
speed is the manufactured tolerance of the slowest component.

Hard-wired logic
is a function permanently built into the circuitry. Often this is an integrated
circuit designed to control the function. Such functions are immediately
available when switched on and cannot be altered by the user. This ensures
that the device will always be in the same initial state when switched on.

Integrated circuit (IC)

including: chip, Large Scale Integration (LSI) and Very Large Scale Integration (VLSI), Small Scale Integration (SSI), Medium Scale Integration (MSI)

is a solid state micro-circuit in which all the components (such as transistors and capacitors) are formed within a very thin slice of silicon. The popular name for an integrated circuit is a '(silicon) chip'.

Most integrated circuits used in computers are produced using *Large Scale Integration (LSI)* or *Very Large Scale Integration (VLSI)* which are techniques for producing integrated circuits of very high density. These have large numbers of components (transistors, diodes etc.) and circuits (decoders, flip-flops etc.) combined as a single integrated circuit.

Small Scale Integration (SSI) has up to 20 logic gates on a chip; typically they are used for (hard) wired logic circuits.

Medium Scale Integration (MSI) has 20 to 100 logic gates or less than 1000 memory bits on a chip; these are also used for (hard) wired logic.

Large Scale Integration (LSI) has 100 to10000 logic gates or up to 16000 memory bits on a chip; used for computer logic or memory.

Very Large Scale Integration (VLSI) has more than 10000 logic gates or more than 16000 memory bits on a chip; used as standard for computer manufacture.

Bistable

including: flip-flop

is a device that has two stable states. Since each state is stable the device effectively forms a memory which can differentiate between two pieces of data. Whatever the technology, which could be electronic, magnetic, liquid or pneumatic, the two states are used to represent the binary digits 0 and 1. This means that mathematical manipulation can be performed on data held in binary form.

The bistable in the integrated circuits used for the main memory of computers is a *flip-flop*, a logic circuit designed to store a single data bit. The receipt of an electrical pulse by the flip-flop will reverse its state, and a series of pulses causes it to flip sucessively between the two stable states.

Latency

including: propagation delay and access time

is the time delay before a component in the computer responds to an instruction, for example the time between data being requested from a memory device and the time when the answer is returned.

Even a single logic gate has a latency (or ***propagation delay***) which will be very small (a fraction of a microsecond) but, with a large number of gates involved, these delays can be significant. The computer cannot work any faster than the limit imposed by latency.

A special case of latency is ***access time***, which is the time delay in retrieving data stored either in main memory or on backing store. Access time is relevant when deciding which backing store should be used in any particular context to produce an acceptably fast computer system.

Logic element
including: logic circuit
is a *gate* (see page 328) or combination of gates needed to perform a logical function as part of the circuitry of a computer. It may be a single *AND gate* (see page 332) or a more complex component such as an *adder* (see pages 294 and 340). Hardware system designers can produce complex circuits using logic elements as modules in the construction of their designs.

A ***logic circuit*** is designed to perform a more complex function, perhaps specific to the system being built, producing a required set of outputs from a given set of inputs.

Programmable Logic Array (PLA)
also known as: Uncommitted Logic Array (ULA)
is an array of standard logic gates, in which each element is identical, manufactured on a single LSI (large scale integration) chip. The logic circuits required for a particular application are created by 'burning out' unwanted connections.

Real-time clock
is an electronic unit that maintains the time of day in a special register that may be accessed by suitable instructions in a computer program. It is powered by internal batteries, and continues to function even when the computer is switched off. For example, the computer can use this time information to label files with the time and date they were created or to trigger timed events such as collecting a weather satellite broadcast.

ZIF socket

or zero insertion force socket

is a socket on a printed circuit board in the computer into which an *integrated circuit* (see above) is plugged. The socket is designed so that no pressure is needed on the component to plug it in (*zero insertion force*) or to remove it. This means that an integrated circuit can be removed and replaced without damage. It also means that a computer can be easily upgraded by having an obsolescent integrated circuit replaced by a new one without risk of damage to the integrated circuits or to the computer itself.

Dual In-Line (DIL) socket

including: Dual In-line Package (DIP)

is a socket which accepts most standard *integrated circuits* (see above). These integrated circuits are constructed with two parallel lines of pins, one at each side of the integrated circuit package. This form of package is known as a *Dual In-line Package* (*DIP*). There are a number of standard sizes of dual in-line packages, which enable flexible design and interchange of components.

DIN socket

is a plug/socket design adopted by Deutsche Industrienorm (the German Standards Organisation) but which is widely used internationally. There are a variety of types of DIN socket with various numbers of pins and layouts. The most common is the '5 pin DIN', which is also widely used in audio systems.

C17   *Communications Technology*

This section is concerned with the principles involved in achieving communication between computer systems, and the conventions that determine how such systems communicate with each other. Related terms can be found in A4 Communications, B6 Networks and B7 Communications Devices and Control Devices

Ways of communicating data between distant places, using electrical energy have been in use for over 100 years, of which the telegraph was the first. Very quickly, machines replaced people and automatic communications became typical. Telephones, tele-printers, radio, and television were all well developed before computers were combined with them to produce the range of global communications that are now available.

Global communications require that there are the same standards for the equipment used in all the countries of the world. Some of these standards have been set by those countries which initially developed the systems, but most have been worked out and agreed by international bodies, sometimes with the direct authority of the United Nations. Each industrial country has a national organisation that sets standards for all kinds of products. These organisations have been setting standards, and revising them, throughout the last 100 years. Thus there are international standards defined by ISO, the International Standards Organisation, and by CCITT, the Committée Consultatif International Téléphonique et Télégraphique of the United Nations, and other standards of a national origin are accepted through organisations like the General Agreement on Tariffs and Trade (GATT).

The specification of standards is a complex and expensive process. The implications of a particular choice can be very far reaching, both for the industries that make products to those standards, and for the consumers of those products. As far as the consumer is concerned, the acceptance of a single manufacturer's standards for some device or system can have limiting effects, particularly when there is severe competition for sales of the product. However in a situation of rapid technical development, the consumer is likely to benefit from clearly defined standards which help to ensure some measure of compatibility between hardware and software originating from different sources. The most important areas of standards definition for the computer and information technology industries are those of input/output specifications and external communications.

Data transmission

including: full duplex, half duplex, simplex; synchronous, asynchronous, start bit, stop bit, parallel, serial transmission; echo
is the passing of data from one device to another. This may be between parts of a computer system or between computers in a network.

Data transmission may have a number of distinct characteristics:

- it may be synchronised or unsynchronised
- it may be serial or parallel
- it may be in both directions at the same time, called **duplex** or **full duplex;** in only one direction at a time, called **half duplex;** or in one direction only, called **simplex**
- checks may be made on the accuracy of transmission (*parity checks*, see page 301, or the use of echo processes)
- data may be *packeted* (see *packet switching system*, below) with the addresses of destinations.

Synchronous transmission is a method of transmitting data between two devices in which all the data transfers are timed to coincide with a clock pulse. Within a computer the timing is provided by the computer's clock. Between computers, the clock in one computer acts as the master clock for the system.

Asynchronous transmission is a method of data transmission, in which a character is sent as soon as it becomes available rather than waiting for a synchronisation signal or a clock pulse. A *start bit* marks the beginning of a character and one or two *stop bits* mark the end of a character.

In *parallel data transmission* the bits for a character are sent simultaneously along separated data lines; thus an 8-bit code will require a minimum of 9 *channels* (see below) for parallel transmission (8 data and at least one ground, return channel).

In *serial data transmission* the bits for a character are sent one after another along the same data line; thus serial transmission requires two wires (a data line and the ground, return line).

Echo is a feature of data transmission in which the data received is returned to the point of origin for comparison with the original data in order to check it.

Signal routing

including: message switching, message queuing
is the choice of route for a particular message through a network. In *ring* and *star networks* (see pages 146 and 147) there is little choice of route. But

more complex network topologies provide many possible routes for any message. If the direct connection between two nodes is unavailable, perhaps because of some fault or because the connection is busy, then the intelligence in the *routers* (see page 158) at the nodes sends the message forward in a direction which is available. Since the time for a message to travel between nodes is often nearly the same regardless of the distance apart, this is more efficient than waiting for the direct link to become available. For example, it is possible that a message from London to Manchester may be routed via a satellite to Los Angeles and then on to Manchester. The computer in London which sent the message and the computer in Manchester have no control over the route used, nor has the computer in Los Angeles through which it may have passed. The next part of the message may go by some completely different route. See also *Figure A4.2, The life story of an E-mail message*, page 20.

Message switching is a method of batching, organising and storing sections of data, so that they can be transmitted economically in a network; it is usually applicable to networks with many computers. Each section of a message is sent from node to node with each node responsible for the choice of route for the next part of the journey. This requires that the nodes are intelligent. A message will be accepted at a node and, if necessary, stored until it can be transmitted onwards. Finally, all the sections of the data are assembled, in the correct order, at their destination

Message queuing is a method of passing messages in a network in which a host computer stores a message for a terminal until it is ready to receive the message. This is a system appropriate to *star networks* (see page 147).

Packet Switching System (PSS)
including: packet
is a method of sending data over a *wide area network* (see page 145). Packet switching networks are available for general use in most countries.

A *packet* is a group of bits, made up of control signals, error control bits, coded information, and the destination address for the data. In a given situation the size of a packet may be fixed.

Since each packet occupies a channel for only a short time, this arrangement provides for very efficient use of the system. Error checking should ensure that errors are detected, and appropriate procedures can be automatically started. If there is an error, it will only be in a small part of the data, and this can be retransmitted quickly.

Collision detection
including: Carrier Sense Multiple Access/Collision Detection (CSMA/CD)
is a method of managing data traffic on a *local area network* (see page 144).
Individual computers are responsible for waiting for the network to be free
before sending a message. If two messages are sent at the same time, a
collision occurs. It is detected and the messages have to be retransmitted
when the network is free.

The network interface in each computer is watching all the messages being
sent over the network and waits if it detects a message being transmitted.
When no traffic is detected by the computer, any message awaiting
transmission can then be sent. As it is likely that several computers are
waiting to transmit messages and that they will do so at the same time,
message corruption will result. The network interfaces detect this corruption
(or collision) and are designed to wait for a short time before trying again.
This staggers the load on the network.

Carrier Sense Multiple Access/Collision Detection (*CSMA/CD*) is a
protocol for implementing this process used on Ethernet local area networks.
See also *token ring network*, page 148.

Communications protocol
including: File Transfer Protocol (FTP)
is a standard set of rules describing the transfer of data between devices. It
specifies the format of the data, and the signals to start, control and end the
transfer. Many current protocols have been specified by the United Nations
communications committee, CCITT (Committée Consultatif International
Téléphonique et Télégraphique). See also *Open Systems Interconnection*
(*OSI*), below.

File Transfer Protocol (*FTP*) defines the way files are transmitted over a
network. The files are generally split into blocks with the file transfer
protocol defining block structure and error-checking procedures.
Z modem is a file transfer protocol for networks in general, but principally
on the Internet.
Kermit is an early file transfer protocol for networks in general, which is
simple to implement and is still often used.
X.25 is the CCITT standard for public *packet switching system (PSS)* (see
above) networks.
X.400 is the CCITT standard for *E-mail* (see page 20).
V.22bis is the CCITT standard for 2400 bps modems.
V.32bis is the CCITT standard for 14400 bps modems.
V.34 is the CCITT standard for 28800 bps modems, formerly called V-fast.
V-fast is the early name for the current V34 protocol.

V.42 is an error control and correction protocol.

V.42bis is the data compression protocol which includes V42 error correction. The data compression and decompression are automatically provided by a suitable modem. The compression can reduce data to a quarter of its original size, reducing transmission time.

TCP (*Transmission Control Protocol*) is a data transmission protocol defined for high-speed communications within networks.

TCP/IP (Transmission Control Protocol/Internet Protocol) is a set of protocols for data transfer within and between networks. It was defined by the US Government for the transfer of data across a range of networks, the original Internet.

SMTP (*Simple Mail Transport Protocol*) is an international standard for *E-mail* (see page 20).

MNP (*Microcom Network Protocol*) is a set of protocols for error correction and data compression.

Open system

including: Open Systems Interconnection (OSI), ISO 7
is a set of protocols allowing computers of different origins to be linked together. The standards relating to open systems are called *Open Systems Interconnection (OSI)*.

ISO 7 is the seven-layer design for the OSI protocols established by the International Standards Organisation (ISO). It enables manufacturers to design equipment and software for a particular layer. These systems will interconnect with equipment designed for the layer above and the layer below. A brief summary of some of the aspects covered by ISO 7 is given in Table C17.1, page 319.

The relations between the levels of TCP/IP (Transmission Control Protocol/Internet Protocol) network protocol 'family' and ISO 7 are shown in very simple form in Figure C17.2, page 320. See also *TCP/IP*, above.

Channel

is a path for a signal. The path may be provided by wires, fibre optic cable or microwave (radio or infra-red) links. The material and design of the means of providing the channel will determine the range of frequencies that the channel can carry. See also *bandwidth*, below.

OPEN SYSTEMS INTERCONNECTION (OSI)

7 LAYER NETWORK ORGANISATION MODEL (ISO 7)

level	level name	some functions specified within the level descriptions
Level 7	Applications	specific applications, for example data transfer, messaging, distributed databases; operating system functions and end-user interface
Level 6	Presentation	data transformation, syntax adjustments and formatting for output devices; data encryption and compression
Level 5	Session	establishes and maintains session dialogues; synchronises data exchange; provides access control and protection of higher levels from low-level functions
Level 4	Transport	establishes and maintains communications between users; levels out the data flow; provides greater flow control than the data link layer
Level 3	Network	routing/addressing between open systems; preventing packets from getting lost when crossing networks; multiplexing and physical network access
Level 2	Data Link	error-free connections to networks; error recognition and correction; creating and synchronising data blocks
Level 1	Physical	how bit sequences are to be sent; there is no error correction

Table C17.1: *ISO 7 model*

RELATIONSHIP BETWEEN OSI and TCP/IP PROTOCOLS

OSI	TCP/IP
Application	FTP
Presentation	TELNET
Session	SMTP
Transport	TCP
Network	IP
Data Link	Ethernet
Physical	

OSI	Open Systems Interconnection
TCP/IP	Transmission Control Protocol/Internet protocol
FTP	File Transfer Protocol
TELNET	TELetype NETwork
SMTP	Simple Mail Transport Protocol

Table C17.2: OSI and TCP/IP equivalents

Bandwidth

including: broad band, narrow band

is the difference between the highest frequency and lowest frequency in a range of frequencies. For example, the bandwidth of audio frequencies is 19,985Hz, the difference between 20,000Hz and 15Hz. However, the term is also used to describe the signal capacity of a *communications channel* (see page 154), in which case it is often measured in bps.

> ***Broad band.*** The numerical value assigned to the term broad band has changed over time; a few years ago it was used to mean a frequency greater than 4 kHz, which equates with up to 12 Kbps depending on the method of data transmission. It is now generally taken to be a communication rate not less than 34 Mbps, which equates with frequencies between 11.3 and 34 MHz. Broadband is also used to describe equipment which works at communication speeds greater than 34 Mbps.
>
> ***Narrow band*** is the description of bandwidths less than the smallest recognised broad band bandwidth. The term is frequently used to mean fractions of a broad band, since a broad band channel is often divided into a number of narrow band channels.

Signal

including: carrier signal, carrier wave

is electrical or electromagnetic energy transmitted from one point in a circuit to another along the *channels* (see above) connecting them. A signal can carry data of either analog or digital origin. A basic ***carrier signal*** consists of a constant-frequency electro-magnetic wave. This wave, the ***carrier wave***, is modified by combining it with a representation of the data in a way that can be reversed to extract the data after transmission. This process is called *modulation,* see below.

Modulation

including: amplitude modulation (AM), frequency modulation (FM), phase modulation, demodulation

is the process of introducing variations into the shape (the waveform) of a *carrier wave* (see above). The modulation is used to superimpose data onto the carrier wave.

Figure C17.1: *Unmodulated carrier wave*

There are three forms of modulation used for the transmission of digital data, amplitude modulation, frequency modulation and phase modulation:

Amplitude Modulation (AM), in which the amplitude, that is the height, of the carrier wave is used to represent 0 and 1. The simplest form of amplitude modulation is to switch the carrier wave on for a 1 and off for a 0.

Figure C17.2: *Modulation by switching the wave off*

Other forms involve increasing above a chosen height and decreasing below a chosen height to represent 1 and 0.

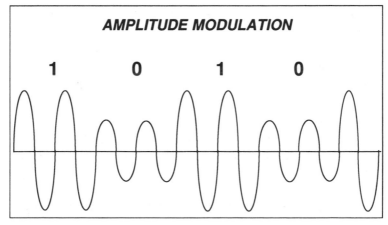

Figure C17.3: *Modulation by changing the amplitude*

Frequency Modulation (*FM*) combines two different frequencies with the carrier wave to produce a wave form which is made up of high and low frequency parts. This is a very common form of modulation for lower speeds of transmission.

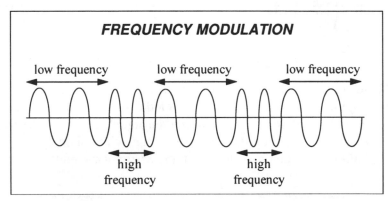

Figure C17.4: Modulation by changing the frequency

Phase modulation combines the carrier wave with an identical wave which is out of phase with it. Two-phase modulation combines two waveforms to provide patterns which are used to represent 0 and 1, shown in Figure C17.5. Four-phase modulation combines four waveforms to provide patterns which are used to represent 00, 01,10 and 11. Four-phase modulation transmits two data bits for each element of the wave, and thus sends data at twice the bit rate of two-phase modulation. Eight-phase modulation provides for three bits (000 to 111) for each wave pattern and sends data at three times the bit rate of two-phase modulation.

Figure C17.5: Modulation by adding another wave

Demodulation is the extraction of the modulating data from the modulated carrier wave signal. The circuits to do this are similar to those used in radio receivers to convert the received signals into sound signals.

Interference

including: Electromagnetic Interference (EMI), Radio Frequency Interference (RFI)

is the introduction of unwanted variations into a transmitted signal. These variations may be caused by faulty design of communications equipment or by external energy sources. Interference can sometimes occur inside a computer system, but more usually effects external communications. At any place there is a large variety of electromagnetic signals, many of which are unintentionally generated by equipment such as electric motors. These signals may be picked up by wire conductors carrying electronic communications. and become part of the signal that reaches the receiver. In addition there is an increasingly high density of intentionally transmitted signals (for example from portable phones), which may cause interference on equipment for which these signals are not intended.

Electromagnetic Interference (***EMI***) is the general term for interference caused by electromagnetic radiation at any frequency, whether continuous or intermittent.

Radio Frequency Interference (***RFI***) is interference which is generated at typical radio frequencies, in the range 10 KHz to 100000 MHz. Radio frequencies are at the lower end of the electromagnetic frequency spectrum and are more prone to interference than the higher frequency radiations such as infra red and light.

Noise

including:signal-to-noise ratio

is electrical disturbances affecting the transmission of intended signals. The existence of noise generally has the same effect on the accurate transmission of signals that people experience when listening to a person talking in a room with other people who are also talking. This is the basic origin of the term. When the noise level is too high, effective transmission ceases. The comparison of the strength of the signal with the level of noise is called the ***signal-to-noise ratio.***

On-line service

is a type of telecommunications service, for example electronic mail or public access database, that can be accessed via a modem.

Public Telephone Operator (PTO)

is any provider of publicly available telephone service such as BT, Mercury, cable companies and cellular telephone companies.

Public Switched Telephone Network (PSTN)

is the traditional analog telephone network, which is being replaced by digital services which are elements of ISDN (integrated services digital network) (see below).

ISDN (Integrated Services Digital Network)

including: ISDN (basic, primary, broadband) service rates, B-channel, D-channel

is a CCITT definition for (global) digital data communications. Its purpose is to ensure that people, computers and other devices can communicate over standardised connection facilities. The criteria include the setting of standards in such a way that users will have access through a limited set of multi-purpose interfaces. This really amounts to the establishment of world-wide digital communications for speech, and other data, with the simplicity of access that current telephone dialling systems provide. ISDN has definitions for the data transmission speeds, or capacities, of channels and the number of channels in each service.

The capacity of channels is set at:

B-channel is 64 Kbps and provides a good quality speech channel.

D-channel is 16 Kbps and is intended for signalling and control data.

ISDN service rates are:

rate name	number of channels	total capacity
Basic	2 B- and 1 D-	$2 \times 64 + 16 = 144$ Kbps
Primary	30 B- and 1 D-	$30 \times 64 + 16 = 1936$ Kbps
Broadband		more than 34 Mbps

The proposed broadband rates are 150 Mbps and 600 Mbps

Dialcom

is the BT (British Telecommunications) name for its ISDN service; the successor to Datel, which was the name for the British Telecom data transmission services in the UK.

Video data compression

including: JPEG, MPEG, delta compression

is the use of electronic methods to reduce the amount of data that has to be included when video data, either for still or moving pictures, is stored or transmitted. For moving pictures (video), the principles involve identifying those parts of the picture which change from one scan to the next, and sending data only about the changes, which is known as ***delta compression***. This alone will save a significant amount of transmission and storage capacity. Periodically a complete new whole picture will need to be sent. The Joint Photographic Expert Group (***JPEG***) has defined standards for still picture compression, and this format for storage or transmission is called JPEG. These standards have been extended by the Motion Picture Expert Group (***MPEG***) to cover moving images. These proposals are currently being used for video compression on CD-ROM, and the system is referred to as MPEG.

Very Small Aperture Terminal (VSAT)

is a satellite communication system using dishes less than 3 m in diameter. It is primarily for down-linking (receiving satellite transmissions), but it can be used for up-linking (transmission to satellites).

High Definition Television (HDTV)

is a proposed form of television transmission which will provide a wider picture of much clearer quality than present standards. HDTV transmission will require much greater bandwidth but data compression techniques will be possible. For the decompression of picture data, considerable computer processing power will be needed in HDTV receivers.

C18   *Truth Tables and Logic Gates*

Binary logic is important in computing because the truth values, True and False, can be represented as the binary digits 1 and 0. All integrated circuits are designed using Boolean logic. They respond to the binary patterns they receive and produce the required outputs as binary patterns. Binary logic influences not only hardware design, but also the design of algorithms and programming languages, for example the way a test such as "If the month is February *and* if it is a leap year" is programmed in a high-level language.

Boolean algebra

is named after the mathematician George Boole (1815–1864) and is a set of rules for manipulating truth values according to truth tables.

Gate

is an electronic device to control the flow of signals. The output of a gate will depend on the input signal(s) and the type of gate. The components of a computer system can all be seen as combinations of a number of gates, each with a number of possible inputs and a single output. For details of gates see *logic gates* below.

Truth value

also known as: Boolean value
including: true, false
The truth values in Boolean algebra are True and False (abbreviated to T and F), often represented by the binary digits 1 and 0. In electronics, these are usually represented by different voltages.

Truth table

is a notation used in Boolean algebra for defining the output of a logic gate or logic circuit for all possible combinations of inputs. Examples can be found in the *logic gates* and *logical equivalence and combination of gates*, below.

Logical equivalence

exists when two logic circuits have the same output(s) for given inputs. Two equivalent circuits will do the same thing even though their designs are different. One result of this is that it is possible to construct all logic circuits using only NAND gates or only NOR gates. This is very useful because it allows the use of a single form of component for a variety of purposes. See also *programmable logic array*, page 313. Some examples of logical equivalence are given in *logical equivalence and combination of gates*, below.

Karnaugh map

is a method of displaying and manipulating the relationships between Boolean operations. Karnaugh maps are mainly used to reduce logic expressions to their simplest form. They make use of the fact that all logic can be expressed as the 'AND' of 'ORs' or the 'OR' of 'ANDs'.

In the three-input logic table below, the rows for which the output is 1

represent the logic expression $A.B.C + A.B.\overline{C} + \overline{A}.B.\overline{C} + \overline{A}.\overline{B}.\overline{C}$

INPUT (A)	INPUT (B)	INPUT (C)	OUTPUT (P)
1	1	1	1
1	1	0	1
1	0	1	0
1	0	0	0
0	1	1	0
0	1	0	1
0	0	1	0
0	0	0	1

The Karnaugh map contains those elements for which the output is 1.

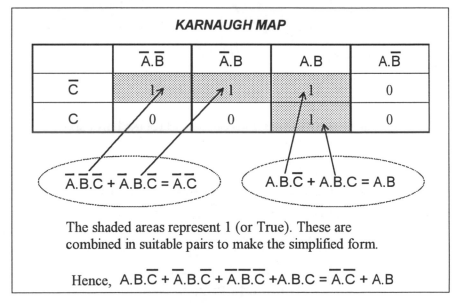

KARNAUGH MAP

	$\overline{A}.\overline{B}$	$\overline{A}.B$	$A.B$	$A.\overline{B}$
$\overline{C}$	1	1	1	0
C	0	0	1	0

$\overline{A}.\overline{B}.\overline{C} + \overline{A}.B.\overline{C} = \overline{A}.\overline{C}$ $A.B.\overline{C} + A.B.C = A.B$

The shaded areas represent 1 (or True). These are combined in suitable pairs to make the simplified form.

Hence, $A.B.\overline{C} + \overline{A}.B.\overline{C} + \overline{A}.\overline{B}.\overline{C} + A.B.C = \overline{A}.\overline{C} + A.B$

Figure C18.1: Karnaugh map

Venn diagram

is a way of representing the relationships between sets in diagrammatic form. There is a close connection between set operations and logic operations. For example, in Figure C18.2(a), below, the hached area represents the set operation corresponding to 'XOR'. When the rules for manipulating Venn diagrams are known, it can be seen that this diagram also establishes the logical equivalence

A XOR B = (A OR B) AND NOT (A AND B).

Figures C18.2 (b) and (c) illustrate the same relationships between the two sets.

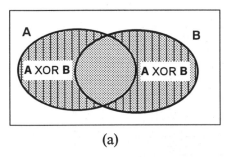

(a) the hatched area is: A XOR B
(b) the hatched area is: A OR B
(c) the hatched area is: A AND B

Hence: A XOR B =

(A OR B) AND NOT (A AND B)

(a)

(b)

(c)

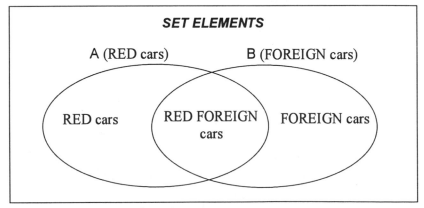

Figure C18.2: Venn diagrams

Logic symbol

is a symbol used to represent a logical operation. In addition to circles with words in them, there are standard symbols which are conventionally used to denote logic operations. These symbols are shown in *logic gates*, below.

LOGIC GATES

including: NOT gate, OR gate, AND gate, NOR gate, NAND gate, XOR gate, XNOR gate

Some important simple logic gates are described below.

For each, the following information is given:

- the name of the gate
- a brief description of its function
- how it may be written (there are several notations in common use)
- its truth table (showing how the output changes with different inputs)
- how it may be represented in diagrams (there are several methods, some using different shaped boxes for different gates).

NOT gate

including: inverse, inverter

The output of a NOT gate is the *inverse* of its input. If the input is TRUE then the output is FALSE and if the input is FALSE then the output is TRUE.

NOT gates have only one input and one output.

A NOT gate is also known as an *inverter*.

It may be written as: P = NOT A

other notations express this as: $P = \overline{A}$, or P = ˜A

INPUT (A)	OUTPUT (P)
0	1
1	0

Figure C18.3: NOT gate

OR gate

The output of an OR gate is TRUE if any input is TRUE, otherwise the output is FALSE.

OR gates have two or more inputs and one output.

It may be written as: $P = A$ OR B

in other notations as: $P = A + B$ or $P = A \vee B$

INPUT (A)	INPUT (B)	OUTPUT (P)
0	0	0
0	1	1
1	0	1
1	1	1

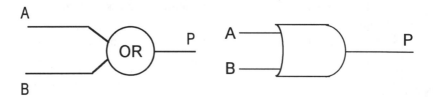

Figure C18.4: OR gate

AND gate

The output of an AND gate is TRUE if all inputs are TRUE, otherwise the output is FALSE.

AND gates have two or more inputs and one output.

It may be written as: $P = A$ AND B

in other notations as: $P = A \cdot B$ or $P = A \wedge B$

INPUT (A)	INPUT (B)	OUTPUT (P)
0	0	0
0	1	0
1	0	0
1	1	1

Figure C18.5: AND gate

NOR gate

The output of a NOR gate is TRUE only if all inputs are FALSE, otherwise the output is FALSE.

NOR gates have two or more inputs and one output. They are important because all logic circuits can be constructed from NOR gates alone.

It may be written as: P = A NOR B

in other notations as   P = NOT (A + B)   or $P = \overline{A + B}$

It is equivalent to: P = NOT (A OR B)

INPUT (A)	INPUT (B)	OUTPUT (P)
0	0	1
0	1	0
1	0	0
1	1	0

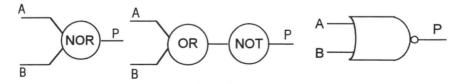

Figure C18.6: NOR gate

NAND gate

The output of a NAND gate is FALSE only if all inputs are TRUE, otherwise the output is TRUE.

NAND gates have two or more inputs and one output. They are important because all logic circuits can be constructed from NAND gates alone.

It may be written as: $P = A \text{ NAND } B$

in other notations as $P = NOT (A.B)$ or $P = \overline{A.B}$

It is equivalent to: $P = NOT (A \text{ AND } B)$

INPUT (A)	INPUT (B)	OUTPUT (P)
0	0	1
0	1	1
1	0	1
1	1	0

Figure C18.7: NAND gate

XOR (Exclusive-OR) gate

including: EOR gate, NEQ gate, non-equivalence gate
The output of an Exclusive-OR gate is TRUE if the two inputs are different, the output is FALSE if the inputs are alike.

XOR gates have only two inputs and one output.

The Exclusive-OR gate is also known as EOR gate or NEQ (Non-EQuivalence) gate.

It is written as: $P = A \text{ XOR } B$ $P = A \text{ EOR } B$

$P = A \text{ NEQ } B$ or $P = A \oplus B$

INPUT (A)	INPUT (B)	OUTPUT (P)
0	0	0
0	1	1
1	0	1
1	1	0

Figure C18.8: XOR or NEQ gate

XNOR (Exclusive-NOR) gate

including: EQ gate, equivalence gate

The output of an Exclusive-NOR gate is TRUE if the two inputs are the same, the output is FALSE if the inputs are different.

XNOR gates have only two inputs and one output.

The Exclusive-NOR gate is also known as EQ (EQuivalence) gate.

It is written as: P = A XNOR B   P = A EQ B

$$P = \overline{A \oplus B}$$

INPUT (A)	INPUT (B)	OUTPUT (P)
0	0	1
0	1	0
1	0	0
1	1	1

Figure C18.9: XNOR or EQ gate

LOGICAL EQUIVALENCE AND COMBINATION OF GATES

All logic circuits can be constructed in many different ways, using different combinations of gate circuits. In particular all logic circuits can be constructed using only NAND gates, or only NOR gates. Choosing the easiest, or cheapest, to make can influence the manufacture of computer circuits. The following examples are only a small set.

Equivalence for NOT logic

A NOT gate can be made by connecting together both inputs of a NAND gate:

INPUT (A)	A NAND A	NOT A
0	1	1
1	0	0

$$P = \overline{A.A} = \overline{A}$$

$$P = A \text{ NAND } A = \text{NOT } A$$

Figure C18.10: A NAND A = NOT A

A NOT gate can also be made by connecting together both inputs of a NOR gate:

INPUT (A)	A NOR A	NOT A
0	1	1
1	0	0

$$P = \overline{A + A} = \overline{A}$$

$$P = A \text{ NOR } A = \text{NOT } A$$

Figure C18.11: A NOR A = NOT A

Equivalence for AND logic

A AND B is equivalent to NOT (A NAND B):

INPUT (A)	INPUT (B)	A NAND B	NOT (A NAND B)	A AND B
0	0	1	0	0
0	1	1	0	0
1	0	1	0	0
1	1	0	1	1

$$P = A.B = \overline{\overline{A.B}}$$

Figure C18.12: A AND B = NOT (A NAND B)

Equivalence for NOR logic

A NOR B is equivalent to (NOT A) AND (NOT B):

INPUT (A)	INPUT (B)	NOT A	NOT B	(NOT A) AND (NOT B)	A NOR B
1	1	0	0	0	0
1	0	0	1	0	0
0	1	1	0	0	0
0	0	1	1	1	1

$$P = \overline{A + B} = \overline{A}.\overline{B}$$

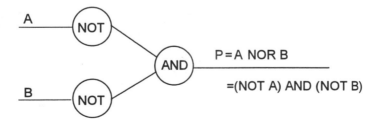

Figure C18.13: A NOR B = (NOT A) AND (NOT B)

Equivalence for XOR logic

1)   A XOR B is equivalent to (A OR B) AND NOT (A AND B):

A	B	A OR B	A AND B	NOT (A AND B)	(A OR B) AND NOT (A AND B)	A XOR B
1	1	1	1	0	0	0
1	0	1	0	1	1	1
0	1	1	0	1	1	1
0	0	0	0	1	0	0

$$P = A\ XOR\ B = (A + B) . \overline{(A . B)}$$

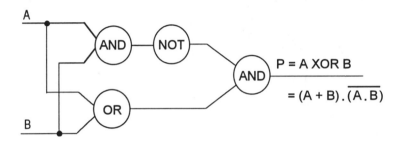

Figure C18.14: A XOR B = (A OR B) AND NOT (A AND B)

2) A XOR B is equivalent to (A AND NOT B) OR (B AND NOT A):

A	B	NOT A	NOT B	A AND NOT B	B AND NOT A	(A AND NOT B) OR (B AND NOT A)	A XOR B
1	1	0	0	0	0	0	0
1	0	0	1	1	0	1	1
0	1	1	0	0	1	1	1
0	0	1	1	0	0	0	0

$$P = A\ XOR\ B = (A . \overline{B}) + (\overline{A} . B)$$

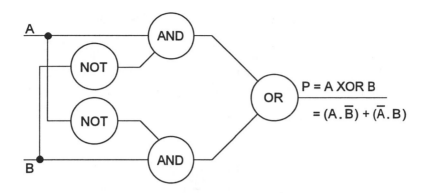

Figure C18.15: A XOR B = (A AND NOT B) OR (NOT A AND B)

3)   A XOR B can be constructed entirely from NAND gates

A	B	A NAND B (Q)	A NAND Q (R)	Q NAND B (S)	R NAND S (P)	A XOR B
1	1	0	1	1	0	0
1	0	1	0	1	1	1
0	1	1	1	0	1	1
0	0	1	1	1	0	0

$$P = A\ XOR\ B = \overline{R.S} = \overline{\overline{A.Q}.\overline{Q.B}} = \overline{\overline{A.\overline{A.B}}.\overline{\overline{A.B}.B}}$$

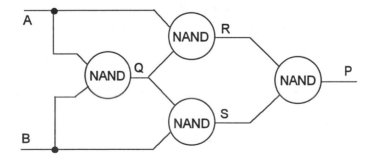

Figure C18.16: XOR circuit constructed from NAND gates

EXAMPLES OF STANDARD LOGIC NETWORKS

Half adder

The half adder can add two bits together to produce a sum output (**SUM**) and a carry output (**Cout**). See also *adder*, page 294.

These are defined as:

SUM = A XOR B

Cout = A AND B

bit A	bit B	Cout	SUM
1	1	1	0
1	0	0	1
0	1	0	1
0	0	0	0

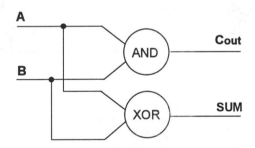

Figure C18.17: *Half adder*

Full adder

The full adder can add together two bits and a carry input (**Cin**) to produce a sum output (**SUM**) and a carry output (**Cout**). See also *adder*, page 294.

These are defined as:

SUM = (A XOR B) XOR Cin

Cout = (A AND B) OR (A AND Cin) OR (B AND Cin)

A	B	Cin	Cout	SUM
1	1	1	1	1
1	1	0	1	0
1	0	1	1	0
1	0	0	0	1
0	1	1	1	0
0	1	0	0	1
0	0	1	0	1
0	0	0	0	0

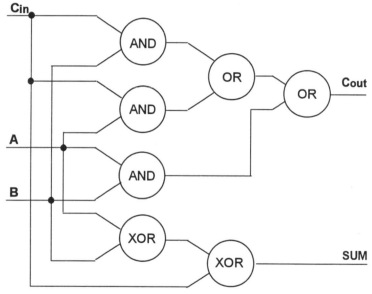

(a) constructed from individual gates

More helpfully, a full adder can be seen as a combination of two half-adders.

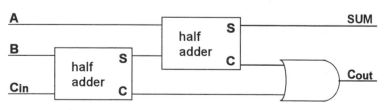

(b) made up from two half adders and an OR gate

Figure C18.18: *Full adder*

Decoder

A decoder circuit is used to select one of several inputs. Address lines are used to indicate the source to be selected. n address lines can handle 2^n sources (e.g. 2 address lines for 4 sources, 3 address lines for 8 sources).

$$P = \overline{A}.\overline{B}.S_0 + \overline{A}.B.S_1 + A.\overline{B}.S_2 + A.B.S_3$$

Figure C18.19: Decoder logic circuit

Address switching

A single source can be switched to one of several destinations by a logic network using address lines to indicate the destination.

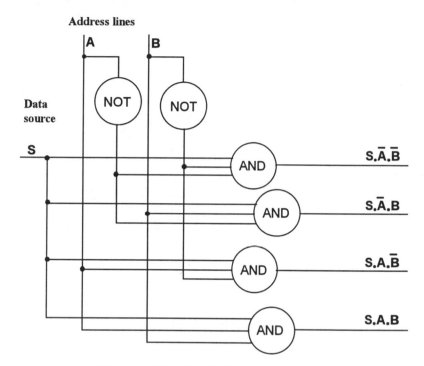

Figure C18.20: *Address logic circuit*

Part D: Appendices

D1   *Acronyms and Abbreviations*   *346*

D2   *Units*   *357*

One characteristic of modern life, and particularly any form of technological activity, is the use of abbreviations, acronyms and other 'jargon' by those who are involved in any specialised activity. This use of words, terms and acronyms when writing for or talking to others involved in the same activity can be a way of economically passing information between like minded people, but on the other hand it can also be a barrier to understanding for those who do not know the meanings of the strange new words. Computer users have always made great use of a vocabulary containing many abbreviations and acronyms. Over time this vocabulary has changed as new ideas are developed and old ones are no longer appropriate.

No list would ever be complete or up-to-date, but in section D1 there is an extensive list of acronyms and abbreviations whose use is either commonplace throughout most computing activities or is specific to a particular aspect of computing. The list is alphabetic and includes many terms which are treated in the main body of the Glossary, for these terms the appropriate page references are given. For terms which have no page reference, the only information provided is the expansion of the acronym and for some an indication (in brackets) of the context in which they may be met.

D1   *Acronyms and Abbreviations*

Where a page number is given, it indicates where additional information can be found. Brackets are used to indicate the context in which the acronym or abbreviation may be met.

A-to-D	analog-to-digital *159*
A/D	analog-to-digital *159*
ACC	accumulator *293*
ACIA	asynchronous communications interface adapter
ACK	acknowledgement (ASCII character)
ACM	Association for Computing Machinery
ADC	analog-to-digital converter *159*
ADC/MPS	analog-to-digital/microprocessor system
ADFS	Advanced Disk Filing System *284*
ADSR	attack, decay, sustain, release (sound) *52*
AFIPS	American Federation of Information Processing Societies
AI	artificial intelligence *67*
ALGOL	ALGOrithmic Language *254*
ALU	arithmetic logic unit *293*
AM	amplitude modulation (communications) *322*
ANSI	American National Standards Institute *267*
APL	A Programming Language *254*
APT	automatically programmed tools (machine tool language)
AQL	acceptable quality level
ARU	audio response unit
ASCII	American Standard Code for Information Interchange *267*
ASDR	Attack Sustain Decay Release (sound) *51*
ASIC	application specific circuit
ASR	automatic send-receive
AT	advanced technology (bus) *307*
ATM	asynchronous transfer mode
ATM	automatic teller machine *20*
BA	bus available
BABT	British Approvals Board for Telecommunications
BASIC	Beginners All-purpose Symbolic Instruction Code *254*
BBC	British Broadcasting Corporation
BBS	bulletin board system *18*
BCC	block check character
BCD	binary coded decimal *276*
BCS	British Computer Society
BDOS	basic disk operating system

BEAB	British Electrical Appliances Board	
BEL	bell (buzzer) (ASCII character)	
BiMOS	bipolar-MOS	
BIOS	basic input output system	*286*
bit	binary digit	*272*
BNF	Bachus-Naur form	*251*
bpi	bits per inch	*119*
BPP	bits per pixel	
bps	bits per second	*159*
BS	back space (ASCII character)	
BSI	British Standards Institution	
CAD	computer aided design	*29*
CAD	computer aided drafting	*29*
CAD/CAM	computer aided design and manufacture	*39*
CAI	computer assisted instruction	
CAL	computer assisted learning	*64*
CAM	computer aided manufacture	*39*
CAN	cancel (ASCII character)	
CASE	computer aided software engineering	
CBT	computer based training	*64*
CCA	Central Computing Agency	
CCD	charge coupled device	
CCITT	Committée Consultatif International Téléphonique et Télégraphique	
CCP	console command processor	
CCR	condition code register	
CD	compact disc	*121*
CD-I	compact disc interactive	
CD-ROM	compact disk read-only memory	*121*
CDI	collector diffusion isolator	
CEG	Computer Education Group	
CEPIS	Confederation of European Professional Informatics Societies	
CGA	colour graphics adapter	*130*
CIR	current instruction register	
CISC	complex instruction set computer	*292*
CMI	computer managed instruction	*64*
CML	computer managed learning	*64*
CMOS	complementary MOS	*120*
CMYK	cyan, magenta, yellow, key (black)	*136*
CNC	computer numeric control	*40*
COBOL	COmmon Business Oriented Language	*254*
COM	computer output on microfilm	*107*
COMAL	COMmon Algorithmic Language	*254*
CP gate	comparator-gate (=XOR)	*334*

CP/M or	control program monitor or
CPM	control program for microcomputers *284*
CPE	central processing element
cps	characters per second *159*
CPU	central processing unit *291*
CR	carriage return (ASCII character)
CR/LF	carriage return/line feed
CRC	cyclic redundancy check
CROM	control ROM
CRT	cathode ray tube
CSCD	carrier sense collision detection
CSCW	computer supported co-operative work *19*
CSMA-CD	carrier sense multiple access collision detection *318*
CSV	comma separated variables (file) *266*
CTRL	control (ASCII character)
Ctrl	control (ASCII character)
CTS	clear to send
CUA	common user access *289*
CUG	closed user group *20*
CWP	communicating word processors
D-to-A	digital-to-analog *159*
DAC	digital-to-analog converter *159*
DAC	data acquisition and control
DAT	digital audio tape
DBA	database administrator *91*
DBMS	database management system *26*
DC1	device control 1 (ASCII character)
DC2	device control 2 (ASCII character)
DC3	device control 3 (ASCII character)
DC4	device control 4 (ASCII character)
DCD	data carrier detect
DCE	data communications equipment
DCS	telephone data carrier system
DD	double density *119*
DDE	direct data entry *4*
DDL	data description language *27*
DEL	delete (ASCII character)
DES	data encryption standard *43*
DFS	disk filing system *284*
DIB	data input bus
dil	dual in-line *314*
DIL	Dual In Line *314*
DIN	Deutsche Industrienorm *314*
DIP	dual in-line package *314*
DLE	data link escape (ASCII character)

DLT	digital linear technology
DMA	direct-memory access *296*
DML	data manipulation language *256*
DOS	disk operating system *284*
DP	data processing *2*
DRAM	dynamic random access memory *120*
DSR	data set ready
DSS	decision support system *6*
DSW	device status word
DTE	data terminal equipment
DTL	diode-transistor logic
DTP	desk top publishing *9*
DTR	data terminal ready
E-mail	electronic mail *20*
EA	extended addressing
EAN	European article number *3*
EAROM	electronically alterable read only memory *120*
EB disk	electronic book disk *121*
EBCDIC	extended binary coded decimal interchange code *267*
EBR	electron beam recording
ECD	electrochromeric display
ECL	emitter-coupled logic
ECMA	European Computer Manufacturers Association *227*
EDP	electronic data processing
EDS	exchangeable disk storage *113*
EEPROM	electrically erasable PROM *120*
EFT	electronic funds transfer *20*
EFTPOS	electronic funds transfer at point of sale *20*
EGA	enhanced graphics adapter *130*
EIA	Electrical Industries Association (USA)
EISA	extended industry standard architecture *307*
EM	end of message (ASCII character)
EM character	end-of-medium character (ASCII character)
EMI	electro-magnetic interference *325*
ENQ	enquiry (ASCII character)
EOF	end of file *265*
EOM	end-of-message
EOR	exclusive OR *334*
EOT	end of transmission (ASCII character)
EPOS	electronic point-of-sale *20*
EPROM	erasable programmable read-only memory *120*
EPS	encapsulated postscript
EQ	equal
EQ	equivalence *335*
ESC	escape (ASCII character)

ESDI	enhanced systems drive interface
ETB	end of text block (ASCII character)
ETX	end of text (= end of last block) (ASCII character)
FAM	fast access memory
FAST	Federation against software theft *97*
FAT	file allocation table *123, 182*
fax	facsimile *22, 154*
FD	floppy disk *113*
FDD	floppy disk drive *113*
FDDI	fibre distributed data interface *147*
FDM	frequency division multiplexing (communications) *155*
FET	field effect transistor
FETMOS	field effect transistor metal-oxide-semiconductor
FF	form feed (ASCII character)
FFT	fast fourier transform
FIFO	first in, first out *262*
FM	frequency modulation (sound, communications) *50, 322*
FORTRAN	FORmula TRANslation *254*
FPA	floating-point accelerator *297*
FPU	floating-point unit *297*
FROM	fusible ROM
FS	file separator (ASCII character)
FSK	frequency shift keying
FSM	frequency shift modulation
FTP	file transfer protocol *318*
Gb	giga byte
GDU	graphical display unit *129*
GIGO	garbage-in garbage-out
GND	ground (connection)
GPIB	general purpose interface bus
GPR	general purpose register
GS	group separator (ASCII character)
GUI	graphical user interface *71*
HCI	human-computer- interaction/interface *71*
HD	high density *119*
HDD	high density disk *119*
HDTV	high definition television *327*
HEX	hexadecimal *278*
HMOS	high-performance metal-oxide-semiconductor
HRG	high resolution graphics *128*
HT	horizontal tabulation (ASCII character)
Hz	Hertz
I/O	input/output *105*
IAM	immediate access memory *111*
IAR	instruction address register *295*

IAS	immediate access store *111*
IC	integrated circuit *312*
IDE	integrated device electronics *309*
	or intelligent device electronics *309*
IEE	Institute of Electrical Engineers (UK)
IEEE	Institute of Electronic and Electrical Engineers (USA) *309*
IFIP	International Federation for Information Processing
IGFET	insulated gate field effect transistor
IIL	integrated injection logic
IKBS	intelligent knowledge based system *68*
IO	Input/Output *105*
IOP	input/output processor
IORQ	input/output request line
IPL	initial program loader
IR	instruction register *295*
IR	infra red
IR	index register *294*
IS	information systems
ISA	industry standard architecture *307*
ISAM	index sequential access method *183*
ISBN	international standard book number *3*
ISD	international subscriber dialling
ISDN	integrated services digital network *326*
ISM	Industry Structure Model *93*
ISO	International Standards Organisation *319*
ISR	interrupt service routine
IT	information technology *4*
ITDM	intelligent time-division multiplexing *155*
JANET	Joint Academic Network *20*
JCL	job control language *287*
JFET	junction field effect transistor
JPEG	Joint Photographic Expert Group *327*
JSD	Jackson structured design *165*
JSP	Jackson structure programming *165*
Kb	kilo-bit, kilo-byte
KBS	knowledge based system *68*
LA	linear arithmetic (sound) *50*
LAN	local area network *144*
LCD	liquid crystal display *129*
LED	light emitting diode *129*
LEO	Lyons Electronic Office *102*
LF	line feed (ASCII character)
LIFO	last in, first out *262*
Lisp	LISt Processing *254*

LPT	(line) printer
LQ	letter quality *138*
LRC	longitudinal redundancy check
LSB	least significant bit *270*
LSI	large scale integration *312*
MAR	memory address register *296*
Mb	mega byte
MBR	memory buffer register *296*
MCA	micro channel architecture *307*
MDA	monochrome display adapter *130*
MDR	memory data register *130, 296*
MICR	magnetic ink character recognition *106*
MIDI	music instrument digital interface *53*
MIPS	million instructions per second 300
MIS	management information system *5*
MMI	man-machine interface/interaction *71*
MMU	memory management unit *296*
MNP	Microcom network protocol *318*
modem	Modulator/Demodulator *154*
MOS	metal-oxide-semiconductor *120*
MOS	machine operating system
MOSFET	metal-oxide-semiconductor field effect transistor
MPEG	Motion Picture Expert Group *327*
MPS	microprocessor system *292*
MPU	microprocessor unit *292*
MPX	multiplex *155*
MREQ	memory request
ms	millisecond
MS-DOS	Microsoft DOS *284*
MSB	most significant bit *272*
MSD	most significant digit
MSI	medium scale integration *312*
MTBF	mean time between failures
MTF	mean-time to failure
MUX	multiplexor *155*
NAK	negative acknowledgement (ASCII character)
NAND	Not AND *334*
NEQ	Not Equivalent *334*
NFS	Network Filing System *152*
NLQ	near letter quality *138*
NMI	non-maskable interrupt
NMOS	n-channel metal-oxide-semiconductor
NOR	Not OR *333*
ns	nanosecond
NTSC	National Television Standards Committee (USA)

NUL	null (do nothing)
OCR	optical character recognition *106*
OEM	original equipment manufacturer *107*
OLE	object linking and embedding
OMR	optical mark reader *106*
OOD	object oriented design *166*
OOL	object oriented language *166*
OOP	object oriented program(ming) *168*
OS	operating system *284*
OSI	Open Systems Interchange *319*
OV	overflow *188*
PABX	private automatic branch exchange *154*
PAL	phase alternating line *127*
PBX	private branch exchange *154*
PC	personal computer (IBM-PC compatible) *100*
PC	program counter *295*
PCB	printed circuit board
PCI	programmable communications interface
PCI	peripheral component interconnect *307*
PCM	pulse-code modulation
PCMCIA	personal computer memory card international association *308*
PD	phase distortion (sound) *50*
PDA	personal digital assistant *100*
PDM	pulse duration modulation
PIA	peripheral interface adapter
PID	personal identification device
PILOT	Programmed Inquiry, Learning Or Teaching *254*
PIN	personal identification number *83*
PIO	parallel input/output
PIXEL	picture element *127*
PL/1	Programming Language 1 *254*
PLA	programmable logic array *313*
PLC	programmable logic circuit
PMOS	p-channel metal-oxide-semiconductor
POS	point of sale *20, 150*
ppm	pages per minute
PRN	printer *135*
PROLOG	PROgramming in LOGic *254*
PROM	programmable read-only memory *120*
PRR	pulse repetition rate
PRT	program reference table
PSN	packet switching network *317*
PSS	packet switching system *317*
PSTN	Public Switched Telephone Network *326*
PSU	power supply unit

PSU	program storage unit
PSW	program/processor status word
PTO	public telephone operator 326
QBE	query by example 253
QD	quad density (disks) 119
QIC	quarter-inch cartridge
QWERTY	conventional typewriter keyboard 71
R/W	read/write 183
RAID	redundant array of independent (or inexpensive) disks 116
RAM	random access memory 120
RD	read 183
RDBMS	relational database management system 27
REM	remark(s)
RF	radio frequency
RFI	radio frequency interference 325
RGB	red green blue 129
RI	ring in
RISC	reduced instruction set computer 292
RJE	remote job entry 287
ROM	read-only memory 120
RPG	report program generator 253
RS	record separator (ASCII character)
RSA	Rivest, Shamir, Adleman (algorithm) 44
RTF	revisable or rich text format(file) 266
RTL	resistor-transistor logic
RTS	request to send
SAA	systems applications architecture 289
SAR	store address register
SBC	single board computer
SCR	sequence control register 295
SCSI	small computer systems interface 309
SDR	store data register
SHF	super high frequency
SI	shift in (ASCII character)
SIC	silicon integrated circuit
SID	standard interchangeable data (file) 266
SIMM	single in-line memory module
SIMS	Schools Information Management System
Simula	SIMULAtion 254
SIO	serial input/output (controller)
SLSI	super large scale integration
SMPTE	Society of Motion Picture and Television Engineers (USA) 58
SMTP	simple mail transport protocol 318
SNA	network architecture 289
SNOBOL	StriNg Oriented SymBolic Language 254

SO	shift out (ASCII character)
SOH	start of header (ASCII character)
SOS	silicon on sapphire
SOT	start of text (ASCII character)
SP	stack pointer
SQA	software quality assurance
SQL	structured query language *253*
SSADM	structured systems analysis and design method *169*
SSI	small scale integration *312*
STD	subscriber trunk dialling
STX	start of text (ASCII character)
SUB	substitute (ASCII character)
SVGA	super video graphics array *130*
SWR	status word register *195*
SYN	synchronisation character (ASCII character)
sysop	system operator *18*
TCP	transmission control protocol *321*
TCP/IP	transmission control protocol/internet protocol *321*
TDM	time division multiplexing (communications) *155*
TEMP	temporary
TP	teleprocessing *167*
TP	transaction processing *166*
TP	twisted pair *156*
TPA	transient program area
TPI	tracks per inch
TRL	transistor-resistor logic
TSV	tab separated variables (file) *266*
TTL	transistor-transistor logic
UART	universal asynchronous receiver/transmitter
UHF	ultra high frequency
UJT	unijunction transistor
ULA	uncommitted logic array *313*
UPC	universal product code *3*
UPS	uninterruptable power supply
US	unit separator (ASCII character)
USART	universal synchronous/asynchronous receiver/transmitter
USRT	universal synchronous receiver/transmitter
UTP	unshielded twisted pair *156*
UV	ultra violet
VANS	value added network service *152*
VDG	video display generator
VDT	video display terminal
VDU	visual display unit
VESA	Video Electronics Standards Association *307*
VGA	video graphics array *130*

VHF	very high frequency
VLSI	very large scale integration *312*
VM	virtual memory *123,296*
VMOS	vertical-current-flow metal-oxide semiconductor
VR	virtual reality *36*
VRAM	volatile read only memory *132*
VRR	vertical refresh rate *132*
VSAT	very small aperture terminal *327*
VT	vertical tabulation (ASCII character)
WAN	wide area network *145*
WIMP	windows icons mouse pointer *72*
WORM	write once, read many *121*
WP	word processing *8*
WR	write
WS	working store *123*
WYSIWYG	what you see is what you get *12*
XGA	extended graphics array *130*
XNOR	exclusive NOR *335*
XOR	exclusive OR *334*
ZIF	zero insertion force *314*
4GL	fourth generation language *225*

D2 UNITS

Symbol	Prefix	Meaning	Decimal	Power of ten
T	tera	one million million	1 000 000 000 000	10^{12}
G	giga	one thousand million	1 000 000 000	10^{9}
M	mega	one million	1 000 000	10^{6}
K	kilo	one thousand	1 000	10^{3}
		one	1	10
m	milli	one thousandth (1/1 000)	0. 001	$10^{-3} = 1/10^{3}$
µ	micro	one millionth (1/1 000 000)	0. 000 001	$10^{-6} = 1/10^{6}$
n	nano	one thousand-millionth (1/1 000 000 000)	0. 000 000 001	$10^{-9} = 1/10^{9}$
p	pico	one million-millionth (1/1 000 000 000 000)	0.000 000 000 001	$10^{-12} = 1/10^{12}$

In computer storage terms, the symbols K, M, G and T have particular values related to the powers of 2, not to the powers of 10:

K is 2^{10} = 1 024, thus 8K bytes of store is 8 x 2^{10} = 8 192 bytes

M is 2^{20} = 1 048 576, thus 4Mbytes (4Mb) is 4 x 2^{20} = 4 194 304 bytes

G is 2^{30} = 1 073 741 824, thus 60 Giga-bytes (60 Gb) is 60 x 2^{30} = 64 424 509 440 bytes

T is 2^{40} = 1 099 511 627 776, thus 2 Tera-bytes (2 Tb) is 2 x 2^{40} = 2 199 023 255 552 bytes

Index

A-to-D converter *159*
Abort *246*
Absolute address *191*
Absolute code *199*
Absolute reference *17*
Abuse - computer *94*
Acceptance testing *168*
Access time *312*
Accumulator *293*
Action bar *73*
Active device *160*
Active system *38*
Active window *72*
Actual parameter *216*
Actuator *160*
Ada *254*
Adapter
  - display *127*
  - graphics *127*
  - terminal *154*
  - video *127*
Adder *294, 340*
Additive synthesis *51*
Address
  (programming) *191*
  (spreadsheet) *16*
  (storage) *111*
  absolute *191*
  base *191*
  bus *298*
  calculation *294*
  field *197*
  modification *294*
  register *295*
  relative *191*
  switching *343*
Addressing *198*
ADFS *285*
ADSR *52*
Advanced disk filing system *285*
Advanced technology bus *307*
Adventure game *63*
AI *67*
Algebraic notation *192*
ALGOL *254*

Algorithm *42*
  - program *192*
  pseudo-code example *192*
Alpha test *164*
Alphanumeric data *265*
ALU *293*
AM *322*
American standard code for information interchange *267*
Amplifier - signal *158*
Amplitude modulation *322*
Analog
  computer *102*
  sensor *160*
  signal *158*
  sound generation *50*
  synthesiser *51*
Analog-to-digital converter *159*
Analysis
  - lexical *282*
  - syntax *282*
Analyst - systems *92*
Analyst/designer *92*
AND *196*
AND Equivalence *337*
AND gate *332*
Animation *30*
ANSI character set *267*
APL *254*
Append *183*
Appletalk *152*
Applications
  package *163*
  program *163*
  programmer *91*
  software *163*
  system design *163*
Archive file *6, 185*
Argument *216*
Arithmetic logic unit *293*
Arithmetic operator *224*
Arithmetic register *293*
Arithmetic shift *196, 302*
Arithmetic unit *293*
ARM (microprocessors) *292*

Array *258*
   (machine-code programming) *191*
   bound *258*
   dimension *258*
   - one-dimensional *258*
   processor *298*
   - programmable logic *328*
   - two-dimensional *258*
Arrow key *74*
Article number *3*
Artificial intelligence *66, 67*
ASCII *267*
ASCII file *266*
Assembler *282*
Assembler program *282*
Assembly *282*
Assembly language *250,282*
Assignment *194*
Associative storage *122*
Asynchronous transmission *316*
AT bus *307*
Atlas *102*
ATM *20*
Attack (sound) *52*
Attribute *25*
Audio controller *54*
Audit trail *3, 163*
Authoring language *63, 250*
Authoring system *63*
AUTOEXEC.BAT *281*
Automatic Teller Machine *20*
Automation *38*

— B —

B-channel *326*
Backbone *147*
Background job *289*
Background processing *289*
Backing store *111*
Backup file *6, 185*
Backus-Naur form *251*
Badging *107*
Bandwidth *322*
Bank switching *296*
Bar code *3*
Bar code reader *106*
Bar code scanner *106*
Barrel printer *137*
Base address *191*

BASIC *254*
Basic input output system *286*
Basic rate - ISDN *326*
Batch file *281*
Batch processing *166*
Batch total *187*
Baud *159*
Baud rate *159*
BCD *276*
Benchmark *164*
Beta test *164*
Bi-directional printer *135*
Big-bang *167*
Bigtrack *65*
Binary Coded Decimal *276*
Binary
   digit *272*
   notation *272*
   operator *224*
   search *184*
   tree *260*
BIOS *286*
Bistable *312*
Bit *272*
   map *298*
   - parity *301*
   rate *159*
   - start *316*
   - stop *316*
   - sum *294, 340*
Bits per inch *119*
Bits per second *159*
Block *123, 220*
   (spreadsheet) *16*
   diagram *181*
   - parameter *216*
structured language *220*
Blocked *244*
Blocking factor *262*
Blocking ring *124*
BNF *251*
Boolean
   algebra *328*
   data *265*
   operator *224*
   value *328*
Booster - signal *158*
Boot file *281*
Booting *281*
Bootstrap *281*

Bottom-up programming *170*
Box
  - dialogue *76*
  - list *76*
  - operation *231*
  - process *231*
  - text *76*
bpi *119*
bps *159*
Branch *210, 260*
Breaking *206*
Breakpoint *242*
Bridge *158*
Broad band *322*
Broad band rate *326*
Brouter *158*
Browse *61*
Bubble jet printer *136*
Bucket *123*
Buffer *298*
  - circular *262*
  - printer *142*
Buffering *298*
Bug *240*
Buggy *64*
Bulletin board *18*
Bureau *3*
Bursting *139*
Bus *298*
  (microcomputer) *307*
  - expansion *309*
  interface *309*
  - local *307*
  network *145*
  - PCI *307*
  - VESA *307*
  - video *307*
Buses *306*
Button
  - screen *77*
  - mouse *75*
Byte *269*
Bytes per second *159*

— C —

C *254*
Cable *157*
  - coaxial *156*
  - copper *156*
  - fibre optic *156*
  TV *157*
Cache *112*
  - disk *112*
  memory *112*
CAD *29*
CAD/CAM *39*
CAL *64*
Call *214*
  by reference *216*
  by value *216*
CAM *39*
Cambridge ring *148*
Campus 2000 *18*
Card
  (HyperCard) *61*
  - expansion *308*
  - interface *308*
  - memory *308*
  - PCMCIA *308*
Caret *74*
Carrier board *307*
Carrier - data *154*
Carrier sense multiple access/collision
                              detection *318*
Carrier signal *322*
Carrier wave *322*
Carry bit *294*
Carry flag *195*
Cartridge *120*
  - font *137*
  - ink *136*
  - print *136*
  - tape *117*
Case statement *209*
Cash dispenser *20*
Cassette - tape *117*
CBT *64*
CD - multisession *121*
CD - photo *121*
CD-ROM *121*
  drive *113*
  jukebox *113*
  server *151*

Ceefax *23*
Cell
    (memory) *111*
    (spreadsheet) *16*
Cellular phone *19*
Central processing unit *291*
Central processor *291*
Centring *10*
Centronics port *308*
CGA *130*
Chain printer *137*
Changes file *5*
Channel *299, 310*
    - data *154*
    - MIDI *53*
    - music *57*
    number *299*
Character *267*
    code *267*
    data *265*
    printer *135*
    recognition *106*
    set *267*
Characters per second *159*
Check
    (of variables) *241*
    digit *6, 187*
    - range *187*
    sum *6, 187*
Chip *312*
Cipher *42, 43*
Cipher breaking *43*
Circular buffer *262*
Circular queue *262*
CISC *292*
Clicking *76*
Client station *150*
Client-server relationship *150*
Clip art *29*
Clipboard *8*
Clock *311*
    mark *108*
    rate *311*
    track *108*
Closed loop feedback *39*
Closed subroutine *214*
Closed user group *20*
Cluster *148*
Cluster controller *148*
CMI *64*

CML *64*
CMOS *120*
CMYK *136*
CNC *40*
Coaxial cable *156*
COBOL *254*
Code *42, 193*
    - absolute *199*
    breaking (see cipher breaking) *43*
    generation *282*
    - intermediate *252*
    - machine *253*
    - MIDI *53*
    - operation *197*
    page *267*
    - position independent *199*
    - program *193*
    - relocatable *199*
    - SMPTE *58*
Coders *91*
Coding sheet *194*
Cognitive science *67*
Cold start *246*
Collating sequence *268*
Collision *188*
Collision detection *318*
Colour graphics adapter *130*
Colour monitor *126*
Column (spreadsheet) *16*
COM *107*
COMAL *254*
Combinations of gates *336*
Combinatorics *43*
Comma separated variable file *266*
Command file *281*
Command line interface *79*
Command line interpreter *281*
Command sequence *79*
Common user access *289*
Communication - wireless *157*
Communications *18*
    channel *154*
    devices *153*
    protocol *318*
    technology *315*
Compact disk read-only memory *121*
Compilation *282*
Compilation error *240*
Compiler *282*
Complementary MOS *120*

Complementation 274
Complement 274
Completed 244
Complex instruction set computer 292
Complex type 273
Composite key 264
Compression
- data 186
- delta 327
- video data 327
Computer 102
abuse 94
aided design 29
aided design and manufacture 39
aided drafting 29
aided learning 64
- analog 102
animation 30
assisted learning and training 62
assisted manufacturing 39
based music system 57
based training 64
bureau 3
conferencing 19
configuration 103
engineer 92
generations 102
graphics 30
- home 102
- hybrid 102
hygiene 96
languages 254
- laptop 102
- mainframe 102
managed instruction 64
managed learning 64
- micro 102
- mini 102
Misuse Act 94
- multimedia 102
- notebook 102
numeric control 40
operator 90
output on microfilm 107
- palmtop 102
personal 102
personnel 90
- portable 102
service engineer 92
- super 102

support personnel 90
supported co-operative work 19
system 103
types 100
Concentrator 155
Concept keyboard 84
Condition-controlled loop 206
Conditional jump 210
Conferencing 19
CONFIG.SYS 281
Configuration 103
Configuration management 164
Connector symbol 229
Connector - wire 156
Constant 223
Content-addressable storage 122
Continuation symbol 229
Continuous stationery 139
Control 38
character 267
devices 153
panel 89
structure 204
total 3, 187
unit 293
Controller
- audio 54
- cluster 148
- musical instrument 54
- network 91
Conversational interface 80
Conversational mode 79
Copper cable 156
Co-processor 297
Copyright 97
Correspondence quality 138
Corruption 188
Count-controlled loop 205
CP/M 285
cps 159
CPU 291
Crash 246
Crash - head 116
Cross-assembler 282
Cross-compiler 282
Cross-referencer 241
Cryptanalysis 43
Cryptography 43
CSCW 19
CSMA/CD 318

CSV file *266*
CUA *289*
CUG *20*
Cursor *74*
Cursor movement key *74*
Cut and paste *8*
Cut sheet feeder *139*
Cybernetics *67*
Cycle *300*
   - fetch-execute *293*
   - instruction *293*
   time *300*
Cyclic shift *302*
Cylinder *113*

— D —

D-channel *326*
D-to-A converter *159*
daisy wheel printer *135*
Data *257*
   bus *298*
   capture *4, 39*
   carrier *154*
   channel *154*
   compression (text) *186*
   compression (video) *327*
   description language *27*
   dictionary *26*
   directory *26*
   encryption standard *43*
   flow diagram *173*
   flowchart *173*
   glove *36*
   input symbol *174*
   input/output symbol *174*
   logging *39*
   manipulation language *256*
   model *25*
   output symbol *174*
   preparation *4*
   preparation staff *91*
   processing *2*
   processing manager *91*
   processing symbol *175*
   protection *94*
   Protection Act *95*
   Protection Officer *92*
   representation *257*
   retrieval *26*

structure *258*
symbol *175*
terminator *201*
transmission *154, 316*
type *265*
type - numeric *273*
validation *5*
validation *187*
verification *5*
vetting *5*
vetting *187*
Database *24*
   administrator *91*
   - distributed *26*
   - hierarchical *26*
   management system *26*
   - relational *27*
   server *151*
Databases and information retrieval *24*
Date data *265*
Daughterboard *307*
DBMS *26*
DD *119*
DDE *4*
Deadly embrace *244*
Debit card *20*
Debugger *241*
Debugging *241*
Debugging tool *241*
Decay (sound) *52*
Decision
   box *230*
   support specialist *91*
   support systems *6*
   symbol *230*
   table *228*
Declaration *220*
Decoder *342*
Decollate *139*
Default *164*
   option *164, 195*
   value *164*
Defragmentation *290*
Deinstall *89*
Delta compression *327*
Demodulation *322*
Denary notation *272*
Density *119*
DES *43*
Design *28*

Design structure diagram *228*
Designer - systems *92*
Desk-top presentation *9*
Desk-top publishing *9*
Detailed design *168*
Developing Programs *238*
Developmental testing *164*
DFS *285*
Diagnostic aid *241*
Diagnostic program *241*
Dialcom *326*
Dialogue box *76*
Dictionary *9*
Dictionary - data *26*
Digital
   plotter *138*
   sampler *160*
   sensor *160*
   signal *158*
   sound generation *50*
   sound system *57*
   synthesiser *51*
Digital-to-analog converter *159*
Digitising *159*
Digitizer *30*
Dimension *258*
DIN socket *314*
DIP *314*
DIP switch *88, 148*
Direct access *183*
Direct addressing *294*
Direct changeover *167*
Direct data entry *4*
Direct memory access *296*
Directive *224*
Directory *82*
  - data *26*
  file *82*
Disassembler *284*
Disinfection *96*
Disk *113*
   access time *116*
   array *116*
   cache *112*
   density *119*
   drive *113*
   file symbol *175*
   filing system *285*
  - floppy *113*
   format *114*

formatting *114*
- hard *113*
- hard-sectored *114*
- laser *121*
- magneto-optical *121*
map *123, 298*
operating system *284*
pack *113*
- phase change optical *121*
- RAM *120*
- silicon *120*
- soft-sectored *114*
unit - fixed head *113*
verification *114*
- video *121*
Diskette *113*
Display adapter *127*
Display devices *125*
Distributed database *26*
Distributed network *144*
Distributed processing *150*
DMA *296*
DML *256*
Do loop *205*
Docking station *310*
Document output symbol *174*
Document reader *106*
Documentation
  - maintenance *172*
  - program *227*
  - technical *172*
Dongle *89*
DOS *284*
Dot matrix printer *136*
Dot pitch *128*
Double buffering *298*
Double clicking *76*
Double precision *273*
Down time *247*
Download *188*
DP *2*
Draft quality *138*
Drafting *29*
Drag *77*
Drag-and-drop editing *77*
DRAM *120*
Drawing package *31*
Dry run *242*
DSS *6*
DTP *9*

Dual in line package *139, 314*
Dual in line socket *314*
Dummy variable *222*
Dump *242*
Duplex *316*
Dynamic RAM *120*
Dynamic variable *221*

— E —

E-mail *20*
EAN *3*
EAROM *120*
Ease of maintenance *200*
Ease of use *200*
EB disk *121*
EBCDIC *267*
Echo *316*
ECMA symbols *227*
Econet *149*
Editor *280*
EDSAC *102*
EDVAC *102*
EEPROM *120*
EFT *20*
EFTPOS *20*
EGA *130*
EISA bus *307*
Electrically
    alterable read-only memory *120*
    erasable programmable memory *120*
Electro-magnetic interference *325*
Electronic
    book disk *121*
    funds transfer *20*
    funds transfer at point-of-sale *20*
    mail *20*
    signature *96*
Else *208*
Embedded keyboard *71*
EMI *325*
Emulation *34*
Emulator *284*
Encryption *4, 96*
End of file marker *265*
Engineer *91, 92*
Enhanced graphics adapter *130*
ENIAC *102*

Entity *25*
    -relationship *172*
    -relationship diagram *25, 172*
Enumeration *43*
Envelope *52*
Environment
    - user *71*
    - WIMP *72*
EOF marker *265*
EOR gate *334*
EPROM *120*
EQ gate *335*
Equivalence gate *335*
Erasable PROM *120*
Error *240*
    - logical *241*
    message *82, 240*
    - rounding *189*
    - structure *241*
    - syntax *241*
    - truncation *189*
Escaping *206*
Ethernet *149*
European Article Number *3*
Even parity *301*
Event *194*
Event - mouse *75*
Exchangeable disk pack *113*
Exclusive-NOR gate *335*
Exclusive-OR gate *334*
Execute phase *293*
Execution *240*
Execution error *240*
Executive program *290*
Exit *214*
Expansion
    bus *309*
    card *308*
    slot *308*
Expert system *66, 68*
Explanation *68*
Exponent *275*
Export *9, 188*
Extended binary coded decimal
                interchange code *267*
Extended graphics adapter *130*
Extended industry standard
                architecture bus *307*

— F —

Facsimile machine 154
Facsimile transmission 22
False (truth value) 328
Fan-fold paper 139
FAST 97
FAT 123, 182
Father file 4, 186
Fax 22
    groups 22
    machine 154
    modem 154
FDDI 147
FDDI backbone 147
FDM 155
Feasibility study 163
Federation Against Software Theft 97
Feed mechanism 139
Feedback 39
Fetch phase 293
Fetch -execute cycle 293
Fibre distributed data interface 147
Fibre optic cable 156
Field 263
    - address 197
    - key 264
    name 263
    - operand 197
    - operation 197
    - response 80
    type 265
    type - numeric 273
FIFO 262
Fifth generation computer 103
File 4, 185
    access 183
    allocation table 123, 182
    - backup 6
    - batch 281
    - command 281
    - directory 82
    - father 4, 186
    - grandfather 4, 186
    name extension 185
    operations 182
    - reference 7
    - scrap 123
    - scratch 123
    server 151

- son 4, 186
symbol 175
- transaction 185
transfer protocol 318
type 266
- work 123
- working 123
First generation computer 102
First in first out 262
Fixed format record 265
Fixed head disk unit 113
Fixed-length record 265
Fixed-point notation 275
Flag 195
    - carry 195
    - overflow 195
Flash PROM 120
Flat file 26
Flat-bed plotter 138
Flexibility 200
Flip-flop 312
Float type 273
Floating-point accelerator 297
Floating-point notation 275
Floating-point unit 297
Floppy disk 113
Floppy disk drive 113
Flow line 173, 227
Flowchart 173
    - data 173
    - program 227
    - system 173
Fly by wire 39
FM 322
FM (sound) 50
Folder 82
Font 129, 137
Font cartridge 137
For loop 205
For..next loop 205
Foreground job 289
Foreground/background processing 289
Formal methods 165
Formal parameter 216
Formal specification 165
Format
    (disk) 114
    (display) 202
    - record 262
Forms dialogue interface 80

Formula *16*
FORTH *254, 256*
FORTRAN *254*
Fourth generation computer *103*
Fourth generation language *252*
FPA *297*
Fragmentation *290*
Frame *117, 127*
Freeware *97*
Frequency division multiplexor *155*
Frequency modulation *322*
Frequency modulation (sound) *50*
Friction feed *138*
Front-end processor *103*
FTP *318*
Full adder *294, 340*
Full duplex *316*
Full justification *10*
Function *16, 212*
Function key *71*
Functional specification *163*

— G —

G (giga) *357*
G-code *39*
Garbage collection *290*
Gate *328*
Gate (combinations of) *336*
Gateway *152*
GDU *129*
Generation - sound *50*
Generations - computer *102*
Generic software *163*
George Boole *328*
Giga (units) *357*
Global variable *221*
Glove - data *36*
Golf ball printer *135*
Grandfather, father, son files *4, 186*
Graph plotter *138*
Graphical display unit *129*
Graphical user interface *71*
Graphics *28, 30*
    adapter *127, 130*
    pad *30*
    tablet *30*
Greek alphabet *267*
Group - fax *22*
GUI *71*

— H —

Hacking *95*
Half adder *294, 340*
Half duplex *316*
Handshake *158*
Hard
    copy *139*
    disk *113*
    disk drive *113*
    space *9*
    -sectored disk *114*
    -wired logic *311*
Hardware *104*
    documentation *87*
    platform *200*
Hash table *188*
Hash total *6, 188*
Hashing *6, 188*
HCI *71*
HD *119*
HDTV *327*
Head
    crash *116*
    - print *135*
    - read/write *116*
Headset *37*
Help desk *92*
Help system *88*
Hercules graphics adapter *130*
Heuristic program *197*
Heuristics *68*
HEX *278*
Hexadecimal notation *278*
HGR *128*
Hierarchical database *26*
High definition television *327*
High-level language *252, 253*
High-resolution graphics *128*
Highlighting *75*
Highway *298*
Hit *184*
Hit rate *184*
Home computer *100*
Hot key *79*
Hot line *92*
Hub *147*
Human-computer interaction *71*
Human-computer interface *71*
Hung *246*

Hybrid computer 102
Hybrid manager 91
Hygiene - computer 96
HyperCard 61
Hypermedia system 60
Hypertext system 60

— I —

I/O device 105
IAR 295
IAS 111
IBM 360 series 103
IC 312
ICL 1900 series 103
Icon 73
IDE interface 309
Identifier 223
IEEE interface 309
If statement 208
IKBS 68
Ikon 73
Immediate access store 111
Immediate addressing 294
Immediate mode 247
Impact printer 135
Implementation 167
Implementation (software life cycle) 168
Import 9, 188
Incremental plotter 138
Index
    file 186
    hole 113
    mark 108
    register 294
    sequential access 183
Indexed addressing 294
Indirect addressing 294
Industry standard architecture bus 307
Industry structure model 93
Inference engine 68
Inference processor 68
Infinite loop 206
Infix notation 192
Information 4
    processing 4
    retrieval 24, 26
    systems engineers 91
    systems manager 92
    technology 4

Infra-red communication 157
Initial value 195
Initialise 195
Ink cartridge 136
Ink jet printer 136
Input device 105, 106
Input symbol 174, 229
Input/output device 105
Input/output symbol 174, 229
Insert 183
Install 89
Instruction
    address register 295
    cycle 293
    decoder 293
    - macro 213
    - multiple address 198
    - one-address 198
    set 197, 293
    - two-address 198
Int type 273
Integer 273
Integer type 273
Integrated
    circuit 312
    circuit memory 120
    manufacturing 40
    package 165
    services digital network 326
Integration 168
Integrity 95
Intelligent knowledge based system 68
Intelligent time division multiplexor 155
Inter-block gap 117
Interaction - human-computer 71
Interaction - man-machine 71
Interactive
    computing 79
    input symbol 174
    processing 167
    video 61
Interface
    (hardware) 300
    board 308
    card 308
    - command line 79
    - graphical user 71
    - human-computer 71
    - man-machine 71
    - menu selection 74

Interface (continued)
- MIDI *53*
- RS232/432 *308*
- SCSI *309*
- user *71*
Interfaces and buses *306*
Interference *325*
Interlace *127*
Interlaced scan *128*
Interleaving *289*
Intermediate code *252*
Internal character code *267*
International standard book number *3*
Internet *20*
Interpreter *283*
Interrupt *300*
Inverse *331*
Inverse video *75*
Inverter *331*
IO device *105*
ISA bus *307*
ISAM *183*
ISBN *3*
ISDN *326*
ISDN service rate *326*
ISM *93*
ISO 7 *319, 320*
ISO 8859 *267*
IT *4*
Iteration (flow of execution) *204*
Iteration (mathematical) *44*

— J —

Jackson structured development *165*
Jackson structured programming *165*
JANET *20*
JCL *287*
Job *287*
    control language *287*
    queue *287*
John von Neumann *305*
Joint academic network *20*
Joint photographic expert group *327*
Journal file *163*
JPEG *327*
JSD *165*
JSP *165*

Jump *210*
- conditional *210*
- unconditional *210*
Jumper *89*
Junk Fax *22*
Justification *10*

— K —

K (Kilo) *357*
Karnaugh map *329*
KBS *68*
Key *264*
    (for code) *43*
    - arrow *74*
    - composite *264*
    - cursor movement *74*
    disk *89*
    field *264*
    field order *264*
    - primary *264*
    - quick *79*
    - secondary *264*
    - sort *264*
Key-to-disk system *107*
Key-to-tape system *107*
Keyboard *71*
    - concept *84*
    - embedded *71*
    - music *53*
    - qwerty *71*
    - touch sensitive *84*
Keypad - numeric *71*
Keystrip *88*
Keyword *223*
Kilo (units) *357*
Kimball tag *5*
Knowledge
    acquisition *68*
    base *68*
    based system *68*
    elicitation *68*
    engineer *68*

— L —

LA 51
Label 223
LAN 144
Language
 - assembly 250
 - authoring 63, 250
 - data description 27
 - data manipulation 256
 - high-level 252
 - low-level 253
 - machine-oriented 253
 - page description 137
 - problem-oriented 252
Laptop computer 100
Large scale integration 312
Laser disk 121
Laser printer 136
Last in first out 262
Latency 116, 312
Latex 12
Latin1 alphabet 267
Law and administration 94
LCD 129
Leaf node 260
Least significant bit 272
LED 129
Left justification 10
LEO 102
Letter quality 138
Lexical analysis 282
Library 280
 program 280
 routine 280
 - subroutine 214, 280
Licence - software 97
Life cycle (software) 168
LIFO 262
Light Emitting Diode 129
Light pen 84
Line
 art 31
 break 10
 editor 280
 printer 137
Linear arithmetic 51
Linear search 184
Link editor 283
Linked List 262

Linker 283
Linking 283
 error 240
 loader 283
Liquid crystal display 129
Lisa 100
Lisp 254
List 258
List box 76
Listing 228
Listing file 240
Loader 283
Local area network 145
Local bus 307
Local variable 221
Log
 in 83
 off 83
 on 83
 out 83
Logging
 in 83
 off 83
 on 83
 out 83
Logic
 array - programmable 328
 circuit 313
 element 313
 gates 331
 networks 340
 symbol 331
 -seeking 135
Logical
 data 265
 equivalence 328, 336
 error 241
 operation 196
 operator 224
 record 262
 shift 196, 302
Logo 254
Look-up table 197
Loop 204
 - do 205
 - for 205
 - for..next 205
 network 146
 - repeat..until 206
 - while 206

Low-level language 253
Low-resolution graphics 128
LQ 138
LSB 272
LSI 312
Lyons Electronic Office 102

— M —

m (milli) 357
M (mega) 357
Machine Architecture 291
Machine
    code 253
    -code instruction 197
    code subroutine 213
    cycle time 300
    -oriented language 253
    readable 106
Macintosh 100
Macro 213
    assembler 282
    instruction 213
    recording 79
Magnetic
    disk 113
    disk drive 113
    disk file symbol 175
    disk storage 111
    ink character recognition 106
    tape 117
    tape drive 116
    tape file symbol 175
    tape storage 112
Magneto-optical disk 121
Magneto-optical storage 112
Mailbox 20
Mailmerge 10
Main store 111
Mainboard 307
Mainframe 100
Maintenance 168
    (of programs) 201
    documentation 172
    engineer 92
Man-machine interaction 71
Man -machine interface 71
Management and manipulation of data 182
Management information systems 5

Manager
    - data processing 91
    - hybrid 91
    - information systems 92
    - network 91
Mantissa 275
Manufacturing - integrated 40
Map
    - bit 298
    - disk 298
    - screen 298
MAR 296
Mark - clock 108
Mark - index 108
Mark sense reader 106
Mask 196
Masking 304
Mass storage 111
Master file 5, 185
Maths co-processor 297
Matrix 258
MBR 296
MCA bus 307
MDA 130
MDR 296
Measurement of software 164
Media 139
Medium scale integration 312
Mega (units) 357
Memory 109, 111
    address register 296
    buffer register 296
    - cache 112
    card 308
    cell 111
    data register 296
    management 296
    management unit 296
    map 123
    - non-volatile 124
    - permanent 124
    refresh 120
    - virtual 123
    - volatile 124
Menu 73
    bar 73
    - pop-up 73
    - pull-down 73
    selection interface 74
Merge 188

Message 166
    concentrator 155
    - error 82
    queuing 316
    switching 316
Metafont 12
Metal-oxide-semiconductor 120
Metric 168
MICR 106
Micro
    (computer) 100
    (units) 357
    channel architecture bus 307
    -code 301
    -instruction 301
    -program 301
    -spacing 11
Microcom network protocol 318
Microcomputer 100
Microfilm (computer output on) 107
Microprocessor 292
Microwave transmission 157
MIDI 53
    channel 53
    code 53
    interface 53
    standard 53
milli (units) 357
Million instructions per second 300
Mini-computer 100
Minitel 22
mips 300
MIS 5
Misuse Act - computer 94
Mixer - sound 57
MMI 71
MMU 296
Mnemonic 198
MNP 318
Model 34
Modelling 33, 34
Modem 154
Modular design 165
Modulation 322
Module 165
    design 168
    production 168
    testing 168
Monitor 126
Monitor program 290

Monochrome display adapter 130
Monochrome monitor 126
Monte Carlo method 46
MOS 120
Most significant bit 272
Motherboard 307
Motion picture expert group 327
Motor - stepper 160
Mouse 75
    button 75
    event 75
    pointer 74
MPEG 327
MS-DOS 285
MSB 272
MSI 312
Multi-access 166
Multi-part repeater 158
Multi-tasking 288
Multi-timbral synthesiser 53
Multimedia 61
Multimedia computer 100
Multipart stationery 139
Multiple address instruction 198
Multiplexor 155
Multiprocessor system 104
Multiprogramming 288
Multiscan monitor 126
Multisession-CD 121
Multisync monitor 126
Music
    channel 57
    keyboard 53
    synthesiser 51
    workstation 57
Musical instrument controller 54
Musical instrument digital interface 53

— N —

n (nano) 357
Name table 284
NAND gate 334
nano (units) 357
Narrow band 322
Near letter quality 138
Negative numbers 274
Neq gate 334
Nested loop 204

Network 144
    accounting software 152
    - bus 145
    controller 91, 104
    - distributed 144
    - FDDI backbone 147
    - local area 144
    - loop 146
    manager 91
    number 149
    operating system 152
    - peer-to-peer 150
    - ring 146
    - star 147
    station 150
    - token ring 148
    terminal 150
    topology 145
    - wide area 145
Networks 143
Neural net 67
Next instruction register 295
Nexus 147
NFS 152
NLQ 138
Node 260
Noise 325
Non-breaking space 11
Non-equivalence gate 334
Non-interlaced scan 128
Non-volatile memory 124
NOR Equivalence 337
NOR gate 333
Normal form 26
Normalise 276
NOT 196
NOT Equivalence 336
NOT gate 331
Notation
    - binary 272
    - denary 272
    - fixed-point 275
    - floating-point 275
    - infix 192
    - octal 277
    - postfix 192
    - prefix 192
Notation - reverse polish 192
Notebook computer 100
Notepad 8

Novell Netware 152
Numeric
    control 40
    data representation 270
    data type 273
    field type 273
    keypad 71
    overflow 188
    variable type 273
Numerical analysis 46
Numerical computing 42

— O —

Object 166
    oriented design 166
    oriented language 166
    oriented programming 166
    program 239
OCR 106
Octal notation 277
Odd parity 301
OEM 107
Off-line processing 167
Offset 191
OMR 106
On-line data file symbol 175
On-line processing 167
On-line service 325
One's complement 274
One-address instruction 198
One-dimensional array 258
One-way function 44
OOD 166
OOL 166
OOP 166
Open loop feedback 39
Open subroutine 214
Open system 319
Open systems interconnection 319
Operand 197
Operand field 197
Operating system 284
Operating system - network 152
Operation
    (software life cycle) 168
    box 231
    code 197
    field 197
    symbol 231

Operational mode *166*
Operator *224*
   - binary *224*
   - computer *90*
   - logical *224*
   - relational *224*
   - string *224*
Operator's console *108*
Optical
   character recognition *106*
   disk storage *112*
   fibre *156*
   mark reader *106*
   storage *121*
OR *196*
OR gate *332*
Oracle *23*
Original Equipment Manufacturer *107*
OS/2 *285*
OSI *319, 321*
Output device *105, 107*
Output document symbol *174*
Output symbol *174, 229*
Outsourcing *92*
Overall design *168*
Overflow *188*
Overflow flag *195*
Overlay *198*
Overtype *11*
Overwrite (document) *11*
Overwriting *189*

— P —

p (pico) *357*
PABX *154*
Package *163*
Packet *317*
Packet switching system *317*
Packing *200*
Packing density *119*
Pad
   character *11*
   - graphics *30*
   - pressure *84*
   - scratch *123*
Page *296*
   description language *137*
   faults. *296*
   make-up system *11*

   printer *136*
   turn *296*
Paging *123, 296*
Painting package *32*
PAL *127*
Palette *127*
Palmtop computer *100*
Pane *72*
Paper
   feed mechanism *138*
   tape *40*
   tape punch *40*
   tape reader *40*
Parallel
   data transmission *316*
   port *308*
   processing *298*
   running *167*
Parameter *216*
   - actual *216*
   block *216*
   - formal *216*
   passing *216*
Parent node *260*
Parity bit *301*
Parity check *301*
Park (disk) *116*
Parsing *284*
Pascal *254*
Passing parameters *216*
Passive device *160*
Passive system *38*
Password *83*
Paste *8*
Patch *242*
Pattern recognition *67*
PBX *154*
PC *100*
PC-DOS *285*
PCI bus *307*
PCMCIA card *308*
PD *51*
PDA *100*
Peer-to-peer network *150*
Pentium *292*
Performance of software *164*
Peripheral device *105*
Peripherals *105*
Permanent memory *124*

Personal
    computer *100*
    digital assistant *100*
    identification device *83*
    identification number *83*
Phase alternating line *127*
Phase change optical disk *121*
Phase distortion *51*
Phase modulation *322*
Phased implementation *167*
Phoneme *59*
Photo-CD *121*
Physical components *311*
Physical record *262*
pico (units) *357*
PID *83*
PILOT *254*
Pilot running *167*
PIN *83*
Pin printer *136*
Pipelining *301*
Piracy *95*
Pixel *127*
Pixel graphics *128*
PL/1 *254*
PLA *313*
Platform *200*
Plotter *138*
Plug and go *108*
Plug compatible *108*
Point-of-sale *20*
Point-of-sale terminal *150*
Pointer *74*
Polling *304*
Polyphony *51*
Pop *262*
POP-2 *254*
Pop-up menu *73*
Portability *200*
Portable computer *102*
Ported *200*
POS *20*
POS terminal *150*
Position independent code *199*
Post mortem routine *242*
Postfix notation *192*
Postscript *137*
Power series *46*
Pre-printed stationery *139*
Prefix notation *192*

Presentation manager *285*
Pressure pad *84*
Pressure switch *84*
Prestel *23*
Pretty printer *202*
Primary key *264*
Primary rate ISDN *326*
Primary store *111*
Prime numbers *47*
Print
    buffer *310*
    cartridge *136*
    hammer *137*
    head *135*
    job *286*
    quality *138*
    queue *286*
    spooler *286*
    - voice *58*
PRINT USING *202*
Printer *135*
    - barrel *137*
    - bi-directional *135*
    - bubble jet *136*
    buffer *142*
    - chain *137*
    - character *135*
    characteristics *140*
    - daisy wheel *135*
    - dot matrix *136*
    driver *137*
    - golf ball *135*
    - impact *135*
    - ink jet *136*
    - laser *136*
    - line *137*
    - page *136*
    - pin *136*
    server *151*
    spooler *286*
    types *140*
    - thermal *136*
Printers *133*
printf *202*
Printout *139*
Privacy *95*
Private automatic branch exchange *154*
Private branch exchange *154*
Problem-oriented language *252*
Procedure *212*

Process
    box 231
    control 40
    state 244
    symbol 175
Processing mode 288
Processor 291
    cycle time 300
    - sound 57
Product code - universal 3
Productivity tool 163
Program 219
    algorithm 192
    characteristics 200
    code 193
    counter 295
    documentation 226, 227
    execution 240
    flowchart 227
    flowchart diagram 227
    flowchart symbol 229
    - heuristic 197
    library 280
    listing 228
    loop time 300
    maintenance 201
    - object 239
    - re-entrant 217
    - self-documented 199
    - source 239
    statement 220
    suite 219
    syntax 219
    syntax error 241
Programmable logic array 328, 313
Programmable read-only memory 120
Programmed by example 213
Programmer 91
Programming (flow of execution) 204
Programming (subprograms) 211
Programming concepts 190
Programming languages 248
PROLOG 254, 256
PROM 120
Prompt 83
Propagation delay 312
Protocol - communications 318
Pseudo random-number generator 48
Pseudo-code 227
Pseudo-code example 235

PSS 317
PSTN 326
PTO 326
Public key cryptography 44
Public switched telephone network 326
Public telephone operator 326
Puck 30
Pull 262
Pull-down menu 73
Punched paper tape 40
Push 262

— Q —

QBE 253
QD (quad density) 119
Quality (of print) 138
Query by example 253
Query language 26, 253
Queue 262
Queue - circular 262
Quick key 79
Qwerty keyboard 71

— R —

Radio frequency interference 325
RAID 116
RAM 120
    - dynamic 120
    - Static 120
    disk 120
Random
    access 183
    access memory 120
    number generation 48
Range check 6, 187
Raster 128
Raster graphics 128
Raw data 189
Re-entrant
    program 217
    subprogram 217
    subroutine 217
Read 183
    head 116
    -only access 183
    -only memory 120
Read/write head 116

Reader
- document *106*
- mark sense *106*
- optical mark *106*
Readme file *88*
Ready *244*
Real
number *273*
-time clock *313*
-time entry (music) *58*
-time system *167*
type *273*
Recalculation *17*
Record *262*
- fixed format *265*
- fixed-length *265*
format *262*
- logical *262*
- physical *262*
- variable-length *265*
Recording - macro *79*
Recovery *246*
Recursion *46*
Recursive subprogram *215*
Red green blue *129*
Reduced instruction set computer *292*
Redundant array of independent disks *116*
Redundant array of inexpensive disks *116*
Reel - tape *117*
Reference
- absolute *17*
- call by *216*
file *7, 186*
- relative *17*
Refresh rate *132*
Register *295*
- address *295*
- instruction address *295*
- memory address *295*
- memory buffer *295*
- memory data *295*
- next instruction *295*
- sequence control *295*
Relational database *27*
Relational operator *224*
Relationship (entities) *25*
Relative address *191*
Relative reference *17*
Release (sound) *52*
Release (of software) *168*

Reliability *200*
Relocatable code *199*
Relocation *199*
Remote access *167*
Remote job entry *287*
Repeat..until loop *206*
Repeater *158*
Replacement rules *251*
Replication *17*
Report generator *256*
Report program generator *256*
Request (verification) *124*
Requirements specification *172*
Reserved word *223*
Reset *246*
Response field *80*
Return *214*
Reverse polish notation *192*
Revisable text format file *266*
RFI *325*
RGB *129*
Rich text format file *266*
Right justification *10*
Ring network *146*
RISC *292*
Risc-OS *286*
Rivest, Shamir, Adleman algorithm *44*
RJE *287*
Roamer *65*
Robot *40*
Robot arm *40*
Robotics *67*
Robustness *200*
Rogue terminator *201*
Rogue value *201*
ROM *120*
Root node *260*
Rotation *302*
Round-robin *288*
Rounding *189*
Rounding error *189*
Router *158*
Routine *214*
Row (spreadsheet) *16*
RPG *254, 256*
RS232 interface *308*
RS432 interface *308*
RSA algorithm *44*
RTF file *266*
Rulebase *68*

Run *244*
  -time *244*
  -time error *240*
  -time system *244*
running programs *238*

— S —

S100 bus *307*
SAA *289*
Sample data *265*
Sampler *160*
Sampler - Sound *54*
Sampling
  (control) *39*
  rate *54*
  resolution *54*
Satellite communication *157*
Scan *128*
Scan frequency *128*
Scanner *30*
Scheduling *288*
Schema *27*
Scientific computing *42*
Scope *222*
SCR *295*
Scrap file *123*
Scratch
  file *123*
  pad *123*
  tape *123*
Screen
  button *77*
  dump *242*
  editing *83*
  editor *280*
  map *298*
  refresh *132*
  resolution *128*
Scroll bar *78*
Scrolling *78*
SCSI interface *309*
Search *184*
Second generation computer *102*
Secondary key *264*
Secondary storage *111*
Secret messages *43*
Sector *114*
Security *95*
Seek time *116*

Segment *289*
Segmentation *289*
Self-documented program *199*
Semantics *220*
Semiconductor memory *120*
Sensor *160*
Sequence control register *295*
Sequencer *58*
Sequential access *183*
Serial
  access *183*
  access storage *117*
  data transmission *316*
  port *308*
  search *184*
Server *151*
Service engineer *92*
Servo *160*
Set *195*
Shareware *97*
Sheet feeder *139*
Shell (artificial intelligence) *68*
Shift *196, 302*
SID file *266*
Sign and magnitude *274*
Sign and modulus *274*
Sign bit *274*
Signal *322*
  amplifier *158*
  booster *158*
  concentrator *155*
  converter *158*
  level *158*
  routing *316*
Signal-to-noise ratio *325*
Silicon disk *120*
Simplex *316*
Simula *254*
Simulation *33, 34*
Single-address instruction *198*
Single
  buffering *298*
  precision *273*
  stepping *242*
  -tasking *288*
Slot *16, 308*
Small computer systems interface *309*
Small scale integration *312*
Smalltalk *254*
Smart card *83*

SMPTE codes *58*
SMTP *318*
SNA *289*
SNOBOL *254*
Soft space *9*
Soft-sectored disk *114*
Software *168*
   copyright *97*
   documentation *86*
   library *280*
   licence *97*
   life cycle *168*
   measurement *164*
   metric *168*
   performance *164*
   requirements *168*
   support staff *92*
   theft *97*
Son file *4, 186*
Sort key *264*
Sorting *185*
Sound *49*
   controller *54*
   data *265*
   generation *50*
   generator *54*
   mixer *57*
   processor *57*
   sampler *54*
   source *54*
   synthesis *50*
   system - digital *57*
Source language *239*
Source program *239*
Specification - formal *165*
Specification - system *163*
Speech recognition *58*
Speech synthesis *59*
Spelling checker *11*
Spool - tape *117*
Spooler - print *286*
Spooling *286*
Spreadsheet *13, 17*
SQL *253*
SSADM *169*
SSI *312*
Stack *262*
   (HyperCard) *61*
   overflow *189*
   underflow *189*

Standard
   function *217*
   interchangeable data file *266*
   logic networks *340*
   - MIDI *53*
Star network *147*
Start bit *316*
Start/stop symbol *232*
Statement syntax error *241*
Static RAM *120*
Static variable *221*
Station *150*
Station number *149*
Statistical multiplexor *155*
Status
   bar *73*
   byte *195*
   word *195*
Step mode *242*
Step-time entry (music) *58*
Stepper motor *160*
Stepping motor *160*
Stepwise refinement *170*
Stop bit *316*
Stop Symbol *232*
Stopped *244*
Stopping condition *215*
Storage *111*
   - magnetic disk *111*
   - magnetic tape *112*
   - magneto-optical *112*
   - mass *111*
   - optical disk *112*
   - secondary *111*
   - virtual *123*
Store *111*
   - work *123*
   - working *123*
Store location *111*
Streamer - tape *119*
String data *265*
String operator *224*
Strongly typed language *221*
Structure diagram *179, 228*
Structure error *241*
Structured
   planning technique *170*
   programming *170*
   query language *253*
   systems analysis and design method *169*

Stylus *30*
Sub-directory *82*
Subprogram *214*
Subprogram - re-entrant *217*
Subroutine *214*
   library *214*
   - machine code *213*
   - re-entrant *217*
   symbol *232*
Subschema *27*
Subscript *258*
Subscripted variable *258*
Subtractive synthesis *50*
Sum bit *294, 340*
Super computer *100*
Super video graphics adapter *130*
Supervisor program *290*
Support personnel *90*
Support staff *92*
Suspended *244*
Sustain (sound) *52*
SVGA *130*
Switch
   - dip *88, 148*
   - pressure *84*
   - touch *84*
Symbol
   - (magnetic) disk file *175*
   - (magnetic) tape file *175*
   - connector *229*
   - continuation *229*
   - data *175*
   - data processing *175*
   - decision *230*
   - document output *174*
   - ECMA *227*
   - input/output *174, 229*
   - on-line data file *175*
   - operation *231*
   - output document *174*
   - process *175, 231*
   - program flowchart *229*
   - start/stop *232*
   - subroutine *232*
   - system flowchart *173*
   table *284*
Symbolic addressing *198*
Synchronous transmission *316*
Syntax *219*
   analysis *282*

error *241*
Synthesis - sound *50*
Synthesiser *51*
   - music *51*
   - speech *59*
Sysop *18*
System
   - authoring *63*
   crash *246*
   development cycle *169*
   flowchart diagram *173*
   flowchart symbol *173*
   life cycle *169*
   operator *18*
   requirements *168*
   specification *163*
   testing *168*
Systems
   analysis *163*
   analyst designer *92*
   application architecture *289*
   design *163*
   design and life cycle *162*
   designer *92*
   documentation *171*
   network architecture *289*
   program *280*
   programmer *91*
   software *279*
   specification *163*

— T —

Tab separated variable files *266*
Table *258*
   (relational database) *27*
   - file allocation *123*
   - hash *188*
   - look-up *197*
Tablet - graphics *30*
Tape
   cartridge *117*
   cassette *117*
   drive *116*
   file symbol *175*
   punch *40*
   reader *40*
   reel *117*
   - scratch *123*
   spool *117*

Tape (continued)
    streamer 119
TCP/IP 318, 321
TDM 155
Technical documentation 172
Technical support staff 92
Tele
    -commuting 22
    -conferencing 23
    -processing 167
Telecommunications 22
Telemetry 41
Teletext 23
Teletext character set 267
Terminal 150
    adapter 154
    - network 150
    node 260
    - point-of-sale 150
    - POS 150
Terminator
    (data) 157
    (network) 201
Test
    data 244
    plan 244
Testing
    (software) 164
    programs 238
TeX 12
Text
    box 76
    editor 12, 280
    file 266
Thermal printer 136
Thesaurus 12
Third generation computer 103
Threshing 296
Time division multiplexor 155
Time slice 155, 288
Time -sharing 166
Timer 300
Timing information 108
Toggle 78
Token 148
Token ring network 148
Tool 78
Toolbar 78
Toolbox 78
Top-down programming 170

Topology - network 145
Touch
    keyboard 84
    sensitive keyboard 84
    switch 84
Touchpad 84
Touchscreen 84
TP 156
Trace table 242
Track
    (disk) 113
    (tape) 117
    - clock 108
Trackball 75
Trackerball 75
Tractor feed 138
Transaction
Transaction file 5, 185
Transaction processing 166
Transducer 159
Translator 281
Transmission
    - asynchronous 316
    control protocol/internet protocol 318
    - data 316
    - parallel data 316
    - serial data 316
    - synchronous 316
Transparency 85
Trapdoor function 44
Tree 260
Tree - binary 260
Trojan (horse) 96
True (truth value) 328
Truncation 188
Truncation error 189
Truth table 328
Truth value 328
TSV file 266
Turnaround document 5
Turtle 64
Tutorial 88
Twisted pair 156
Two's complement 274
Two-address instruction 198
Two-dimensional array 258
Types of computer 100

— U —

ULA *313*
Unary operator *224*
Uncommitted logic array *313*
Unconditional jump *210*
Underflow *189*
Univac I *102*
Universal Product Code *3*
Unix *152, 286*
Unset *195*
Unshielded twisted pair *156*
UPC *3*
Update *183*
Update file *5*
Uploading *188*
User
    defined data type *265*
    documentation *86, 88*
    environment *71*
    friendly *85*
    interface *70*
    transparent *85*
Utility program *280*
UTP *156*

— V —

Validation *5, 187*
Value added network service *152*
    - call by *216*
    - initial *195*
    - rogue *201*
VANS *152*
Variable *221*
    check *241*
    - dynamic *221*
    - global *221*
    - local *221*
    - static *221*
    - subscripted *258*
    type *265*
    type - numeric *273*
Variable-length record *265*
Vector *294*
Vector graphics *129*
Vectoring *304*
Venn diagram *330*
Verification (of data) *5*
Verification (request) *124*

Verifier *5*
Verify (disk) *114*
Vertical refresh rate *132*
Very large scale integration *312*
Very small aperture terminal *327*
VESA bus *307*
Vetting *5*
Vetting (of data) *187*
V-fast *318*
VGA *130*
Video
    adapter *127*
    bus *307*
    clip *61, 265*
    -conferencing *23*
    data *265*
    data compression *327*
    graphics adapter *130*
    RAM *132*
Videodisk *121*
Videotex *23*
View (relational database) *27*
Viewdata *23*
Virtual
    memory *123, 296*
    reality *36*
    reality system *37*
    storage *123*
Virus *96*
Virus checking *96*
VLSI *312*
Voice print *58*
Volatile memory *124*
von Neumann architecture *305*
von Neumann concept *305*
von Neumann machine *305*
VR *36*
VR system *37*
VRAM *132*
VRR *132*
VSAT *327*
V.22bis *318*
V.32bis *318*
V.34 *318*
V.42 *318*
V.42bis *318*
V24 interface *308*

— W —

WAN 145
Wand 106
Warm start 246
What you see is what you get 12
While loop 206
Wide area network 145
Wildcard 81
WIMP environment 72
Winchester disk drive 113
Window 72
Windows
    (Microsoft) 286
    for Workgroups 152
    icons menus pointer
        environment 72
Wire connector 156
Wireless communication 157
Wizard 85
Word 269
   length 269
   processing 8
   processor 104
   - reserved 223
   wrap 12
Work file 123
Work group 19
Work station 151
Work station - music 57
Work store 123
Working file 123
Working store 123
WORM 121
Worm (virus) 96
WP 8
Write 183
   head 116
   inhibit ring 124
   permit ring 124
   protection 124
Write-once, read-many 121
WYSIWYG 12

— X —

XGA 130
XNORgate 335
XOR 196
XOR Equivalence 338

XOR gate 334
X.25 318
X.400 318

— Z —

Z modem 318
Zero insertion force socket 314
ZIF socket 314
Z80 292

— # —

186 292
286 292
386 292
486 292
4GL 252
6502 292
68000 292
8086 292